Voices from the Circle

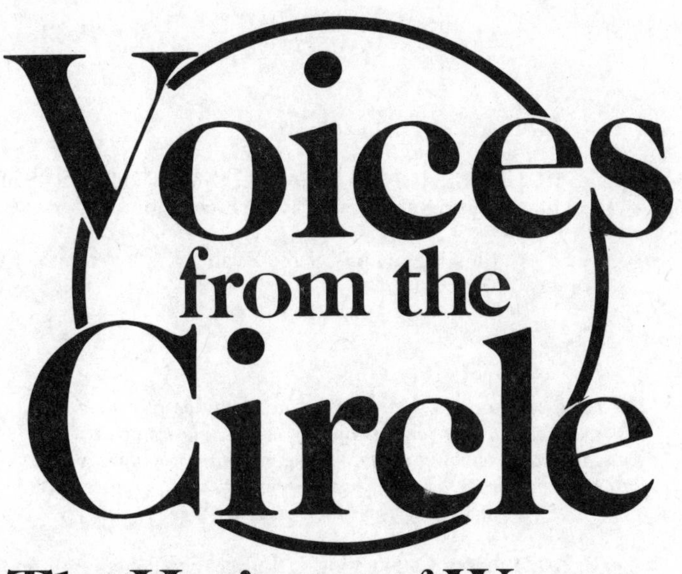

Voices from the Circle

The Heritage of Western Paganism

Edited by
PRUDENCE JONES
and
CAITLÍN MATTHEWS

THE AQUARIAN PRESS

First published 1990

Illustrations by Nicole Ryan

British Library Cataloguing in Publication Data

Voices from the circle.
1. Paganism
I. Jones, Prudence II. Matthews, Caitlín
291

ISBN 0-85030-785-6

The Aquarian Press is part of the Thorsons Publishing Group, Wellingborough, Northamptonshire, NN8 2RQ, England.

Typeset by MJL Limited, Hitchin, Hertfordshire.
Printed in Great Britain by Woolnough Bookbinding Limited, Irthlingborough, Northamptonshire

1 3 5 7 9 10 8 6 4 2

To all who sing the circle
Thanks to our ancestors
Joy to our successors

Contents

Preface 9

Introduction: The Pagan World 13
Prudence Jones & Caitlín Matthews

Circles of Earth, Circles of Heaven 41
Prudence Jones

Why Druids Now? 55
Philip Carr-Gomm

The Initiation 65
Vivianne Crowley

The Medicine Circle of Turtle Island 83
Greg Stafford

Pictish and Keltic Shamanism 93
Kaledon Naddair

She of Many Names 109
Beth Neilson & Imogen Cavanagh

Breaking the Circle 127
John Matthews

Of the Voices of Animals 137
Gwen Blythe

The Woman of the Birds 149
R.J. Stewart

The Weaving Goddess 165
Felicity Wombwell

In a Circle of Stone 177
Caitlín Matthews

Contributors' Biographies 195

Glossary 201

Bibliography 213

Preface

The idea of this book was conceived in September 1987. I was lying awake thinking of the unsatisfactory state of Pagan publishing and of how little of the real teachings ever reached the public. I lay wishing that someone would do something about the low public profile which the primal traditions had in Britain. As I have been trained in the practical school of 'if you want something doing, then do it yourself,' I closed my eyes and looked into that inner reality which we all have access to.

I began to visualize a great fire about which sat all the many traditions of Western Paganism. I fondly recalled the intensity of belonging which attends any meeting of Pagans who gather in a circle to share their tradition, to do magical work and to worship the gods. It seemed to me that I heard the many separate voices harmoniously blending together. This small piece of visualitive magic needed to be earthed — as a book. The title 'Voices From the Circle' leapt to mind immediately.

Although my association with Prudence Jones was of very short duration, I felt that such a book might work well with two editors to shepherd it. I had been struck by her articulate and reasoned thinking shortly before when Prudence and I had both appeared together in a BBC radio interview whose results proved very unsatisfactory. Although all contributors had given positive and stimulating interviews, stressing the beneficial and spiritual aspects of the diverse Pagan traditions, the programme's editor had cut the tape together to include interviews from hardline clergy and hearsay on the negative effects of Paganism, specifically witchcraft, on certain unbalanced individuals. This material, inserted with no right of reply, made all those interviewed sound suspect, if not downright evil.

Prudence and I were very angry about this incident, though

we were hardly surprised, since this kind of negative representation occurs frequently in both the media and the press who have their own axes to grind. They rarely enter into dialogue, but use the guerrilla tactics of hearsay and invective. It had been with great heart-searching that we had agreed to appear at all, but we had been given to believe that the programme was going, at long last, to present Paganism in its spiritual and ecumenical light.

It made us all the more determined to present a forum of informed opinion which was neither simplistic nor apologetic, but which fairly and squarely presented the contemporary Pagan world at work. Most of the books currently on the market at that time concerned themselves with naïve explanations of ritual activity or hazy justifications for spiritual belief in the Pagan gods. They seemed firmly entrenched in the serious business of vindicating Paganism as a life-affirming discipline, which necessarily made them defensive, cautious and simplistic.

Of course, for practitioners and believers working in the Pagan world, there are no such problems. We already live our beliefs, worship our gods and perform our rituals just like any other Christian, Jewish, Hindu or Moslem citizen within our constitutional rights. To us it seems perfectly natural that we should follow our spiritual path. No one thinks it sinister when a Catholic neighbour goes into a church to light a candle for her sick child, or when a Moslem friend at work goes on *haj* to Mecca, so why was it considered peculiar to light a candle to the Goddess in the evening or to go to a sacred site to observe one of the seasonal festivals?

It seemed to us that ecumenical parity hardly ever entered into the field of Western Paganism. For, while it was possible to publish, say, a collection written by Sufi writers, Aboriginal elders, Native American teachers or Shinto believers, a similar collection from Western Pagan hands was virtually unthinkable.

The conceptual problems, which will be manifest from the following introductory essay, were immense, but we persevered undaunted. Why should we not bring together a collection of diverse writers practically working in the many fields of Western Paganism, exactly as though we were putting together an anthology of mystics, theologians or philosophers? There were already enough apologists representing the Pagan tradition. Why not invite a circle of believers and writers who have made significant contributions to their field and get them to share their views, stories and traditions around the communal fire of our book?

Mystical experience is a natural phenomenon, common to all human beings. It is not reserved exclusively for the professionally religious – nuns, monks, priests and the like. The 'everyday ecstasy' of life is frequently experienced by people with no specific spiritual vocation or tradition. Whether we feel the deep joy of a sunset or the more intense wonder of love after a period of emptiness, we are fulfilling our normal human activity. It seemed that, while such experiences might be allowable in professional mystics within classified religious traditions, it was this very normality of spiritual vision that was so hard to establish within Paganism. It was the absence of any idea of 'what goes on in their heads' that made the Pagan publishing market so hollow. For Pagans are animated by ecstasy and insight just like other believers.

This book presents the relaxed, creative, mystical, anecdotal face of Paganism. It is written from within the heart of the Pagan tradition by people who have families, jobs, gardens, pets, and cars; people who work at a variety of skills such as computing, performing, weaving, teaching, psychology or writing. They are concerned with New Age or traditional values, with ecology, with the quality of inner and outer life.

Many would see themselves primarily as human beings enacting a spiritual vocation rather than as 'Pagans', for that word has its pejorative connotations in the outside world. Several contributors are fulfilling an individual spiritual vocation, while others are concurrently teaching or running groups and courses. The sole fact that they also have a spiritual persona at all marks them as unusual because our present age is not renowned for its high spiritual profile. But Paganism is not content to keep its spiritual life separate from 'the real world', it seeks to find ways of earthing its traditions in the world which we all know.

Whether readers are within or outside the Pagan tradition, they will hopefully gather a measure of the breadth and depth of our Western Pagan heritage, which does not seek to proselytize or convert, but which nevertheless abides as the basis for native spirituality.

Those who are unfamiliar with the background and history of the Pagan re-emergence will find the introduction instructive and enlightening. Unfamiliar words and concepts are illuminated in the glossary at the end of the book.

This book cannot hope to cover the full range of Western

Paganism, though we hope that it will stimulate a greater consciousness of Paganism's central contribution as a practical spiritual path. The primal traditions upon which it draws are neither evil nor recondite, but based firmly on the affirmative and creative patterns of life itself. All who have sat at the circle know this and celebrate its wisdom and serenity in their lives.

It is that sense of wonder, joy and harmony that we wish to share with you, for we have ever welcomed all people of goodwill to our fire.

May you be welcome and blessed as you enter the circle!

Caitlín Matthews
La Fheile Bride
1 February 1989

Introduction

Prudence Jones & Caitlín Matthews

The Pagan World

Western Paganism Today

The re-emergence of Paganism as a spiritual way within the West has been generally greeted with stunned disbelief or with hilarity. Paganism seems to be an impossible archaism within the twentieth-century context. What is it all about?

We had better begin by defining Paganism itself, for the word is used by insiders and outsiders in different ways. Commonly, the word 'pagan' is used to denote a person of secular interests, an unbeliever. Within the Pagan resurgence itself, 'Pagans' are people who follow the Old Religion, the native religious tradition of Europe which predates more abstract world religions such as Christianity, just as the Bön religion of Tibet predates Buddhism there. The new Pagans are also explicitly Nature-worshippers, enthusiastically espousing the root meaning of their name; *pagani*, of the countryside.

Paganism has re-emerged within Western twentieth-century society for a good reason, for though it draws upon the past, it is designed for living in the present. Its reappearance at this time is as a spiritual corrective to what many see as the headlong hurtle towards planetary destruction — a pace which has been set by Western economic ethics, with their philosophy of scarcity, competition, and the need for possession and control of natural resources. Pagans are concerned with the natural world, and also with the world of the spirit; for until the current ecological crisis, the world's major religions have not shown responsible guardianship of planetary resources.

More critically, Paganism has reappeared in the West at this time when the numinous and mystical aspects of spirituality have been suppressed. In particular we must point out the absence of the Goddess, the Divine Feminine principle, from Western spirituality ever since the demise of the native Pagan faiths. Her absence has had dubious consequences for our society, for we are a people who have grown up without their mother — a factor which is usually taken into consideration in the juvenile courts when dealing with delinquents!

So in a sense the new Pagans are neo-Pagans, since they derive their impetus from a spiritual re-emergence and restatement of ancient Pagan principles. But in another sense they are simply drawing attention to a native spirituality which has been submerged but not suppressed by the new religion (which in time-honoured fashion decried its predecessor as evil), and whose traces remain apparent in the landscape and life of the whole of Europe. So we shall not call ourselves neo-Pagans, but simply Pagans, bearers of the ancient Nature-tradition.

Paganism has been crucially important in laying the ground for the Goddess to come among us again. Under her aegis, Pagans and many others within the New Age movement, seek to restore the ancient harmonies — intellect and intuition, matter and spirit, earth and heaven, head and heart, for the Goddess naturally presides over the principle of union in Nature.

The Goddess also leads us to respect and participate in the physical world, for women are always seen as being associated with physical life, perhaps because of the unmistakably physical nature of a woman's fertility cycle, perhaps simply because most people alive today took their first physical nourishment from the breast of a woman. We are unlikely to develop a proper respect for Nature in the present ecological crisis without at the same time recognizing the divine archetype in women, the Goddess in whose image they are formed.

In its espousal of joyful, creative values, of trust in Nature and the intuition if these are rightly followed, Paganism offers a way of freedom from oppression and the strange psychic dislocation from which our world suffers. Why a return to the ancient Pagan values should have been necessary today is a long story, and it is a history which few non-Pagans have ever read. To set the record straight and to comprehend consequent developments, it is necessary to return to the beginning.

The Ancient Pagan World

The ancient world was the first to be called 'Pagan', i.e. rustic, by the newly-emerging urban Christians. Rustics, for them as for us, were country people who were out of date, still following the Old Ways. However, these particular Old Ways, the Native religions of the Mediterranean world, were in fact far from backward; indeed they had produced the sophisticated cultures of Egypt, Greece and Rome, with their arts, sciences and organized administrations. What the Christians thought was backward about their Pagan neighbours was the latter's 'idolatry', their perception of spirits in streams and rocks and groves, their acceptance of the whole process of Nature as a manifestation of divinity. Pagan deities sometimes presided over general processes such as war, inspiration, love etc., sometimes they were specific to one place, but often migrated from one place to another as their adherents recognized the same general principles at work behind different images of deity. For example, Minerva, whom we know as the Roman goddess of war and wisdom, equivalent to Greek Athene, in fact developed out of an Etruscan Underworld goddess whose festival followed the Ides of March each year. Minerva later lent her name to the cult of the goddess Sul in Bath, once the Roman Empire reached Britain. Deities changed and interchanged in a rich kaleidoscope of shifting attributions.

While remaining faithful to the basic human reaction of awe and wonder to the natural world about us, Pagan religions are nevertheless capable of as much complexity as other thought systems. One of the oldest surviving native Pagan religions, now called Hinduism, was given a name only 200 years ago (by the British, after Hindustan, the country in which this form of worship prevailed). Hinduism of course has yielded a complex corpus of theology, psychology, mathematics and cosmology which is now at last being appreciated by the dominant Western world-view. Tibetan Buddhism is another Pagan religion which has a great deal of subtle theology to offer the West. Chinese Taoism, with its yin-yang polarity and its observation of the subtle breaths and energies of Nature, is a Pagan way of being; and Shinto in Japan is basically a polytheistic Nature-venerating Pagan religion.

Around the Mediterranean there were sporadic departures from the universal Pagan religion. In Egypt in the fourteenth century BCE the pharaoh Akhenaton introduced the worship of the abstract solar deity alone. This innovation was however unsuccessful; the old religion reasserted itself after the pharaoh's death. In Persia, some time before 600 BCE, Zarathustra introduced the idea of an evil opponent of the supreme deity, and the stalemate of dualism was introduced to world thought. In Palestine, the followers of the Jewish tribal god, Yahweh, waging a bitter war for supremacy against the Canaanite Asherah and her consort Baal, developed a monotheistic cult which was enforced with the utmost rigour. In these religious experiments, modifications of the fundamental Pagan outlook, we see an increasing awareness of the importance and responsibility of the individual rather than of the community as a whole. This brought with it an emphasis on the masculine, separative principle of divinity, rather than on the feminine principle of union, and so the creative polarity of Goddess and God which brings about change in the Pagan universe was replaced by the life and death struggle of God versus anti-God, the good-evil dualism of our own dominant culture.

In the Mediterranean world at the beginning of the Christian era, personal contact with deity was being sought increasingly in the Mystery cults which were growing at the time. The Mysteries sought to put the individual worshipper into direct touch with the divine presence, and thus to change and 'perfect' the soul by awakening the latter's spiritual faculty. This search for autonomy, illumination and personal responsibility was easily able to accommodate the teachings of Jesus of Nazareth, and those Christians who preferred secrecy to martyrdom soon formed a Mystery cult alongside the others of the time. Whether this was ever the intention of their founder is of course a matter of considerable controversy.

However, it was Christianity rather than any of the other fringe religions which eventually took over from the old State Paganism. After the conversion of the Emperor Constantine in 312 CE, the cult of the emperor was easily replaced by the even more centralized worship of the Father God, whose administrator the emperor became in matters secular. Such a father god ruled entirely alone, without a council of the Olympians to speak for the other aspects of nature and human nature, and without a Mother Goddess to counterbalance his overpowering masculine image. So Christianity emphasized the isolation of the individual, following the trend of the time, but because it saw the material world as fallen, it denied that there could be any virtue in the underlying Pagan unity with nature.

However, popular cultural practices are always slow to change. So although un-Christian spiritual teachings were denounced as anathema and heresy, nevertheless the older Pagan practices continued in popular custom. The Roman midwinter feast of Saturnalia, for example, gave Christendom its chosen date for the birth of Jesus, so that the Pagan practices of feasting, misrule, decking the halls with evergreens, and other practices celebrating the return of the light, could be incorporated within the official religion rather than chafing against it. Evidently, the Pagan Nature religion would not be stamped out!

In addition, the worship of the Egyptian goddess Isis, at the time the most popular religion in the Mediterranean world, was soon incorporated into Christianity as the cult of the Virgin Mary. Elements of the Mysteries of the Great Mother and her dying and reborn son, the god Tammuz who is cut down in his prime, mourned for by his mother, and then reborn, also found echoes in the drama of the crucifixion. Hence, Pagans could see Christianity as a version of their own broader religion, and likewise they found some space within the official cult. Thus missionary Christianity was set to expand. In 410 CE the Roman Empire collapsed, and to the Roman Church fell the burden of continuing the Empire by other means.

Meanwhile in the more northerly parts of Europe, the Pagan religion still flourished in its many local forms. Gaul had been Romanized to a great extent, but in Britain the Christianity brought by the Romans soon amalgamated with the religion of the native Britons to form Celtic Christianity, including a Druidical sect, the Culdees. The original Celtic religions flourished alongside this, and were later augmented by the religions of the invading Saxons, Jutes and Angles. The religion of the warlike Celts had a strong Goddess component, as did that of the Saxons at the time of Caesar. The Celts had goddesses of war, of fertility, of magic, and of course the Mother of the Gods, Danu or Anu. There was often a local goddess of the land, and a god of the tribe, so that the tribe would 'marry' the land over which it roamed, for the Celts were largely nomadic. There were tribal gods, warriors, protectors of the people, and there were gods who were sons of mothers, specialized expressions of the goddesses. The Celts loved war, poetry and song, and lived in a magical consciousness where the Otherworld was always close at hand.

The Saxon tribes remained untouched by official Christianity until Charlemagne invaded in 772. Symbolically, he overthrew their national monument, an icon called Irminsul or the pillar of heaven, testimony to their worship of the sky god, Tiwaz. The humiliation of the Saxons is still visible in a sculpture at the site of Charlemagne's victory, depicting Irminsul itself bowed over as a footstool, receiving the body of Jesus from the cross. Irmin, Iring, Tiwaz, Thunor and the other Germanic gods, rather than goddesses, were recorded at the time, but we also know that at the time of Tacitus (c. 99CE), the Saxons had worshipped the goddess Nerthus, Mother Earth. Caesar too had told how the women of the Germanic tribes used to read the omens and were listened to by their warrior menfolk with great respect. This was worth pointing out at a time when women in Rome were relegated to home under the jurisdiction of their husbands.

Caesar also tells us that the greatest festival of the Germanic tribes took place at the time of the first winter frosts. This season is called by the Gaels Samhain, 'Summer's End'. By mediaeval times its cultic activities had become associated with the feasts of Hallowe'en and Martinmas, not to mention, in more recent times with the secular British Guy Fawkes' Night, itself a Summer's End feast of death and remembrance of the ancestors, the rightful king and his ever-reborn opponent. Samhain had a sound practical purpose, for at this time the grazing flocks and herds were brought down from the high pastures to field and byre, and any old or ailing animals had to be slaughtered in preparation for the feed shortages of winter. Even today, Pagans' Samhain bonfires consume the dead branches of autumn pruning.

There was an even more abstract purpose for the importance of Samhain. Without awareness of the coming winter and of the precautions which had to be taken against it, no tribe in these regions could survive. Death, or rather the awareness of death, was the hidden teacher which forced the tribes to develop social organization and forward planning, on pain of extinction. As Carlos Castañeda's mentor Don Juan reputedly said, it is the awareness of death which brings us to life. The festival of Summer's End, for modern Pagans especially, is an annual meditation on this fact. This is echoed in Christian culture by All Souls' Day on 2 November, when in many Catholic countries, people picnic ceremonially on the family tomb, communing with the ancestors as their Pagan forebears did, and remembering the fact of mortality.

Northern Paganism proved as difficult to eradicate as Mediterranean Paganism had been. Hence, in the seventh century Pope Gregory the Great instructed his bishops not to destroy Pagan sites but to convert them to Christian usage, so that the Pagans would have nowhere to hold their own rituals. More Pagan feasts were incorporated into the Church calendar, and so the principal Christian holiday of Easter took on the attributions of the Northern goddesses: the hare, or Easter bunny, and Easter eggs perhaps originally belonging to the goddess whom Bede called Eostre. Other customs were less easily assimilated. In the eleventh century the Christian king of Norway ordered the north door of every church to be walled up, preventing Pagan members of the congregation from gathering there and offering salute to Odin, the Lord of the Wild Hunt who had his seat in the North. The north door of a church is sometimes called the 'Devil's door' for this reason, reflecting the widespread Christian habit, dating at least from St Paul, of calling other people's gods and goddesses by the name of the Christian anti-god.

Away from this battle of the faiths, in areas such as Lapland and Siberia, where people remained nomadic, without an urban culture, traditional shamanism flourished — in some parts until this century. The shaman or shamanka, mediator between the ordinary people of the tribe and the gods, was a full-time mystic and witch-doctor (in modern terminology), whose responsibility was solely to the transpersonal realm, rather than to the proprieties of conventional life or organized religion. Such a figure defies all conventional boundaries between genius, inspiration and madness, and although pure shamanistic culture has almost died in Europe and Western Asia, that of the North American Indians is far from dead, and is re-inspiring the new Pagans of our own culture once more, as a corrective to what many see as Western society's career towards ultimate ecological destruction.

In the Christian missions of Europe, priests took part (and still do) in adapted Pagan rituals which were part and parcel of community life, such as blessing the village plough on Plough Monday (the first Monday after Twelfth Night), when it is taken out of its winter storage and paraded around the village, with mumming and merriment. In sixteenth-century Iceland the priest would lead the traditional procession around the churchyard on the Wednesday before Ascension Day, presenting the crozier to each of the eight sacred (Pagan) directions of the compass and commending the community to God (Christian) at each of them. Other ritual perambulations, 'beating the bounds', are still carried on today, usually by the parish council and often still with benefit of clergy. In the cider country of south-west England, 'wassailing' the apple trees still occurs, the trees being doused with cider and sung to, with much merriment, firing of shotguns, and subsequent drinking of the local brew. This practice was originally to ensure the fruitfulness of the cider trees in the coming year.

Few such native rituals are carried on by people of European descent in European-settled countries abroad now. For one thing the settlers often come of Protestant stock which resists such 'superstition and Popery', but mostly it is because Native religion always links the people with the land: so the gods take different forms in different places, and the remaining European rituals found no place in the new colonies. The Christian settlers, unlike their forebears in the Pagan empires of long ago, never made a connection between their religion and that of the natives of the new land. Only now are the new Pagans of European origin beginning to make the links between their own implicit tradition and the continuing tradition of the indigenous inhabitants of their adopted land. But that is to run ahead.

In Britain, official Christianity came and went with the waves of invasions. It was the Pagan revival of London and Essex from 614 to 655 which expelled Abbot Mellitus from St Paul's to Canterbury, with the result that the major see of Britain is still there rather than in London. In the early eighth century too, Redwald, King of the East Saxons, apparently recognized both religions and, according to the Venerable Bede, 'in the same temple had one altar to sacrifice to Christ, and another small one to offer victims to devils'. (By 'devils', of course, Bede means the deities of the Old Religion.) It is quite false to say that Britain has been entirely Christian and not Pagan since Roman times.

In the seventh century, pressure of population in Scandinavia led to the Viking movement, and soon Scandinavian influence had affected all the North Sea and Atlantic seaboard. The deities of the Vikings, as aggressive expansionists, were fierce, male and militaristic. Enough is known of Odin and Thor not to need rehearsing here, but less is known of the goddesses, who were 'no less sacred [than the gods] and no less powerful'. Chief amongst them seems to have been Freya, herself a deity of a more ancient pantheon adopted into the new warrior caste, and in many ways co-equal with Odin. In the twelfth century there was a resurgence of Freya worship, and on an inside wall of Schleswig cathedral is a mural from that time depicting Freya riding naked on a giant cat (a reference to her traditional chariot pulled by cats), alongside Frigga (the consort of Odin), in similar aspect, riding what appears to be a broomstick, no doubt symbolic of her role as guardian of the hearth.

Women too seem to have enjoyed a respected place in Viking society. In the *Song of Atli* we read that King Hniflungr courted Gudrun because she was 'a woman of deeds', and later in the poem she tells how she, her brothers and her husband went a-viking, each commanding their own ship. The Settlement Book of Iceland tells of a Christian lady called Aud the Deep-Minded, an Icelander who married the King of Dublin, and who after his death and that of her son Thorstein the Red sailed around the northern seas, 'with twenty free-born men aboard her ship', forging dynastic alliances and settling once more in Iceland.

We also gather from these sources that it was common for women in particular to have the second sight and to work protective spells for their friends and family. Even the Christian Aud knew when she was going to die, and held a funeral feast, at which she correctly predicted her death three days later. Such occurrences were taken as natural in Pagan society, but official Christianity declared them to be demonic, thus putting ordinary people in fear of their own human nature. The rejection of what we now call the paranormal powers of the human mind has also affected modern science, which grew up against a background of persecution by the Church, and so now our scientific model of the human psyche has no place for abilities such as Aud's foreknowledge of her death, or the second sight still common on the Celtic borders of Britain. We have had to go to countries which have retained their Pagan heritage, such as India and Japan, to seek a model of how such abilities might be possible. Our native Pagan lore is largely forgotten or else strangely unrecognized.

As Britain became England, the Danelaw, and Wales, the Anglo-Saxon kings passed laws which explicitly forbade the practices of the Pagan religion. King Edgar (959-975) ruled:

[We enjoin] that every priest zealously promote Christianity, and totally extinguish every heathendom; and forbid well worshippings and necromancies, and divinations, and enchantments, and man worshippings, and the vain practices which are carried on with various spells, and with froth-splots, and with elders and with various other trees, and with stozes, and with many various delusions, with which men do much of what they should not. And we enjoin, that on feast days there be complete abstinence from heathen songs and devil's games.

This gives a lively picture of the old Pagan practices. King Canute extends the ruling (1014):

Heathendom is, that men worship idols; that is, that they worship heathen gods, and the sun or moon, fire or rivers, water-wells or stones, or forest-trees of any kind; or love witch-craft, or promote morth-work in any wise; either by sacrifice, or divining, or perform anything pertaining to such delusions.

What we see here is the veneration of natural icons (well-worshipping etc.), the use of natural clairvoyance (necromancies, divination) and of the subtle powers of the human body and mind (enchantments, witchcraft). Such practices have arrived once more on our shores from other Native cultures, e.g. the martial arts, meditation, 'alternative' medical practices such as acupuncture, and even the newly-imported practice of fire-walking. These are accepted nowadays when brought in from overseas. However, the investigation of our own native magical arts, 'witchcraft', still raises a shudder even in the most liberal circles. The Church's later association of these with 'morth-work', ill-wishing, has sunk deeply into people's minds.

Before these practices were described as evil, however, they were dismissed as delusions. People who had visions or practised the old skills were thought to be deceived by the Devil, to be simple-minded victims rather than dangerous doers of evil. As late as 1258, Pope Alexander IV directed that his inquisitors were not to investigate cases of sorcery, which was a delusion, unless they knew for certain that heresy was also involved. From then until the famous Bull of Pope Innocent VIII, however, which in 1484 gave permission for the dreadful wave of witch hunts which was to kill an estimated nine million people, mostly women, in 200 years, the linkage between the old heathen practices of sorcery and scrying, and the deliberate worship of the Christian Devil, became more and more firmly fixed in churchmen's minds. But in fact, to worship a Devil, a cosmic principle of evil, a person must first believe in such a being; and Pagans do not.

For centuries then, the old magical practices which are common to all Pagan societies existed uneasily hand in hand with the new religion in Europe. The Pagan festivals were partly incorporated into the Church calendar, and even the Virgin Mary had taken over some of the attributes of the goddesses of the Old Religion. The agricultural year, however, could not truly be domesticated. Agricultural life is Pagan, and that is that. The eight festivals of the north European year remained as folk festivities, with or without the help of the clergy. Imbolc, the coldest season of the year, became Candlemas, but country folk in Scotland still sat up all night with last year's corn dolly, waiting for the arrival of St Bridget, i.e. the Goddess Brighid. The spring equinox became Easter, but May Eve was never tamed. In England, lads and lasses spent the night out in the woods, returning with boughs of hawthorn to 'bring in the May', and the priest could do nothing about it. In France, the local priest would sometimes lead the May procession across the fields, perhaps hoping to sanctify it in some way. Midsummer gave some of its festivities to Whitsuntide, when maidens would parade their beauty or even compete in sporting contests in order to be chosen Summer Queen, the embodiment of the Goddess for that day. Lammas, the beginning of the harvest, remained a major festival in Ireland well into this century, and the Church took over the autumn equinox as harvest home. We have already seen how Samhain Eve was assimilated into popular custom as Hallowe'en and Martinmas, and Yule of course had long since become Christmas.

In the rhythms of the land, in isolated folk customs such as the various ritual games of football, Morris dancing, cheese rolling etc., and even in underground movements the old practices prevailed. Wherever in the medieval romances we read of herbal medicine, for example, we are sure to find a reference to the Old Ways. There is a herbalist's prayer from the twelfth century, beginning:

Divine Goddess Earth, Mother of Nature, who generates all

things, and brings forth ever anew the sun which you alone show to the folk upon the earth. You are called by the loving kindness of the gods, the Great Mother, who has conquered the god of mighty name.

Here then is the Goddess, here are the healing powers of Nature, and here is the rivalry between the Old Religion and the new.

Christianity, however, was the up-and-coming religion. In the year 1000, Iceland joined its trading partners and became officially Christian. The last European country officially to adopt Christianity was Lithuania in 1386, but in Lapland, for example, Thor was informally worshipped until the eighteenth century. Further South new movements, not usually Pagan, arose, groups such as the Cathars, which the Church put down with the utmost savagery. In 1215 the Fourth Lateran Council fixed the Church's official line for the indefinite future. Spiritual experiment was forbidden, and contact with the Divine source could only be found through the sacraments of the Church. Meanwhile, as we have seen, the practical, magical, 'witchy' features of the Native religion (as opposed to its institutional features in the agricultural year), were being increasingly vilified as demonic. This process went hand in hand with a fear and hatred of human nature.

The witch-hunts which followed coincided also with the Reformation and the rise of rationalism. The Church had always attempted to suppress science as vigorously as it had attempted to suppress heresy. Perhaps as a backlash, the Reformation drastically pruned all the baroque, ceremonial trimmings of religion, including many remnants of the Old Ways. 'Popery and superstition' were condemned in the same breath, as obscurantism and enemies of free rational thought, and under Protestantism science prevailed. Perhaps the misogyny of the witch trials arose partly because women were seen as representing the hated irrationality which was also seen in organized (Catholic) religion.

Only at this late stage in the twentieth century, with the dissemination of Oriental Pagan cosmologies, can speculative scientists such as David Bohm and Rupert Sheldrake now propose a model of the cosmos which contains a mixture of the religious and the scientific outlooks. Pagans of the European tradition can only applaud this development.

The free spirit of enquiry was also exercised itself in more intuitive ways. The Renaissance brought Classical Pagan texts and artefacts to Christian Europe, and the Hermetic movement began. Divorced from a religious cosmology, Hermetic rituals were sometimes adapted to Christianity, at other times conducted in a world of their own, but never, it seems, fused with the native religion. The opposite process did take place, however, and the professional cunning men of the eighteenth and nineteenth centuries certainly made use of Qabalistic and alchemical rituals.

The English Civil War removed many of the festivals of 'Popery and superstition'. Survivals of the Old Ways disappeared, never to return. For example the familiar white-dressed Morris men were once accompanied by a line of male dancers: the Green Man, the Boy, the Hobby-Horse etc., and also by a line of women: Maid Marian, the Old Crone, and so on. After the Restoration, the women's line never returned. However, the Restoration was at least within living memory of the richer traditions of the past, and some of these were reinstituted.

The Enlightenment can be seen as a reaction against the emotional and fanatical excesses of previous centuries. Witchcraft was soon completely disbelieved in, and the Native tradition largely scorned. Individual wise women and cunning men, hereditary practitioners of the ancient skills, pepper the history of these centuries, from Old Mother Shipton, the sixteenth-century prophetess of Knaresborough, through the Hermeticist Dr John Dee, astrologer to the Crown, to Daddy Witch, the wise woman of Horseheath, who at her death was buried in the middle of the road, and Cunning Murrell, the nineteenth-century magician, herbalist and diviner. The last execution of a witch in England took place in 1735. The old skills were practised only by desperate and poverty-stricken peasants who could not afford better solutions to their ills; the old celebrations continued, but were despised as rustic.

The educated classes, however, were now well-versed in the Pagan outlook of Greece and Rome, and peasant life was sometimes romanticized as an 'Arcadian idyll', e.g. in the landscaping of country estates. Pagan religion too was sought after: the notorious Hellfire Club of Lord Francis Dashwood seems to have included aspects of the Greek Mysteries of the Goddess as well as those of the Christian anti-God. Hermeticism flourished too, with several Druidic foundations on the lines of Freemasonry. Poets took up the cause of ecstatic religion through the Romantic revival and the *Sturm und Drang*, on to Kenneth Graham, D.H. Lawrence and the self-styled Pagan poets of the twentieth century. Drugs and other bizarre experiences were often part of this movement, a way of leaping the widening gap between objective, rational consensus reality and the newly-marginalized subjective world of ecstatic experience. But others have bridged rather than leapt that gulf.

Nature mysticism, in particular, has been a part of British and to a lesser extent German culture since the Reformation. The re-emergence of native Paganism, as opposed to the Classical variety, follows a long Nature tradition in the Anglo-Saxon world. The Metaphysical Poets of Tudor and Stuart England, Shakespeare himself, Thomas Traherne, William Law, the nineteenth-century farmer Richard Jeffries, all gained spiritual insight through meditating on Nature. Jeffries, who described himself as an atheist, wrote:

> *Realizing that spirit, recognizing my own inner consciousness, the psyche, so clearly, I cannot understand time. It is eternity now. I am in the midst of it. It is about me in the sunshine; I am in it, as the butterfly floats in the light-laden air. Now is eternity; now is the immortal life. Here this moment, by this tumulus, on earth, now; I exist in it. To the soul there is no past and no future; all is and will be ever, in now. For artificial purposes time is mutually agreed on, but there is really no such thing.*

The search for this kind of experience has carried right through the twentieth century, the hippy movement and the 'good life', to the modern Western revival. More enquirers write to the Pagan periodicals describing personal experiences (or inklings) of union with Nature, than for any other reason. It is an aspect of Paganism quite independent of any dogmatic or ritual framework, facilitated only by reverence for Nature and a willingness to learn from Her. It brings with itself its own purity: there is no fear of ritual sacrifice or brow-beaten superstition here, because it is an experience of resolution, of that harmony of opposites which expresses the love that binds the universe.

The Recent Roots

The intellectual climate of the late nineteenth century thus contained not only Christianity and the secular faith of social Darwinism (evolutionary meliorism), with the remnants of native skills and the festivals of the agricultural year, plus a sophisticated overlay of the Classical Mysteries and Hermetic magic; but also Spiritualism and Theosophy, a version of Hindu and Buddhist esoteric teaching brought to Europe by H.P. Blavatsky in the 1860s. Psychical research sprang up, under scientific auspices. Celtic studies arose, mostly pursued by folklorists, archaeologists and linguists using the techniques of sound scholarship without any practical esoteric interest in the Celtic field. Alternatives to the Christian worldview abounded.

The Hermetic Order of the Golden Dawn, set up in 1888, incorporated Celtic scholarship and recreated magic, Hermetic, Middle Eastern and Rosicrucian (Masonic) theory, and though not in itself Pagan, it included Egyptian god forms in its ritual structures. It provided a systematic account of the processes of magic and the structure of the psyche. Dion Fortune, a relatively late graduate of the Order, not only pursued her own brand of esoteric Christianity in the orders she set up afterwards, but through her novels gave a powerful impetus to the forthcoming Pagan movement. She called this impulse the 'Green Ray', the spirit of Nature worship, relating it back to Greek religion and to the Celtic tradition.

Other researchers followed the Saxon and Nordic paths, usually with less interest in magic than the Celtic scholars. These two strands of British identity were seen as quite distinct, the Celts sometimes being portrayed as much more peace-loving than in fact they were. William Morris translated some of the Norse sagas, and strong feelings of fellowship between Britain and the Nordic-Germanic nations grew up, based on romanticized history, with overtones of mystical nationalism. Folk-song began to be collected, Morris dancing to be revived where it had not exactly survived, and generally the living heritage of the Old Ways began to be glimpsed as what it was.

As Freudian psychology arose in the early years of the twentieth century to bridge the widening gap between intellect and intuition, interest in the primitive power of 'the unconscious' arose, a scientifically respectable way of probing the mysteries of atavism. The analytical psychology of Jung, though slower to become popular than Freudian psychoanalysis, basically trusted the intuition, which suited would-be Pagans better than did Freud. Jung also emphasized two other psychological processes: the importance of integrating ego and shadow, i.e. one's preferred self and one's unacceptable qualities; and the necessity for the 'sacred marriage' of the male and female images in one's own psyche to complete the process of becoming whole. These two prescriptions echo the processes of the ancient Mystery religions, and are readily harmonized with their modern successors.

Anthropology was also flourishing in the late nineteenth century. Charles Godfrey Leland, an American journalist living and working in Europe, published the beliefs and rituals of some surviving witches from Tuscany, which have since been incorporated into the modern Wiccan Charge of the Goddess, quoted in Vivianne Crowley's article, p. 78. In the cause of pure scholarship, W.H. Evans-Wentz was publishing his research on Celtic and Tibetan religion, and J.G. Frazer his findings about ancient fertility ritual and its modern survivals. These findings made new models of religion available, more suited to the remnants of European Paganism than the Christian model which had dominated hitherto.

The rituals and beliefs recorded by proponents of Frazer's theories have had some influence on modern Wicca, which is thus in many ways a revival of the Mysteries of the Great Mother. Gerald Gardner, the man who brought Wicca into the public eye after the repeal of the last Witchcraft Act in 1951, was a devotee of the Goddess and in 1941 had published his first novel, *A Goddess Arrives*, on the cult of Aphrodite in Cyprus. Gardner suspected that he himself, like the hero of his novel, had in a previous life been a weaponsmith in Cyprus, at a time when Aphrodite, goddess of love, art *and* war, was the national deity. Although Gardner later added elements from traditional witchcraft, which had survived or been revived in the New Forest area, and also from Freemasonry and the magic of the Golden Dawn, the devotional Goddess worship which was and remains a feature of Gardnerian Wicca is unmistakably delineated in that first novel.

Frazer and his followers spanned the last decade of the nineteenth century and the first two decades of this, thus bringing us up to the First World War, a social cataclysm which did a great deal to destroy local traditions in the countries involved, but also, through the development of travel and communications technology, speeding up the process of turning the world into a global village.

In 1921 the distinguished Egyptologist Margaret Murray published her book *The Witch-Cult in Western Europe*, arguing that the people accused of witchcraft in medieval and Renaissance times were not diabolists at all, but followers of the Old Religion. As we have seen, there was some truth in this, but unfortunately, since Professor Murray accepted the evidence of the witch trials, extracted under torture, her conclusions have been heavily criticized. They struck a chord in the psyche of twentieth-century Europe nevertheless, and together with poet Robert Graves' *The White Goddess* provided theoretical backing for the religious choice of the new witches of the 1950s who appeared after the repeal of the Witchcraft Act.

Gardner's new cult, known as 'Wicca', enjoyed great popularity and attracted some rivalry. Its mirroring of the simple life of the naked forest and savanna dwellers with whom the ordinary people of Britain, and not just Colonial administrators like Gardner himself, had come into contact through National Service in the Second World War, might have had some appeal, and in the climate of post-war austerity the glamour of Wicca was no doubt attractive. Perhaps its status as the 'Old Religion' provided a sense of continuity which in outer life the two World Wars had swept away. But most of all, Wicca's veneration of the Goddess, robustly counterbalanced by the Horned God Pan, but central nevertheless, was not only based on Gardner's own mystical contact, a necessary beginning for any religion, but it also answered what was to become a pressing need of the times as the emancipation of women proceeded.

One Trunk, Many Branches

The 1960s saw a rise in awareness of other religions and cosmologies in the English-speaking world. This expansion of consciousness was partially aided by some people's experience of instant insight through drugs which artificially accelerated areas of spiritual insight which might have developed eventually but much more slowly without such a catalyst. The Sixties brought a greater freedom in lifestyle than, perhaps, ever before. The old rules of outer behaviour were no longer sufficient, and the spread of higher education created a generation of people who expected to make up their own minds. Personal experience of the divine or transpersonal realm was recognized as not only possible, but also important, and the new generation became committed to building the future on a radically new foundation, linking subjectivity and objectivity, benevolence and clearsightedness, religion and the secular life, scepticism and certainty.

After Gardner's death in 1964, other traditions of Wicca emerged or were founded, and the umbrella organizations followed in Europe and the USA. In 1975 and 1976, the leaders of two of the main Druid orders died, signalling a shift towards incorporating the recent work of Celtic scholars into this reworked tradition, resulting in more authentic forms and in practical applications. In 1974 the Nordic Old Religion was legally reinstated in Iceland, a country which now has two established faiths. At the same time Asatrú foundations sprang up in Britain and the USA, as this particular spiritual path started to emerge not only from its containment within folklore, but from its unfortunate political entanglements earlier this century.

By the mid-1970s too, three major shifts in the general outlook had taken place. First, the women's movement had matured, and women were discovering the ancient religions of the Goddess, mentioned at the beginning of this section. The Goddess is of prime importance in many Pagan groups, especially in the Craft, as a corrective to the prevailing predominance in orthodox spiritualities of the Male Principle. In Dianic groups, where only women convene, it is solely the Goddess who is venerated. Many, many women, in the last 20-30 years, have reconstructed and reaffirmed the Goddess's mysteries. They have been breakers of boundaries, realizers of long-suppressed dreams, and the inspiration for many other women whose spiritual potential has had no outlet within the religions of revelation where there is no female ministry.

Secondly, Earth Mysteries research had a growing following, spreading general awareness of the sophistication of ancient technology. People started to look at the ancient Britons with fresh eyes, willing to study, observe and record the energy levels, alignments and astrophysical computations of stone circles, pillar-stones and earthworks. The ancient world was no longer dismissed as merely primitive, and some groups started to take their work to the level of guardianship of their country's sacred sites. Most Pagan groups try to celebrate at such hallowed centres and many have a healthy interest in Earth Mysteries as they interrelate with their native spiritual tradition. Thus the continuity of spiritual experience is reaffirmed.

The third shift in consciousness of the Seventies was that acupuncture and many other techniques of alternative medicine aroused general interest. These involve working *with* the healing powers of the body and mind rather than primarily working *against* what has gone wrong with the system, as is the usual way of Western medicine. The 'gentle way' of Oriental fighting arts taught Westerners to follow the body rather than to defy it, as in boxing. Similarly, the Human Potential movement and its 'growth groups' promoted trust in the potential rightness of all psychological processes, and gave training in methods of releasing their healing power. Such skilful trust in Nature is the essence of the Pagan outlook.

Although it might seem that the Pagan resurgence is part of the New Age movement generally, in reality the New Age community, with its own therapies and spiritual diversities, has frequently been averse to association with Paganism, seeing it as atavistic and spiritually unclean. Yet Paganism, derived like many New Age groups from ancient spiritual principles, is at least as concerned with practical application of these principles as is any of its more ethereal neighbours, though it sees the rigid avoidance of 'uncleanliness' as suggesting problems with the Shadow (see p. 28 above) which need examining.

The completely new outlook developed in the 1960s and 1970s could not be entirely satisfied by any of the organized religions. Suddenly the distant past (indigenous Paganism), the recent past (Druidry, Wicca, Oriental mysticism), and the spiritual and philosophical needs of the future were seen as a continuum. They are the Pagan heritage of Europe, indeed of humankind.

Within the past five to 10 years too, the growing influence of two brands of native tradition have been experienced throughout the West; Shamanism and the traditions of the Native American tribes. Shamanism is currently the popular mode of Pagan awareness. Deriving from very many world traditions familiar also from the novels of Carlos Castañeda, Shamanism has none of the opprobrium currently attached to the term 'witchcraft'. It is also of more interest to the many lone individuals who do not feel drawn to a group. With its practices, based in techniques of consciousness changing, of walking between the worlds, of healing and wholistic insight, it is rapidly becoming the most popular brand of Paganism, and already its techniques are being synthesized into Pagan groups.

Of like influence are the traditions of the Native Americans.

Not before time, people have begun to wake up to the fact that native traditions are still being practised in the world by native tribes who also speak English. The Native Americans, despised and persecuted for the last 200 years, still possess their ancestral heritage and have, in most cases, direct traditional memory and lore connecting them to it. This is not the case for those pursuing, say, the Celtic or Saxon traditions who stand at an historical remove of up to 1,400 years!

The particular problems of Westerners adapting or being permitted access to these traditions are being addressed by both white and Native Americans of pure and mixed blood. Whatever is publicly taught by such exemplars of the Native way is necessarily in the process of adaptation for the Westerner who does not live in a tribal society and has no personal experience of non-consumerism. The lessons of the Native American way are being seized by many as the ultimate corrective to Western society's mad career towards ecological destruction. Indeed, it is with salutary humility that we should acknowledge the wisdom of this way, its exponents are, after all, possessed of an immediate tradition which has never had to be reformed because it has never been deformed.

The same might be said of the Aboriginal peoples of Australia and the Maoris of New Zealand: both are natives of lands in which a white population predominates but many are slowly coming to find relevance in these despised Native traditions.

It is almost impossible to chart the rapid expansion of Pagan groups at the present time. Such an overview might be written if the editors were to return in a few incarnations' time, but currently events are moving too fast. A brief glimpse of Margot Adler's *Drawing Down the Moon*, a survey of Pagan groups in the United States, will show that diversity is the order of the day.

Pagans are spiritual seekers who have found viable ways of marrying their spirituality to their everyday lives. And since Paganism allows for individual expression and mythological preference, there will perhaps never be a set of codified traditions.

The Family Likeness

What then are the family likenesses, the factors which differentiate Pagans from the mainstream religions of the present world culture?

One major impetus towards Paganism has undoubtedly been the repressive nature of monotheistic religion, which has distanced its faithful from the source of spiritual power. Contemporary Pagan individuals and groups on the other hand are typified by their easy access to the gods. They are directly in touch with their deities in a way which has been forgotten since the medieval rulings which placed Christian salvation in the hands of the clergy, and the materialistic science which arose as their heir. Paganism has taken the reins of spiritual power into its own hands. It recognizes that for each person contact with divinity is possible. The rituals and disciplines of the closed groups may help this process along; and equally some individuals may choose to serve this power of mediation constantly, taking on the social role of priest of priestess. But there is nothing to prevent any one individual from making that connection and sustaining it.

Most Pagans are well in touch with their own potential for spirituality, creativity and insight. There is no 'sin' about performing a ceremony without the expert assistance of a specially ordained priest or priestess. The society of the spectacle, in which passive onlookers observe the goings on of the influential and powerful, is completely ignored by Pagans. They make their own entertainment, they make their own happenings. Paganism has removed the restraints from the imaginal and creative realms, with a resulting freedom of spiritual expression which is wonderful to experience.

One of the chief factors in this loosening up process has been the return of the Goddess to Western consciousness. The last two thousand years in the West, with only the Divine Masculine as a source of symbolic reference, has led to psychological dependence on a hierarchical authority which restricts personal abilities and desires to a fraction of their potential.

The search for the ancient wisdom leads Pagans into communion with the gods: a concept of polytheism at which outsiders baulk. But there are very few monotheistic religions in the world. Christianity has a triple-aspected male deity, an unavowed goddess figure, and a vast number of saints: Buddhism acknowledges the multidimensional manifestations of the buddhic nature: even mystical Judaism sees the aspects of God through his angelic emanations. The Native traditions perceive a variety of deities, and they also acknowledge a divine source. But strikingly, the polarity of the Goddess and the God in Pagan religion allows for the creative resolution of any dilemma through the interplay of equal and opposite principles, in contrast to the requirement of merely accurate submission to the One True Way which all too easily characterizes monotheistic, hierarchical religion.

What differentiates the Pagan vision is its ecstatic and wholistic character. Theodore Roszak wrote in his illuminating *Where the Wasteland Ends* (New York; Anchor Books, 1979):

> *Prejudice and ethnocentricism aside, what we know for a fact is that, outside our narrow cultural experience, in religious rites both sophisticated and primitive, human beings have been able to achieve a sacramental vision of being, and that this may well be the wellspring of human spiritual consciousness. From that rich source there flow countless religious and philosophic traditions. The difference between these traditions — between Eskimo shamanism and medieval alchemy, between Celtic druidism and Buddhist Tantra — are many; but an essential magical worldview is common to them all. This diverse family of religions and philosophies (represents) the Old Gnosis — the old way of knowing which delighted in finding the sacred in the profane. I regard it as the essential and supreme impulse of the religious life. This is not, of course, religion as many people in our society know it. It is a visionary style of knowledge, not a theological one; its proper language is myth and ritual; its foundation is rapture, not faith and doctrine; and its experience of nature is one of living communion.*

For Pagans, there is no division between matter and spirit. The sacred and the holy are all about us, they are realizable dimensions. The reintegration of spirit and matter is one of the tasks which the Native tradition has set itself, a necessary corrective to the desacralization of the Western world, and indeed of the Eastern world too, where Western economic ethics have been emulated to the detriment of the planet.

The interpenetration of the worlds of the spirit and of creation is an age-old awareness which has been lost sight of in this century. For the medieval magician, magic was the Great Work which brought the macrocosm and the microcosm into harmony with each other. Within the surviving native traditions, we see a mature appreciation both of the created world and the uncreated worlds which is both healthy and moral. It is only among the desacralized civilizations of the West that we see alarming signs of spiritual erosion and perhaps true barbarism.

To ignore the Otherworld — whether one thinks of it as the Inner Planes or Paradise — is very dangerous. Esoterically speaking, all ideas, aspirations and creative actions are born 'on the Inner': humankind is the dreamer, the artist, the shaper who manifests these archetypal urgings. Paganism, along with many other esoterically active groupings, understands and promotes this idea. For unless the heart is first activated and the spiritual purpose understood, no amount of political activism will ever change the world.

Seeing Nature as an expression of divinity means that Pagans naturally have an ecological awareness of the globe. The new Pagans were the first Westerners to incorporate 'green' priorities into their religion: not just by becoming Friends of the Earth but by performing rituals to alleviate starvation, resistance to world peace, and ecological ruin. Pagans in traditional cultures, such as the Native Americans, have been uniformly horrified at the dominant Western culture's abusive attitude towards Nature. The seasonal festivities of Pagan religion, from the eight festivals of the north European year to the differing Native cycles elsewhere in the world, where the climate is not that of Europe, seek to harmonize human activities with the natural rhythms of the cosmos.

Most Pagans also practise some form of meditation, keeping in touch both with the worlds within and with their own spiritual condition. Many practise life-enhancing disciplines and therapies which help them become effective practitioners of their tradition. Without such regular meditation, it is recognized that one is likely to stray from one's spiritual tradition. Such forms of self-knowledge have been a part of all religious paths, from the Apollonian dictum, 'know thyself', to the practice of self-examination within Christianity.

Pagans are also typified by their sense of tribal in-gathering. Most groups meet in circles, a shape conducive to the fluid, informal and yet balanced nature of Pagan spirituality. The great warmth of Paganism which many experience on initiation is reconstituted every time the circle reforms: a mutual bond of love and trust which transcends individual prejudice and dissolves any sense of incongruity or reserve brought in from the desacralized cosmos. And, as in all families, sometimes this accord breaks down into squabbles and downright rows where people walk out, vowing never to return. But such things are normal. Those who sit about the circle bring with them their own unique vision — a vision which each is prepared to substantiate and make manifest if possible. When the time finally comes to share these visions and enter a greater circle, the challenge will then be to find a closer communion with each other.

The Shape of the Circle

About the circle convened in this book are seated a variety of practitioners, priestesses, priests, mediators, and spiritual teachers. Each has his or her own tradition and approach. The insights which they share with us are imparted within the consecrated and demarked meeting place of the circle, the place between the worlds, where the inner and outer worlds conjoin.

Prudence Jones draws attention to the layout of the circle in which we find ourselves Having a sense of direction — both geographically and spiritually — is fundamental to Pagans. Aligning ourselves with the structure of the universe as it impinges upon us is part of the Great Work of harmonizing the outer and inner worlds. As Prudence points out, the Pagan cultures of northern Europe did this deliberately and with some precision, a part of our heritage that most of us have forgotten. Some of the forgotten myths of our culture are recounted here to show how the landscape itself displays the ritual circle's structure as a living mandala, a symbol of wholeness.

Philip Carr-Gomm addresses the problem of re-evaluating one's own tradition. Everyone needs to make periodic assessments of this kind, at least once a year, to establish where one is going: otherwise it is easy to fall into self-complacency and spiritual sloth. Philip goes back to his first experience of sitting in a circle with the Order of Bards, Ovates and Druids. Both he and Vivianne Crowley, whose essay follows his, record the risible and often absurd feeling which comes over most initiates when they first begin esoteric work. The feeling 'what the hell am I doing here, and who are these people anyway?' comes over everyone at one time or another. But in all of us reverence and absurdity are poles against which we measure our tradition. Being able to laugh at one's tradition keeps one's feet on the ground. If we can both love it and laugh kindly at it, then we are truly part of an extended family.

Vivianne Crowley has written about the nature of initiation from the unusual viewpoint of the initiator. Her revealing and humorous piece shows how the high priestess about to 'bring in' an initiate to her circle, must remain completely responsive to the flow of events. From the standpoint of the initiate or the outsider, an experienced practitioner, such as a priest or priestess, may appear to be possessed of great dignity and wisdom, but each was once a nervous initiate trembling at the edge of the circle. Vivianne shows the vulnerability of the priestess, preparing to take responsibility for the new initiate, for contrary to received opinion the Craft does not pull people off the street and make witches of them willy-nilly. Seekers are only accepted after long scrutiny for suitability for they have to be worthy members of the spiritual family. Although the onlooker to a ritual sees only the robes, the incense and the ritual implements, in this essay we gain insight into the participant's direct experience of the inner worlds, of the heart of the circle.

Greg Stafford makes connection with the physicality of the native tradition through the abnegation and physical discomfort of the Native American sweat-lodge. This method of purification was once part of north-west European culture also: saunas are a degenerate echo of this discipline. Here we enter into the experience of the medicine wheel, a great sharing which the Native Americans recall when they enter and leave the lodge saying, 'For all my relations'. This too is the responsibility of the initiate: to undergo and to enhance the hidden unity of all beings.

Kaledon Naddair writes about the initiatory shamanism of the Picts and Kelts (his preferred spelling). His extraordinary experiences show the vast range of abilities which a shaman must employ. His article challenges armchair shamanism and indeed the urban Paganism of many in the present resurgence. The Pagan symbolism of the seasonal ceremonies, performed to aid the natural world and redress the balance of the year, implies that practitioners must remain in touch with the turning of the seasons, and questions whether they can rightly choose to spend their lives in cities.

Imogen Cavanagh and Beth Neilson explore the nature of the threefold Goddess and share the experience of living through the eight festivals of the Pagan year. For those who follow a sacred order, the year takes on a meaning, shape and texture which colours their lives. Here, Imogen reveals the threefold patterning of the Goddess in her own daily life, taking the moods of Brighid, of the Queen of Elfland, and of Cerridwen, as mediators.

John Matthews writes poetically about the Traditional Craft. His article brings up the question of secrecy within the native traditions. Only 38 years ago as of writing (in 1989), the Witchcraft Act still obtained. Unlike the more relaxed and open attitude of the groups which have formed since the re-emergence, Traditional groups, here as elsewhere, still carry a deeply-dyed residue of caution about sharing their traditions with newcomers, and some are now dying out through inability either to transmit their inheritance or to find some new means of adaptation. The timeless quality of John's essay, with its atavistic power and archaic ritual, could as easily convey a scene in the Foretime as in the mid-twentieth century. This is a solitary voice, which now speaks so softly that the rest of the circle now has to bend to hear it at all.

Gwen Blythe writes about the kingdom of the power animal, the totem beast, reminding us that other species too belong in our circle: not the wild animals which live in our forests, but the bearers of ancient heraldic tradition, emblems of the resources of the Otherworld. Although our ancestors lived off the world's resources, they also acknowledged their own share in the planet's ecology, and to this the totem animal is a guide. For those Pagans humble and whole enough to hear them, the voices of the animals offer sure help and powerful guidance.

At the circle there always sits at least one story-teller and singer. R.J. Stewart tells us about the Woman of the Birds in a story based in the Foretime, whose strange, archaic lore is mysteriously linked to our century. It is the creative openness of the artist, musician and story-teller which forges such a link, creating a kind of time corridor down which passed the hidden meaning of the oral tradition. We find ourselves touched by an inspiration not our own, a helping inner spirit which the Greeks knew as the daimon. Here the teachings of the Woman of the Birds may wake a resonance in the mind of those who cannot now be trained by a wise and venerable teacher such as she.

Felicity Wombwell, working with the symbolism of the fourfold Goddess, in contrast to the threefold Goddess of Imogen Cavanagh and Beth Nielsen, here shows how the Old Ways can be rediscovered and restated in utterly practical terms. Her process of inner discovery is available to anyone who is willing to trust their instincts and practise their meditation regularly. Here, the Goddess touches the mundane level of life as powerfully as she does the meditative and magical levels. In a variety of ways, women are approaching the Divine Feminine, and in the process breaking down the tidy barriers which have kept spiritual experience hutched conveniently away from life's real concerns.

In Caitlín Matthews' reflective essay, the component parts of the circle are examined in the light of ancient and modern tradition. Tradition is never static: it must be challenged and reshaped anew by each who would work within it. We may learn from our elders, but each person sitting at the circle must find the animating principles of what they have been taught, and try them anew in the fires of daily life. Whether we stand as new initiate or venerable sage, it is as bearers of tradition that we leave the circle. Caitlín prophesies a time when, with imagination and insight, the circle will indeed be greater.

Our own age, with its technological advances, has not been balanced by respect for the natural wisdom of the planet. The cult of reason too has virtually dismantled the mystical traditions of revealed religion, leaving a spiritual desert in our time. It is in answer to these twin needs that our Pagan tradition has found a new form, of which the people who write in these pages are some of the shapers.

Some people have feared that the new Paganism is an atavistic regression, a flight from the stresses of modern life to some imagined haven of primitive simplicity. This is far from being the case. Paganism also involves an exploration of the creative and mystical capacities of the human mind. Although we may contact our roots by investigating ancient techniques such as the alignment of stars in stone circles, or the shamanic method of walking between the worlds, the idea that Pagans must therefore accept animal or human sacrifice, methods of cursing and ill-wishing, is as ludicrous as the corresponding belief that 'true' Christians really ought to return to the burning of heretics or the crucifixion of disobedient monks, as happened in the Middle Ages.

In looking to our ancestral heritage, we are seeking a spiritual communion with the natural wisdom of the universe. We wish to be the inheritors of what is good, wise and practical for our own times. That is the legacy we shall pass on to our children.

Declaration of Principles

The Pagan religions of Europe, including Druidism, Wicca and Asatrú, are not derived from Christianity and have nothing to do with Satanism, which is a perversion of Christianity, but are an independent religious path, celebrating the Godhead, which all religions seek to contact, particularly in its feminine form of the Great Goddess, Mother of all things. Pagans recognize the divinity of Nature and of all living things. Accordingly, they do not condone blood sacrifice, rape, child abuse, substance abuse or any other activity which would violate the integrity of another living being, but on the contrary would seek to help and protect anyone who had been the victim of such practices.

In particular, black magicians, who wilfully inflict harm on others, are not Wiccans, whatever they may call themselves. Nor do Pagans of any kind draw their power from the Christian Devil. Witches and other Pagans use the natural forces of the mind and the earth for healing and rebalancing, exactly as do Oriental practitioners of meditation, yoga and alternative medicine.

The ancient Nature religions of Europe and around the world have arisen once more in our day to help heal the rift between humankind and our planet. They are working for balance and for harmony, and it behoves us all to help bring the wisdom of the Old Ways into the light in a worthwhile and workable form for the New Age.

Adapted from a declaration issued by Morning Glory Zell of the Church of All Worlds.

Circles of Earth, Circles of Heaven

Prudence Jones

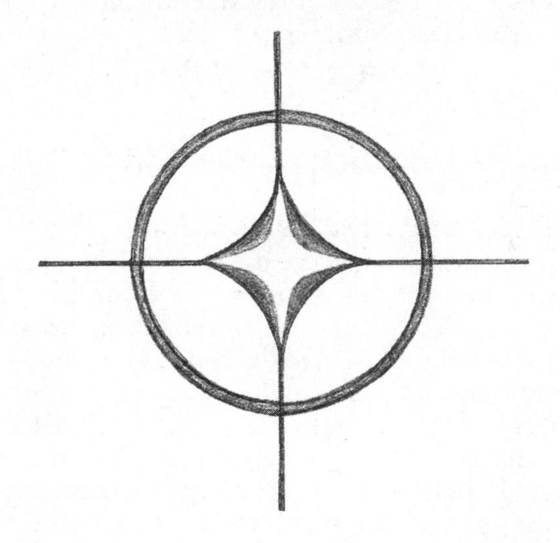

All are but part of one stupendous Whole,
Whose body Nature is, and God, the Soul

Alexander Pope

Why, we might ask, do meditative and magical groups generally work in a circle marked at the four cardinal points of North, South, East and West? What is being imaged by such a sacred space? Why the circle, why the cross? Psychologically, the circle is a place set apart, and yet in its quartering, as we shall see, it is not subjective at all, but a place totally integrated with the rest of the cosmos. Circles for ritual or meditation, celebration or discussion, are always aligned with the four points of the compass. Why? Each of these four quarter points has a symbolic guardian, symbolic attributes. Why? Surely these traditions came from nineteenth-century ceremonial magic: is it worth

Pagans continuing them? Is it even true to say, as a ceremonial magician said to me once, that orientation is purely a matter of personal choice, that for ritual purposes any old compass direction can be taken as, say, East in the circle? In fact it is not. To say this is to overlook a very precise and concrete set of correspondences in the world around us, which locate us in space and in time, and so underlie any possible kind of ritual or myth which attempts to put the isolated human being (or community) back into harmony with the greater rhythms of the universe. These correspondences underpin not only astronomy and geography, but also any religious explanation of the world.

Celestial Orientation of the Circle

Imagine setting up a circle, say in a clearing in a forest. Tie a rope to a knife or a sharpened stick, fix this into the centre of the chosen place, and trace out a circle around it, as broad as we need it to be. Now from the point in the centre of the circle, look up through the clearing to the North Star, sometimes called the leading star, mark star, or lode star. In our time it is the star at the end of the tail of the Little Bear, a constellation called by the Anglo-Saxons Our Lady's Wain. It is the star which almost exactly marks the centre of the turning heavens. The point on the ground directly below that centre is the north point of our circle. Opposite it, on a line drawn through the central dagger, is the south point, and at right angles to this line, on their own axis through the centre, are the east and west points. The circle is now aligned with the cardinal points of the heavens, and of course with the cardinal points of the visible horizon, as we would see if our circle were out in the open on a hilltop. Indeed it is, to all intents and purposes, at the very centre of the visible universe.

The circle we have created is thus a focal point of all the energies of the cosmos, channelled in towards us and out away from us along the four royal roads, once so-called, leading to the cardinal points of the compass, the roads which link earth with heaven. If we look in more detail at the stars now, we will see that our north point is always aligned with the North Star far above it, but that during the course of our meeting, the other three points of our circle and our horizon stay constant against a shifting background of constellations. The northern road leads to the North Star, but the other three roads seem to lead to nowhere in particular.

Yet if we abstract ourselves from this particular time and this particular horizon, and consider the sun's yearly path, the ecliptic, through the belt constellations known as the Zodiac, we realize that this too has its four corners, the places where the sun is found at each of the solstices and the equinoxes. These are also called cardinals, but they are the cardinal points of the year, not of the compass, and they give us not our location in space but our location in time, our proximity to the four great solar feasts of Yule, Easter, Midsummer and Michaelmas. Once a day, in any location in the northern hemisphere, these cardinal points of the year line up with the cardinal points of the horizon, with the spring equinox point due East, the winter solstice point high above the southern horizon, the autumn equinox point in the West, and the summer solstice point invisible below the horizon to the North. This is the magic hour, when the worlds of earth and heaven are in alignment, when the paths which quarter our circle, leading out along the royal roads of the horizon, stretch out to the cardinal points of time itself, the turning points of the solar year which are the solstice and equinox points of the Zodiac.

Now imagine that our meeting in the wood has taken place on the eve of the spring equinox, 20 March. Having danced and feasted all night, we brew a final cup of coffee and file out to the eastern edge of the trees in order to watch the sunrise. From the east point of the horizon, arching over the southern sky, the great path of the constellations of the ecliptic rises above us. The stars above the eastern point are the constellation of Aquarius, the water carrier. As the slow dawn rises before the sun itself, we can no longer see the stars that accompany the sun at its moment of rising, but we are told that they are somewhere right at the end of the constellation Pisces. This celestial point, the border of Aquarius and Pisces, was called by medieval astrologers the Greater Fortune, but nowadays we know it as the dawning of the Age of Aquarius.

Roughly 2,000 years ago, observers would have seen the spring equinox sun accompanied by the last stars in the constellation Aries; 4,000 years ago, by the final stars of Taurus; and so on. The spring equinox point, or indeed any of the other three cardinals, when observed over generations, locates us, on an even greater time-scale.

Six thousand years ago, the spring equinox point lay on the edge of the constellation of Taurus, where the Milky Way, arching through the northern heavens, cuts the ecliptic in the East. The autumn equinox point opposite it was then on the edge of the constellation Scorpio, where the Milky Way cuts the ecliptic in the western sky. At sunset on the eve of the spring equinox and sunrise on the day itself, not only were the quarters of the circle and the horizon lined up with the quarters of the year, the solstice and equinox points, but two of these year points were linked by the great arch of the Milky Way. As the sun set on the west point of the horizon, the Milky Way would build up in the darkness rising from the East, arching overhead and then dropping down below the western horizon, forming a bridge across the whole circle a few minutes after sunset. And next morning just before sunrise, having swung back and forth across the circle with the movement of the Zodiac, the Milky Way would be back in place, forming a bridge from the West to the growing light of the East. Now that phenomenon would have been worth seeing.

Is it coincidental then that 6,000 years ago the first standing stones were erected, precursors of the great stone circles of Europe, so many of which mark the rising and setting points of sun, moon and stars?

The ritual circle, the temple precinct, the sacred space, is thus not a place arbitrarily set apart from the realities of the world, but on the contrary is truly aligned with the essence of the world as we perceive it through the celestial and geographical coordinates of North, South, East and West.

Settlements patterned on cosmos

Many Pagan cultures attempted to model what we would now call their secular affairs on the sacred model of the quartered square or circle, having the main streets of settlements running North-South and East-West, as the Swedish Vikings did in Birka, or in Irish fashion with the four provinces of Ulster, Leinster, Munster and Connaught lying around the central province of Meath, whose capital was the holy city of Tara.

The pattern of the four quarter stations around a sacred central one is reflected in Celtic and Saxon board-games such as Tawlbort and Nine Men's Morris. Here the attacking side's pieces are arranged around the outside of the board; the defence clustered around the king piece in the centre. It is not simply the king who is to be defended, as in chess, but the place on which he stands and which he represents, the centre of the board — the centre of the world.

Settlements too were laid out with a central point marked by a tree or monolith or later a buttercross. In Scandinavia and northern Asia, the cardinal and other points on the horizon visible from this centre might also be marked with a cairn or a pre-existing natural feature such as a tree or hilltop, to register the rising and setting of sun, moon and stars. This was a means of telling both time and season. The central point also served as sanctuary in times of need, the degree of available protection being reduced as the fugitive moved further away from the central marker itself. In Anglo-Saxon England, the king too was surrounded by an area of lawful jurisdiction, the 'King's peace', which moved with him around the country. Here again the secular and the sacred were combined, in a way which we would judge nowadays to be superstitious and restrictive, but which in its essentials put ordinary life into alignment with the comparatively unchanging co-ordinates of heaven.

So to follow my magician friend, and to treat the quarters purely symbolically, with no objective reference, is to destroy the circle's sacred function, the aspect which harmonizes us with the macrocosm. Meditation and ritual then become purely subjective, and the practitioner is no longer aligned with the structure of the cosmos. This might be useful as an exercise in self-determination, but for general work it is, literally, disorienting. I once found myself stumbling over both words and feet when trying to attune to the quarters in a circle which, unknown to me, had been set up out of alignment with the true celestial directions. If the Mystery cults are to be a means of training the intuition, then let us at least train this to be in harmony with what is really going on. An Irishman, a fellow rambler, once swore to me solemnly that he could tell in which direction he was facing without using a compass. If he was facing North, he said, it felt as if he was going uphill. Was this just a touch of the blarney, or did he really pick up on the magnetic current flowing against him from North to South? Our magical, intuitive senses can be taught to align us instinctively with patterns which would otherwise take laborious time and attention to calculate or even to observe.

So the ritual circle is then seen to be a special case of the oriented and quartered environment which the Native Pagan cultures of northern Europe — as indeed of North America and of China and of other Native cultures throughout the world — created wherever they settled. And this environment was not so much *created*, we might say, as *modelled* on what was seen to be there already, in the orientation of the heavens with their centre of rotation marked by the North Star. It is not a matter of symbolism, and certainly not of superstition, but of simple perception.

Cyclical time

The old order changeth, yielding way to new,
And God fulfils himself in many ways,
Lest one good custom should corrupt the world.
Tennyson

To understand our native myths and symbols, it is likewise helpful to keep the physical layout of the environment in mind. In northern latitudes, even as far South as England, France and the USA, the sun rises and sets noticeably farther North on the horizon in summer than in winter, thus giving longer hours of daylight. In Scotland and Canada the difference is unmistakable, even to city dwellers, and in Norway and Iceland the sun can be seen practically all day in the summer months, rising almost due North on the horizon, circling around the eastern, southern and western quarters, and setting again barely West of North. Similarly, around the winter solstice in the far North the sun barely rises at all, rising, culminating and setting over a tiny arc around the southern point of the horizon. But at the equinoxes, anywhere in the world, the sun rises due East and sets due West. So in a way, people might say that the sun goes to bed and rises at each of the quarters on the quarter days. In Norse legend there is what seems to be a curious story about this phenomenon. The *Prose Edda* tells us that the four corners of the horizon were said to be held up by four dwarfs: North, South, East and West by name. Now later on we are also told that the goddess Freya, usually known as the goddess of youth and happiness, desperately wanted to possess a particular gold necklace. Its name was Brisingamen, the Shining One, and it had been made by four dwarfs. These four dwarfs demanded that in payment for the necklace the goddess should spend a night with each of them in turn.

The shining gold necklace can be seen as the circle of the sun's rising and setting points on the horizon throughout the year, and indeed of the sun's flattish daily path through the summer sky in the higher latitudes. Freya, who with her brother Frey, is one of the Vanir, the older race of Nature deities worshipped to this day by the Craft in Norway, seems originally to have been a solar goddess. In Scandinavia she presided over the winter solstice festival, Yule, at which a blazing wheel was rolled down a hill to represent the return of the sun after the long polar night. In Germany, a blazing sunwheel was rolled down the hill at the summer solstice. Freya was said to weep tears of gold over land and amber over the sea, and to fly about the sky in a coat made of falcon's feathers, the far-seeing falcon being generally a solar bird. Although in the myths of the later deities, the Æsir, there is no sun goddess (or god), the sun and presumably the moon being 'made by the gods to light the worlds', Freya's origins are clear. What better way for ordinary folk to remember the solar markers of the seasons, in an age without printed calendars, than by telling the tale of the goddess and the four quarter dwarfs?

Legend also tells us that Freya's brother Frey was once on Odin's high seat at the centre of the world, a place forbidden to him. Looking towards the North, he saw a beautiful woman going towards a large and fine dwelling. Frey was instantly smitten with desire for her, and as she raised her arms to open the door, such radiance filled the world that he was almost blinded.

This story surely describes the midnight sun, which is actually visible on the northern horizon in northern Iceland. Freya and Frey, as sister and brother, are different aspects of the same deity. Freya appeared in the first legend as the sun goddess; in this legend, Frey sees the midnight sun personified as a woman whose radiance is made manifest as soon as she opens the door of her 'house' at the northern point. It is a myth about usurpation: Frey appears to be usurping Odin's high seat, and his lovesickness and subsequent bedazzlement are described as a punishment for this. It is however more likely that he is here reclaiming the status he once shared with his sister Freya. As patriarchal myth took over from matriarchal myth in Nordic lands, Frey became simply the consort of Freya, who somehow retained her status as chief and independent goddess, choosing half the slain after every battle (Odin, as is well known, having the other half), and living independently of the other goddesses in a homestead called Field-of-Warriors. Frey, as her consort, would originally have belonged on the high seat, but by the time of the Eddas this place belonged to Odin, with his consort Frigga.

The North Star, the centre of the turning universe, was seen as Frigga's spindle, with Orion's Belt, low down on the winter horizon, as her distaff. Here we have the Goddess in a different form spinning the fabric of the universe, embodying one of the oldest images of Fate and perpetuating the image of the heavens as an ever-renewed sacred circle, with a circumference and a centre determined by the gods. Sometimes Frigga is said to spin with golden thread, so maybe she was not only the goddess of the night sky, but like Freya she once ruled the solar world.

There are Native seasonal myths too. A Gloucestershire tradition tells how the giant Wandil stole the spring, so that winter became hard and long. The gods finally caught him and made him give back the spring, then threw his body up into heaven, where he became what we call the constellation of Gemini. When his eyes (Castor and Pollux) glare down, there will be a hard frost. There is some truth in this, since as the sun is in the constellation of Gemini in the summer, the constellation itself is only bright enough to 'glare' at us at the dead of night in winter, when the sun is hidden below the earth on the opposite side of the ecliptic. As everybody knows, the stars twinkle brightly when the sky is clear, when the lack of cloud cover can bring frost. But why this particular constellation? Any bright stars in that area of the heavens could serve to predict frost. Could it be that the story dates back 6000 years to the emergence of the spring equinox sunrise from the 'feet' of what we now call Gemini, moving back into Taurus, the time when the first stone circles were built? After all, the children's rhyme beginning 'Matthew, Mark, Luke and John', invoking the four quarter guardians in their cosmological disguise as the constellations of Aquarius, Leo, Taurus and Scorpio, presumably dates from the time when these four constellations marked the year's quarters.

These myths then are both practical and symbolic. They are a vivid shorthand for the rules of calendar-making and orientation in the outside world, as well as referring to the psychological or symbolic reality of the culture that made them. The myth of the golden necklace tells us that in order to receive the necklace, which is a badge of humankind's veneration, the solar goddess must acknowledge her need of the forces of earth and respect their need of her. The sun's path would not be circular if it were not seen from the earth, and in this way the golden circle of the sun's path is indeed forged on earth, as was the necklace of ancient myth.

The solar goddess who weeps tears of gold and amber comes from a different pantheon than the more familiar solar god of modern Wicca with his shining spear of light. The people who worshipped that pantheon would have a different outlook: their sun would be a symbol of fruitfulness rather than of victory, and the central priorities of their culture would be different. The Norwegian witches who worship Freya and Frey, the Old Gods of Scandinavia, see the newer gods as evil, so I am told, and the continuation of the story of Freya's necklace, in which Odin, chief of the newer gods, steals it by guile and then names his price for its return, is clearly a take-over myth. Yet in the Pagan world, all things have their times and cycles. At the end of the age of the Æsir, who are gods of achievement, of guile or intellect, and of light, will come Ragnarok, the Gods' Twilight, in which they will be toppled in their turn by the giants, by the Serpent of Middle Earth, and by the monstrous Wolf, embodiments of the primal stuff of the world. And yet at the end of this cataclysm, we are told in the *Deluding of Gylfi*, a green and fruitful world will rise from the sea, with some of the older gods ruling it, and a new race of mortals.

Now perhaps there are some fundamentalist Pagans who would take this story literally, but it can equally be taken spiritually or psychologically, as an instance of the unity of opposites, the return and transformation of 'the repressed', as Freud would put it. The Æsir were apposite to an age when gaming and riddles and the shrewd intellect were coming into prominence, when the Old Ways of unity with Nature were felt to be oppressive, and so Freya lost her necklace, and so Thor the thunder god was demoted from his chariot at the centre of the heavens, which was thereafter renamed Woden's (Odin's) Wain, and which we moderns have learned to call the Great Bear. To those who cling onto the Old Age, the dawning of each New Age appears monstrous, and perhaps necessarily so, for it should not be accepted without testing. But after the test comes the creative resolution, and time can begin again in a new framework. One of the tasks of the spiritual life is to understand — or to be at one with — and resolve the inevitable clash of opposites in the most constructive possible way.

This framework of the universe, the four corners of the

cosmos, with the North Star above them, marked in our circles and in the ancient layout of settlements, shifts its markers regularly with the precession of the equinoxes. And although for 2000 years we have been in the age when Pisces rises before the Eastern dawn, in fact 1200 years ago, when the Viking Age with its warlike Æsir was beginning, a shift in the Pole Star was taking place. Alpha Draconis, on which the Pyramids were aligned, had long since passed away; Alpha Ursae Minoris, our present North Star, will not be exact until after the year 2000; but around the year 800, the faint star 32 Camelopardalis was at the pole of the heavens. A shift in perspective had occurred, a new steering star had pledged itself to mariners, and the myths had to be rewritten. A culture which navigated by the stars, which oriented itself by the celestial directions, which lay in a starlit Polar night for several months of the year, could not have failed to notice this fact. And once the myths are rewritten, the mind of humanity changes.

As Pagans approaching the Age of Aquarius, an age astronomically determined, which coincides with the second millennium of a calendar based on Christian reckoning, and is thus unconsciously imprinted on the mind-set of the dominant Western culture, we would do well to look out once more at the stars and orient ourselves more consciously with the shift that is taking place. In a few decades the position of our present North Star will be exact on the axis of rotation. It is my guess that as the framework of the cosmos changes, the myths of our age will be rewritten, both the myths of the Zodiac which we have from the Middle East, which have shaped so much of our education and civilization and which give people the notion of the 'Age of Aquarius', and likewise our underlying native myths of the North Star, 'Troja', the turning-point of the heavens, 'Asgard', the fortress of the gods, and the crystal cave of Caer Arianrhod, which are so vividly present to those who remember them here in our northern latitudes. The two sets of myths are not so separate. 'The earth will rise again from the waters', the Edda tells us, and indeed it will be a higher constellation — Aquarius is above Pisces in the Zodiac rising from the East — which will mark the spring equinox, as if the plane of the horizon had shifted up a notch in the East, and tilted down in the West. The star which had once been the spindle of Frigga became known, some time in the Viking Age, as the sword-hilt of Tir. We are also told in the Anglo-Saxon Runesong that Tir is the token of one who never falters, remaining constant above the mists of night. This kenning gives us the image of the sword in the stone, the ritual weapon which fixes the axis of the visible universe and can only be withdrawn by the man who is noble enough to become the new world hero.

The astronomical pattern of the sword in the stone is mirrored by some Traditional groups in their circle layout. The ritual sword, emblem of the element of Air, is placed in the North of the circle, symbolizing the axis of the northern heavens. The stone of destiny, emblem of Earth, is placed in the South, the spear of the light-bearing god placed in the East, and the cup of the waters of life goes in the West. This contrasts with the practice of most modern groups, which take their lead from ceremonial magic and place Air in the East, Earth in the North, and Fire in the South. In the former system, the symbolism of the outer world is brought directly into the circle, with the image of the sword in the stone describing the North-South axis just as it does in greater pattern of the heavens. The circle thus elaborates the pattern of the outer world, intensifying the patterns and forces which surround us, unseen, in everyday life.

So we can look out from our little circle in the woods or on the hilltop and see the greater quartered circle of the horizon containing us, with the mighty celestial circle of the solar year and of the precession, the measure of all usable time, wheeling majestically around even this. Our myths and legends of gods and demigods, beings who are greater than human, take place against this starry background, which before people had thought of analytical psychology was seen as the primary transpersonal realm, the picture-book of the archetypes.

The Centre of the Circle

I know that I hung on that windswept tree
For all of nine nights, wounded by a spear,
And given to Odin, myself to myself,
On that tree of which no-one knows
The roots from which it rises

Havamal

At the very centre of the ritual circle, and symbolically at the very centre of the world, is the secret place in which all times and all places are present. It is the subjective realm of mystic vision, beyond space and time, beyond choice and judgement, beyond all personified goddesses and gods. Just as the four-square layout of the traditional settlement is supposed to harmonize the cycles of earthly activity with those of heavenly activity, so that of the ritual circle aligns the physical, unconscious functioning of each celebrant with the patterns of earth and of heaven, vividly symbolized by the quarter guardians, and thus leaves the abstract mind free to soar unhindered into the realms beyond space and time. In the Northern tradition, we usually place the altar in the North, the direction of the unchanging polar stars, but at other times it is placed in the centre of the circle, especially for a meditative or trance ritual.

We might see the centre as the middle of a maze, where the convolutions of thought and action in ordinary life are suddenly stilled, and where we experience the wholeness of life. The paths of the mizmaze, the unicursal labyrinth or Troytown, lead us in strange directions, we know not where, by some inner logic until, exhausted and giddy, we stand still in the centre and perceive the harmony of the whole. Puzzle mazes, leading us down blind alleys of would-be thought, came into being as the conscious mind learnt through Hermetic studies to perceive in their workings the processes of magic. Either way, conscious and unconscious, sequential and wholistic, are interlinked, and their resolution lies in perceiving the whole.

The centre is the axis of the world, a strange imitation of the pole of the heavens, the spindle or God's nail, the pillar of heaven or the World Tree. In it all things are contained, all time is latent. It is the shining pillar in the observatory of the Castle of Wonders into which Gawain looked when he had conquered the illusions and diversions set to try all seekers who came there. In the magic pillar, all the happenings of the world are reflected, and the world seems to circle around it. There are two ways of seeing true. One is by looking outwards and reading the script in the starry heavens. The other is by looking inwards, and perceiving directly from the centre. But to get to either we have to abstract ourselves from the confusion and experimentation of the middle realm, where most of our life goes on. Looking outwards gives us perspective, but looking in gives us certainty. The axis is also the World Tree, on which Odin hung for nine nights, sacrificed to himself and seeking understanding. He returned to life with the mystery of the runes, that alphabet both practical and magical which enables ineffable thoughts to be somehow set down for all to see.

Objectively, the runic alphabet is said to be derived from the script of Etruria, modern Tuscany, whose civilization preceded that of Rome. In Italy the North Star is lower down in the sky, no model for the axis of the horizon, but the mystery of the centre is still there, in the offering pit which is the road to the Underworld, found in the centre of each of the quartered Etruscan settlements. Myth and mystery were important to the Etruscans, and through the amber routes to the Baltic their culture communicated with that of the North.

The pillar is the God's symbol. The Goddess can shape the centre in a different way, as the spring of life, the cup of sovereignty, the fountain of youth. All things are mixed mysteriously in the cup, the cauldron, all life revivified by the fountain. Under each root of the World Ash Tree was a spring: the spring called Seething Cauldron in the Underworld, a spring of dissolution, of the ending of all separate form. On the middle level, the human level, was the spring of wisdom, from which Odin drank, but had to give up one of his eyes to do so. Which 'I', which identity was it? Was it, as for human beings, the conscious, presentable ego-I? Or was it the eternal I of his foreknowing, the sacrifice of his certainty so that he could learn practical skills and the ability to react?

In the gods' realm, the upper world, is found the spring of destiny, the source of that which cannot be changed, and here the gods hold their council. Three Norns live at the upper spring, spinning the web of fate, alternative personifications of Frigga with her spindle. The middle spring is guarded by a male dwarf, and the Seething Cauldron below is the home of the serpent which grinds down the world. In Britain many springs were guarded by women, Old Mother Shipton, of Knaresborough, being one. Legend has it also that King Arthur went to the Otherworld to seize a cauldron which was guarded by nine maidens. The Goddess appears too as the Sovereignty of Ireland, seated in a crystal chair, having a golden cup at her feet, a golden cup at her lips, and a silver cup with four gold corners before her. The four gold corners are the four sacred directions, the cardinal points. This cup she gives to the successful hero, bestowing on him the right to be High King.

The imagery of the cup is not the clear-cut imagery of the reflecting pillar. The shifting, gyroscopic axis of the turning spindle is not the trusty steadfastness of the World Ash Tree, of the Heart of Oak. The images of the centre shift and develop, it has aspects of both Goddess and God, and their own natures alter through time, from culture to culture, poet to poet. But always the centre is the point of resolution.

So our circles are cosmograms, and also icons, mandalas. They lead our attention out, and they lead it in, by no clearly rational means. The centre and the circumference have had the same meaning all along, but we have had to reach the centre to understand that. If we see it rightly, the whole landscape is a living mandala, whose centre is not to be found in any physical location, but where we make it, in the Otherworld. It is a giant cosmogram, whose polar axis still only symbolizes the centre of the world's being. These hints and clues can lead us on our search, but only we can make sense of all our journeying.

Why Druids Now?

Reflections on the relevance of Druidry to the current crisis faced by humanity and the planet

Philip Carr-Gomm

My father introduced me to the Chief of the Order of Bards, Ovates and Druids when I was 15. His name was Philip Ross Nichols, but I soon came to know him by his mystical name of Nuinn.

Shortly after our first meeting, I accepted his invitation to the Order's celebration of Imbolc on 2 February. That evening, over 20 years ago, as I made my way to Baron's Court, I felt tired and cold. I had spent the afternoon playing football in the wind and the mud, and I had no desire to celebrate the first day of spring. I wanted a hot bath and an early night. But there I was, walking the dark streets of an area of London in which Ouspensky had lived and taught, and in which the dervishes still whirl silently in white as the trains of the District and Piccadilly lines run by, so near, yet caught in another world.

I was greeted by Nuinn and shown into his sitting-room. He asked me to help distribute sherry and peanuts, and within moments my mood had changed. I was soon talking to a journalist from *The Times*, and then with an Irish novelist, feeling very adult as my 15-year-old body sipped sherry and relaxed in the warmth of the room. After a while, a blue-robed Bard appeared, inviting us to descend into the basement. There, in the candle-light, was a circle of chairs which were quickly occupied, leaving late-comers to stand behind. On a central table was a glass dish filled with water and strewn with snowdrops, and out of this water rose eight white candles, all alight.

From an open door, which led in fact to Nuinn's kitchen, the brothers and sisters of the Order emerged in file, Bards robed in blue, Ovates in green, and Druids proper in white. The miracle, the wonderful and extraordinary thing, was that no one burst into laughter. How strange it was to be in a basement room in London's West Kensington, with two dozen people who had, a few minutes before, been engaged in standard ritual behaviour, now awefully and respectfully adapted to a totally new and strange ritual activity. Nuinn had written about this process 20 years before, in 1946, in his book *Cosmic Shape*: 'In festival drama is a possible technique whereby the self-conscious modern may learn to partake of mass dramatic action and music without the entry of that paralysing sense of the ridiculous that checks the outward expression of any form of reverence'. So there we were, and none of us were paralysed — we were fascinated. Nuinn now entered, distinguished as the Chief, by a golden emblem of the Three Bars of Light placed on his head-dress — at the point of the brow chakra, the Third Eye.

'Let us begin by giving peace to the quarters, for without peace can no work be. Peace to the North. Peace to the South. Peace to the West. Peace to the East. May there be peace throughout the whole world.'

After dedications, explanations and a prayer, Nuinn continued: 'See at the centre of man are air and fire. The leaves of the trees speak with air. In the heart of wood is the seed of fire. Guardian of the Fire, is warmth prepared?'

'It is prepared.'

'O Ritualist, is poetry in readiness?'

'It is in readiness.'

'Then I declare that this fire festival of the Bards is open for instruction, for song and for the arts of man.'

A lectern was placed in front of Nuinn, and he began to talk: 'This is the earliest of the spring celebrations, marking the purity of snow, the clearing of the debris of winter, the First Ploughing and sowing. It is the only one of our eight festivals given entirely to the Mother Goddess under many names, Brighid being the central one of three, each representing a season. Imbolc is a quiet ceremony, with water, lights and readings showing the many forms of the feminine in deity. The ceremony is inductive — that is it aims to encourage the sun, to show that light and warmth are increasing. The First Plough means confidence in the future. There is the washing of the face of the earth — the celebration of the Goddess's recovery from giving birth to the new year's Sun God. It is a festival of virginity, as well as a festival of purification after childbirth. In the Christian tradition this celebration becomes the Feast of the Purification of the Blessed Virgin Mary and the time of the Churching of Women. So here we have the use of earth and water and light. The snowdrops are traditionally the first flowers to appear from the snow — they are the flowers of washed purity. We will now celebrate this festival with music, song and readings.'

As we listened to the Celtic harp of a Breton Druid who was staying at that time with Nuinn, I gazed at the eight candle flames and their reflections in the water.....

The other Druids read poems in turn. Then Nuinn again, reading from his long poem *Cosmic Legend:*

The cup is filled the cup has power
the waters of new vision flow,
the crops upstart, and into flower
the later grasses glow.

A reading on the Goddess from Apuleius' *The Golden Ass* brought the festival to an end.

The candles were extinguished ceremonially while Nuinn said: 'As the flames die down, may they be relit in your hearts. May your memories hold what the eye and ear have gained. I declare this fire festival of the Bards of Caer Lud is closed in the apparent world. May it continue within our beings.'

Twenty years on, the memory of that first Druid ceremony shines like a beacon in my consciousness. Each of the following ceremonies has added colour and depth to an inner mandala that acts like a compass, as I move through my life and through each year. Imbolc was followed by Alban Eiler, the Spring Equinox, celebrated looking down upon London from Parliament Hill. Then came Beltane, when on May Day we climbed Glastonbury Tor to perform a ceremony filled with deep and ancient symbolism. We were back at Parliament Hill for the Summer Solstice, which was followed six weeks later by the celebration of Lughnasadh in a private country garden. Alban Elued, the Autumnal Equinox at Parliament Hill, was followed by the inner and magical ceremony of Samhuin at Hallowe'en, which we celebrated in Nuinn's house. The eightfold mandala of the Druid year was completed with the celebration of Alban Arthuan, the Winter Solstice, on December 21.

In 1975 Nuinn died and with his death the Order moved into a period of winter sleep. I began training as a psychologist, and the romantic years of initiations on Glastonbury Tor, and ceremonies on sacred hills, gave way to a decade of academic work and family life. The ability of psychology to address human suffering became my main concern, and the teachings of the Druids seemed to me at that time of little relevance to the problems of the contemporary world. I had seen that the path of the esoteric could provide as many pitfalls and cul-de-sacs as it could provide insights and inspiration, and it seemed that only a thorough analysis of the human mind and character could safeguard one from the escapism and distortions of the occult.

Looking back it seems as if the post-war generations have been accelerated through an unparalleled process of psychic development — the decade of material stabilization of the fifties was followed by the mass initiations of the flower power era in the sixties. No one would deny that the excesses and abuses of the drug culture caught many in a dangerous blind alley, but most of those souls who had been initiated by the expansions of consciousness triggered by either psychedelics or simply the extraordinary energy generated during this era, were carried into the next chapter of their development by the evolutionary wave that moved them in the seventies towards the spiritual guidance of gurus and teachers, who evoked not only devotional qualities in individual souls, but awakened thousands to the power of group consciousness. As the decade drew to a close, the power of the gurus seemed to turn negative, just as the quality of flower power turned bad at the end of the previous decade. But the wave carried on, and although the undertow caught some souls in the cult-trap, the crest of the wave carried the majority forward into the eighties — to a time in which the empowerment of the individual became the prime work. The external way-showers of psychedelics and gurus were no longer appropriate. Human Potential training in all its guises became the dominant vehicle for human transformation. Still seated in a circle, it was no longer the sacred pipe that was passed, nor the guru that was adored, but it was the individual self in relation to all the other selves in the group that was honoured. And what circle will we be seated in, as we move into the final decade of the millennium?

Way back in other lives, we have been seated in tipis and in groves; our grandparents sat in spiritualist circles, and we — as we were hurled through the post-war psychlotron — have sat in occult and psychedelic and new age and growth group circles. But I ask again — which circle will hold us as we move into the nineties?

1984, nine years after Nuinn's death, found me practising as a psychotherapist. Although I had kept all my Druid papers, I had not thought of Nuinn or the Order for years. I was meditating one morning, when suddenly, he was there — six feet in front of me. 'Look around you,' he said. 'There is a place for Druidry now. Man has lost his connection with nature. Anything that can help heal the split is of value. Druidry can offer a way to reunite man with his home, which he is destroying.' He then gave instructions which were to result in the Order beginning a new cycle of activity — with astonishing consequences.

After this experience it became clear to me that the final decade of this millennium would be a decade of the 'Turning Without'. We had been accelerated through 30 years of soul development, of building a knowledge of the inner, precisely so that we would be ready to turn outwards with that awareness, to the planet and to all its kingdoms — human, animal, plant and mineral — in order to redress the imbalance we have created since the scientific revolution.

The only circle that would hold us now would be the circle of the whole earth — and the physical circles that we would sit in, would be formed not only for self-development and support (for those needs will never cease) but would also be for the work of planetary healing and for the building of concrete and specific projects to aid this work.

The fact that in the coming decade we will turn increasingly in our work to resolving the planetary crisis does not mean that we will cease the treading of our spiritual path. Just as outer reflects inner, we step forward on our journey whether that step results from concern for the outer world or concern for the inner. The following notes of an inner experience of guidance by Nuinn will make this clearer.

Deep in a quiet wood in Oxfordshire Nuinn would go for periods of solitude and communion with nature. He owned a small piece of natural woodland that was part of a much larger private forest. He had bought it before the war from friends of my parents, and there he had built a few wooden huts, and there he would cook by an open fire, meditate and walk in the forest, storing up energy in preparation for his return to the city.

One of the main effects of a retreat there came from the utter simplicity of the place. There were very few things. He kept warm at night by using a thick sleeping bag, and in the evenings by making fires of the dead wood he had gathered during the day. It was like camping, but with the pleasant difference of having a dry wooden hut to sleep in, rather than a cramped tent.

The simplicity of surroundings matched the simplicity of diet that I submitted to, during the following experience on the inner planes: 'You will eat nothing but apples for three days, and drink nothing but hot water and apple juice,' announced Nuinn eagerly scrutinizing my face for signs of resistance.

'So that's what that crate of apples was doing in the back of your car?'

'Yes, what more can we need?' he said with a smile.

'Nothing, absolutely nothing' I murmured, thinking that maybe my friends were right and that he was slightly mad. Maybe I'd get ill, or go green.

'I undergo this retreat eight times a year.' I was astonished — he had never mentioned this before. 'For a week before the Solstices and Equinoxes and for three days before each of the Fire Festivals, I come here to rest and fast and be transformed. Do you know how old I am?'

'No. About 50 I suppose.'

'I'm 69. The reason I look younger is because I have followed this practice for years, which was taught me by my predecessor. If you can follow it, you will find it will change your life — increasing your energy, vitality and health, and ultimately your longevity. There's nothing complicated about it, just as there is nothing complicated in Druidry. You just have to remember a few things. Firstly, the psychological and emotional attitude should be one of freedom, detachment and rest. Tell yourself that during this period you will set aside all your worldly concerns and cares. Live in the greatest simplicity — it helps to be without electricity and all which that brings — telephones, televisions and radios. Try not to think overmuch, but commune as much as possible with Nature — with the sun and stars, the trees and the earth. Spend your time watching animals and birds, and allow yourself time to dream.' He said this last phrase with emphasis, looking at me kindly, as if to say 'This is particularly for you'. I was a serious sort of person, and looking back, he was quite right — I needed to give myself the freedom to dream.

'Physically, it should be a period of rest and regeneration and cleansing for your body. We all eat far too much, and the wrong kinds of food. The Ancients have always carried as part of their tradition, a teaching concerning the proper use of fasting and diet. As regards the subtleties of the esoteric doctrine of diet you must wait until the higher grades, but as regards cleansing and fasting, and the elementaries of our understanding of diet, we can begin now.'

As if he realized that he had provoked a fascination within me, he changed tack, and having poked and adjusted the fire, he said 'The whole question of glamour and fascination and mystery must really be thought through by you. You must ask yourself why you are interested in the Druid and Arthurian mysteries, in ley lines, megalithic remains, astral travel, numerology, sacred architecture, alchemy, mythology, ritual, festivals, and all that sort of thing. I would say that this interest has both a healthy and an unhealthy side to it. The healthy or beneficial aspect lies in the fact that these studies can promote self-knowledge, spiritual development and a greater awareness of the wonder and complexity of life. The unhealthy, disturbed, or hindering aspect lies in the possibility that these interests could be a form of escape from the real world, from properly and creatively engaging in the outside world and its challenges. This is a danger we should always bear in mind. It is one of the functions of a spiritual guide to ensure that this happens as little as possible. If you are attentive to your own psyche and to events occurring in your life, you will see that these interests follow cycles — wide patterns like the seasons. There will be times when you will set aside these concerns and work openly and vigorously in the world

— turning towards inner things at such times in your life may even seem distasteful, because your psyche will not need it, and to force it would be like forcing yourself to eat a food that your body reacts against. I sometimes sense these periods as summer times when we are outside working in the sun, intensely aware of the outer world. At other times, autumns and winters of our psychic lives perhaps, we turn towards these inner studies and practices, and we feel depths which were not satisfied by our outer work. And again, if we force ourselves to carry on in our outer way, we will feel uncomfortable. We will sense, even if unconsciously, that we are unbalanced, that our concerns are superficial, that our inner selves are not satisfied. Of course these seasons occur in miniature cycles within the wider ones. In other words, during one day you may well move from one to another; but there is a way in which these patterns also occur over a longer time-scale, lasting months and years, sometimes even lifetimes. If a soul has spent a whole lifetime in contemplation and inner work, as a monk for example, he may spend his next life in almost total outer activity as a compensation.'

This piece of teaching from Nuinn clarified my awareness that we should create forums and vehicles which can express both our need for outer activity and for inner work — with both of these contained within an all-embracing spiritual context. Said another way, for many of us there has been a conflict between our ecological concerns and our spiritual concerns. Some of us opt for outer action in the political, social or environmental arena, having decided that inner concerns are an indulgence we can ill afford in such troubled times. Others of us, knowing that changes in consciousness precede changes on the physical level, opt for inner work and self-development, seeing outer work as labouring with effects rather than causes. The rhythmical seasonal analogies of Nuinn helped me to see that we can integrate both approaches, fulfilling the need for both outer and inner work, and that the 'earth religions', such as Druidry offer a way of doing this. The revival of interest in these 'earth religions' points to the growing awareness of the necessity to combine our spirituality with a reverence and care for the earth.

It is undeniable that there is a renaissance of interest in these natural religions throughout the world. A part of this renaissance reflects the need in the collective unconscious to redress the balance that has been disturbed by the dominance in our religious consciousness of the patriarchal religions of the Judaeo-

Christian and Islamic worlds. This imbalance has resulted in a disturbed relationship to the planet herself, and the renaissance can be seen as the manifestation of human and divine concern that this relationship be made harmonious and the earth be thereby saved. Rather than seeing the revival of interest in earth religions as regressive — harking back to primitive times — the upsurge of interest demonstrates quite the opposite trend — one of progression, in which we meet the old wisdom at a new turn of the spiral and see that we need its sense of the sacredness of all life if we are to survive as a species and planet.

A great deal of interest is currently being shown in Native American Indian ways, and many of their teachings and practices are similar to the western ways of Druidry and Wicca. Druidry and Wicca are distinct and separate manifestations of the Western path, and the best way to consider them are as brothers and sisters — within the same family and therefore sharing family characteristics but also separate, with characteristics peculiar to themselves.

Druidry is biased towards a reverence for the sun, whereas Wicca is biased towards lunar reverence. Wiccan work is often concerned with polarity, whereas Druidry does not stress this aspect to such a degree. Both, however, work in a circle, with the four quarters and four elements, and celebrate the seasonal festivals.

The renaissance of the natural spiritual paths coincides with the world ecological crisis. As half the forests of Scandinavia and Germany are diseased or dying, and as only 30 years remain, according to some estimates, before the world lung of the Amazon forest is totally removed, some of us become concerned with the spiritual power and meaning of trees. As the air and sea and land become polluted, and as the sun's rays become capable of endangering our lives due to the ozone layer damage, some of us look at the four elements in a new light, and want to work with them in a spirit of reverence and respect.

The Old Magic sought to command the elements, but in this age we are seeking not to command or dominate, but to venerate and learn from these forces which we have threatened so severely.

The upsurge of interest in natural ways has its distortions, as does any great movement in consciousness. Just as the flower power, guru and Human Potential movements had their charlatans and their casualties, so too does the new wave of natural spiritual concern have its pitfalls of the escapism or glamour of occult or tribal culture, and a regressive interest in the sexual or spell-working aspects of paganism, but this should not blind us from seeing the purity and urgency of this new movement, for it is not the externals to which we should pay attention, but the inner attitude and direction — which is one of deep concern for the environment and one of following a spiritual way which unites the natural earthly self with the divine, spiritual self.

Seated by the fire in another inner experience of guidance with Nuinn, he helped me to answer my earlier question: 'You ask what circles we will be seated in, as we move through the final decade of the millennium. Perhaps they will be ones which recognize and work with the qualities experienced in the previous decades — with the power of love, the power of reverence and group consciousness, and with the understanding of the needs of the individual, but hopefully there will be no manipulations by charismatic figures, no leaning on externals other than the support of the group and its work. They might use as their compass the mandala of the natural world, which is the mandala of the earth and her seasons. The ecological crisis would act as a focus for both the inner work of the circles, and for particular projects which they may initiate in response to the needs of their local environment. Understanding that crisis precedes evolution, they would be able to work with hope and confidence in the future, but with their feet firmly planted on the ground.'

Now I knew why Nuinn had taken the trouble to pay a visit after he had left this plane. The Druid path was too important to remain hidden in the times that lie ahead, and although it can by no means be treated as a panacea for all the problems we face, it clearly offers a dynamic way of working in the world through this coming decade and beyond.

The Initiation

Vivianne Crowley

We were nearing the end of an introductory course on Wicca. The 18 students who had begun the course had whittled down to a hard core of 12 who were seeking initiation into the Old Religion; to be made Priests and Priestesses of the Goddess. I had talked that night on the meaning of initiation and now it was time for questions.

'What is it like to be initiated?' This was the first and rather predictable question; then came a second and less predictable one. 'What is it like to initiate someone?' I smiled. This question came from one of the most promising of the would-be initiates. Painfully shy when she had first come to the course, she had blossomed over the weeks as she had learned to talk about her innermost feelings and to give of herself in the way that is required of an initiate and a Priestess.

What is it like to initiate? Well, every time it is different, but also the same. One hopes and fears, worries and relaxes, and one offers oneself to the Gods to act as a channel which will bring their power into the rite and make the initiation a thing of beauty and meaning for the initiate. The initiator is the channel, but it is the archetypal forces themselves which perform the initiation. The initiator is the mediator who links the initiate with the Gods. It is they and the initiate who determine what happens.

We were sitting around the living-room fire and as I gazed into the flickering flames, I thought of all the initiations I had carried out. England, Australia, America, Germany — first degree initiations which make the initiate a Priest or Priestess and Witch; second degree initiations, and finally third degree initiations which make the initiate a High Priest and Magus or High Priestess and Witch Queen. How many? I had never counted; but each was different, each individual initiate unique. Gazing at the flames, I remembered how two winters ago I had sat in the same place at much the same time of evening with the man who was now a Priest in our coven.

'I will tell you about one initiation,' I said, 'not because it's particularly special; but because it is very ordinary, and perhaps that is the extraordinary thing about initiation. How it is ordinary people, not men and women of great spiritual gifts or magical and psychic powers, that become Priests and Priestesses and witches, if only we have the courage to try; to dare to change and to grow.'

This is the story I told. I have added to it some of the things which I had already said that night about initiation. I have changed the names of the people involved, but that is all. It is a true story and, as I told our students, a very ordinary one.

We were in the village hall of a small village in Devon which was an unlikely setting for what had just taken place — a performance of Aleister Crowley's Gnostic Mass. The rite had finished and it was time for the feasting. Rob and I sat on two canvas chairs drinking wine.

'Have you thought any more about initiation?' I asked, knowing that he had. He had been toying with the idea for some months.

'Yes, a lot,' said Rob. 'I keep on thinking I want to do it. But I can't quite bring myself to take the final step.'

I looked at him thoughtfully. I had known him for a year. His girlfriend Carol was already in the coven and at first on coven meeting nights he had merely dropped her at the house. Then he began to come in for a drink before going; then later he began to wait downstairs while we had the rite. He seemed to be hovering on the edge of the group waiting for an invitation in.

We had talked before about the meaning of initiation. 'It is a way of opening us up to an expansion of consciousness,' I had explained, 'but it does not automatically bestow "powers" and great spiritual insights. Spiritual growth and the ability to perform magic are gained through hard work and persistence. Initiation is a gateway to a path up a mountain which we must then climb. It is a path which leads to other levels of consciousness, the levels from which psychic and magical powers spring. The initiator can do no more than open the gate. It is you who must then climb the path.'

I had explained the role of the initiator, the mediator, the channel for the force which links the initiate with the Gods. He had understood this. So often people came seeking initiation, having read books which implied that the rite would immediately make them clairvoyant and give them magical powers. Fortunately Rob was too down-to-earth to have such illusions. He also understood the other important point which was that while initiation did not immediately make one the greatest witch since the Inquisition, it did change people. He had watched his girlfriend change in the year that had passed since her own initiation and he understood what initiation could do as well as what it couldn't.

It is because of the changes which initiation brings, that we do not actively encourage people to seek it. It is a decision which they alone can make. Wiccan initiation is something for the few and not for the many. It is the way of Priest of the Elder Gods, the way of the witch. It is a hard path and it must be freely chosen. Initiation strips the soul bare until we see ourselves as we really are; then it makes us change. This process is often painful. One part of us wants change and growth; the other prefers the status quo. The higher self seeks to lead us forward; the ego struggles and resists, afraid to lose its place of dominance.

Now in the aftermath of the Gnostic Mass, I sensed that Rob and I had reached the crunch. He wanted to ask for initiation; but he could not quite bring himself to take the final step.

'Do you think Rob will *ever* come into Wicca,' I had asked Andy, my husband and High Priest, some weeks before.

'Probably not,' he said. 'He'll never make the commitment.'

'I'm not so sure,' I had replied. 'I think in the end he will.

He seems to be working himself towards it. If he does ask, shall we initiate him?'

'Yes,' said Andy, 'if he asks.'

Traditionally, obtaining initiation has always been difficult. If there are obstacles placed in the person's way, it is seen as part of the initiatory process to work to overcome them. Many of the barriers are of our own making — our own doubts and inadequacies and fears. These we must overcome alone. No one could offer Rob initiation; the would-be initiate has to ask.

I had known Rob a year. Suddenly it struck me that this might be significant. There is no set time-limit before a would-be witch is initiated, but the old tradition was that the candidate should wait a year and a day. 'A year and a day' — I began to count mentally the weeks that had passed since I had first met Rob. It was about right. Perhaps the time had come for him to decide.

My level of consciousness made a sudden shift; I was seeing clairvoyant pictures. It was as though I was standing on one side of a steep ditch. Rob stood on the other side, a little below me. He was reaching out his hand, but he was afraid to leap. The other bank was slippery and wet. There was an appeal in his eyes.

Initiation in Wicca is always given to a woman by a man and by a man to a woman. It is the female who must initiate the male. The High Priestess enacts the role of the man's anima; that unconscious feminine part of him which is symbolized by the element of water, the womb, the mother. It is this hidden contra-sexual self which leads us to the Gods. If Rob was to be initiated I must be the one to help him over the threshold. The image of the slippery bank transfixed me. What should I do?

I found myself speaking, 'Supposing I was to say to you that we would arrange your initiation for six weeks time, on Beltane, would you come?'

He hesitated for only a fraction of a second. 'Yes, I think I would,' he said laughing.

'Shall we do that then?' I asked.

'Why not?' he said.

I suddenly realized what I was saying. What had I done? This was against all the rules. The initiate must ask for initiation and he had not. But as a High Priestess I must know when to break the rules, I found myself thinking, and I feel this is right.

'Are you sure?' I asked Rob.

'Yes, it's about time I got on with it,' he said.

'Shall we tell the others?'

'I suppose we'd better,' he replied.

A few minutes later Carol and Andy appeared clutching wine glasses. It was as though they had sensed that something was afoot and had tactfully kept out of the way. Of the two, Carol seemed the more surprised at our news.

'What made you suddenly decide?' she asked Rob.

Given my rather over-proactive role that evening, I felt rather embarrassed. I replied on Rob's behalf, thinking that he might find this question a little difficult to answer. 'Oh, Rob and I had a chat and decided it was about time we got on with it,' I said. 'We're going to do it at Beltane.'

Later that night driving back to London with a heavy orange moon hanging on the Eastern horizon, I wondered if I had done the right thing. 'I think so,' I told myself. 'I think it will be all right.'

Four weeks later, Rob and I sat in front of the fire in my London house. I looked at him and remembered how Andy and I had first met him. It was in a local pub. We were to be introduced to him prior to his girlfriend's initiation. It was a meeting which we had suggested so that he would know who these people were who were to turn Carol into a witch.

We had arrived first and sat at a table with our drinks. Carol came in through the door followed by a figure in a leather jacket, clutching a motor bike helmet. He looked pleasant enough and as I talked to him he came across as bright. Nothing unusual, except perhaps for one thing which emerged during the course of the evening; he was very well-balanced. And now this man who led a very ordinary life — the pub, bike rallies, work, tenpin bowling — was to be made a Priest and a Witch.

How was this transformation to be made? The initiation had the power, this I knew; but it needed great effort and energy to make it work. The person must be lifted out of their ordinary level of consciousness and into the other realm, the realm of possibilities, of magic and of symbol, where one thing could be transformed into another. Could I do this thing for this man, and more importantly, could he do it for himself? Together could we make the link between the *world of men and the realms of the Mighty Ones*? Could I link with Rob so that he could link with the Gods?

We had gone over the requirements of the initiation. I had asked him if he had any questions. He had remarkably few.

'Have you ever had any past life experiences?' I asked to my own surprise. I had no idea what had prompted the question.

'Yes, I think I have,' said Rob. 'It was somewhere on the border between Wales and England. I'm not sure exactly when, sometime about the fourteenth century. I was in a castle which was being attacked. I was a soldier, a fighting man, and I was grappling with another man. We were fighting with swords.'

Images started to come into my mind. I was sharing what he was seeing.

'I was above the other man on a spiral staircase inside the castle. He was trying to force his way up. He was pushing me back up the stairs, hacking his way towards me. I don't remember anything after that.'

We had seen his death. I gazed into the fire. New pictures were coming to me. I began to see something else. It was in Wales as before, but somehow I knew this was a different castle, further South. I was there. Then I realized — I had known this man before. The words of the Samhain ritual came into my mind, 'We shall meet and remember and know them again.'

I was sitting by my husband's side. It was early evening. There was a banquet in the great hall and there were many guests. Suddenly the doors of the hall swung open and the flames of the rush lights flared with the draught. A tall man was ushered in. He was a bard and across his back he carried a harp. On his left shoulder sat a very small and very serious-looking boy with dark hair. How old was he — two, three? It was Rob. Taliesin's son — I remembered now who he was and how I had first seen them — how I had loved Taliesen Bard.

The picture changed in the abrupt way of clairvoyance. I was sitting with some women in the great hall, but this time it was day. It was cold and well into autumn and we sat by a roaring fire. We were doing tapestry work. The door opened and a dark-haired young man entered. He wore a cloak and a sword. A gust of wind came through the door with him and dead leaves blew about the floor of the hall where the door had opened. It was Taliesin's son. He strode across the hall towards us. 'My Lady,' he said bowing and smiling. 'I have come home for a few days to visit my father.'

I did not know what to say. Involuntarily I glanced upward to where his father's harp hung on the wall of the great hall. His son's eyes followed my gaze — he knew. 'Your father died three months ago,' I said. 'It was very peaceful. There was no pain. I'm sorry we couldn't let you know. We tried to get messages to you, but we didn't know where you were.'

The words sounded empty and inadequate, hollow and flat. There was silence and I did not know what to say. Grief distorted his face. I could see that he wanted to cry, but not here. Not in public in the great hall.

The picture changed again. We were sitting together on Taliesin's narrow bed in the tiny room in the turret. Taliesin had liked to be high up where he could see out across the river and watch the trading boats go up and down. The pile of Taliesin's possessions looked pathetically small.

'How little debris a man's life leaves,' I thought.

'I loved him,' said Taliesin's son.

I felt he needed to say it. He never told Taliesin, I thought, so he wants to say it to someone; here in his father's room. 'He knew,' I said, giving what comfort I could.

The picture faded and I came back to the present. I shivered with the cold of that autumn day long ago and drew nearer the fire. I looked at Rob. Had he shared the vision? It was obvious he had not and I should not tell him. If it was a true vision, in time he too would see it. I could then share with him what I had seen and he would know that he was not misled by his imagination, or by mine.

The night of the initiation came and the preparations for the rite began. The rest of the coven arrived first and then Rob came later alone. I spoke with him for a while. He was very tense.

We were to initiate Rob in our London temple. I took him to a separate room to remove his clothes; for in the Gardnerian and Alexandrian traditions of Wicca, the rites are performed naked. In initiation, we must be willing to expose ourselves, both literally and symbolically. We have to be willing to cast aside the persona and to enter the circle as we first entered the world, naked and vulnerable.

With the removal of our clothes, we are like crabs removed from their shells. We feel exposed and endangered. We trust, but there is also an element of fear. This fear is appropriate, for initiation is not a step to be taken lightly. We are afraid of what we will meet within the circle, and so we should be; for what we will meet there is ourselves — good bits and bad, wise bits and foolish, spirit and flesh.

For the initiation we are also blindfolded. Like the child in the womb who has not yet been exposed to the day, we await in darkness our entry into the circle of light. The blindness symbolizes our spiritual state. We have not yet seen ourselves in the mirror of truth, and until we do, the veils of our egos come between us and the rest of creation. We cannot see ourselves or the world as they really are.

At the beginning of the initiation rite, it is the custom in our coven to introduce the blindfolded initiate to each of the five elements: Air, Fire, Water, Earth and lastly Aether, the element that lies behind and beyond matter. Five Priests and Priestesses had been chosen to represent the elements and the divine forces which corresponded to them. I was to be Aether, the fifth and last. I would lead Rob to each of the four cardinal points of the circle and would introduce him to each element in turn. Then at the centre of the circle, he would be confronted with the last element, with Aether.

I took Rob by the hand and led him to the East, the quarter of Air. His hand was cold and stiff. He seemed very alone, very separate and apart. I touched his arm to move him into position before the Eastern quarter and my etheric energy seemed to burn him. I gave Rob's hand to the Priest who bore the censer, the magical weapon of Air. The Priest began:

I am Puck
Youngest of Gods and oldest of men
My Father was Lord of Space and Shadows
My Mother the Goddess of the Night
Who spins the Web of Time
And naught but two gifts they gave me
The Thread and the Sword which cuts it
But they are the power of life and death

In life no one can know me
In death alone will you see my face
I am the masked Way-Shower
Whom some call Anubis
I am the Spell-Master
The Speaker in Riddles
And some call me Orpheus
Singer of songs and magic
But others call me Loki
The Wizard of the Lie

I entice you to the circle
But leave you in the darkness
For at the threshold and turning point
All must stand alone
I am Air.

Puck had released Rob's hand so that he was truly left in the darkness. After a while I reclaimed him and led him to the South where the Fire Priest waited bearing a flaming torch. I gave Rob into the care of Aureus who drew him near to the heat and light of the flame.

I am Aureus
The Golden One
I am the Sun in its heaven
The Vision of Splendour
The Banisher of Darkness
When my golden rays shine upon you
You are no more alone

I am hope in the heart of man
I stepped forth from the light
Which is Father and Mother of us all
No Goddess gave birth to me
I am the Son of the Most High
The Crown of Kingship is upon my brow
I am Fire.

Aureus released Rob's hand and I led him to the West. A Priestess awaited him bearing Water:

I am Circe
The Mother of Magic
The Moon upon the Sea
From my island kingdom I rule the tides
And would have all things turn to me
For I am Mistress of Witchery

I am love in the heart of man
I have been since time began
Dreaming beneath the darkness
And weaving visions in the light
I am uncertainty

In me all things are in flux
I am not what I seem
Yet I shall not deceive you
I am Water.

Then to the North, where a Priestess waited bearing a bowl of Earth. She took Rob's hand and gently laid it upon the smooth cold surface of the soil:

I am Erin
The last but the first
The elder sister of the Lord of Air
My mother, the Lady Time
Spun as I slept
And wove for me a vision
And when I woke
Out of clay I moulded shapes
That came from deep within my dream
My brother the Air
Breathed life into them
And these were my first children
And I called them The Race of Men
For them I made a sister whom I called Nature
I brought her forth from my womb
As fair flowers and fields and trees
That Man and Nature might dwell in harmony
And now I sleep again
To dream a new creation
Time is slow within me
The passing years are as naught
I am as I always was
I am in trees and stones
I endure where all else fails
I am that which sustains you
I am faith in the heart of man
I am Earth

At last I brought Rob to the centre of the circle. To initiate him, we must be sufficiently in tune for me to act as a channel between him and the Goddess. If we were sufficiently linked, he would know the answers to the questions I would ask. I would know now whether the initiation would succeed or fail.

Would he give the right answer? I was uncertain. That night two weeks before, when we had sat before the fire and I had remembered our shared past, I had thought the link would be strong. Now his body seemed rigid as I led him across the circle. He seemed shut in another place, far away.

What if he did not give an acceptable answer? The situation had never arisen. Well soon we would see. I reached out to him with my mind, but he eluded me. There was a barrier. Was it fear, tension, excitement, or was it something else? I did not know. I hesitated for a moment, but I would wait no longer, I would have to go on. I began:

I am Arianrhod
The last of my race
I am without beginning or ending
For before ever time and change began
My mother the Star Goddess
Lay upon the Lord of Darkness
And brought me forth
Darkness and Light are met within me

I dwell behind the veil of matter
I see but cannot be seen
I hear but cannot be heard
I touch but cannot be touched
Men question my existence
And I answer that I am and I am not
But at the end of cycles and seasons
Which some men name Death
But those who have lifted my veil name Life
On the shores of the Sea of Time you will find me
Listening to the wind
Watching the ebb and flow of your being
And walking by the waves of the aeons and waiting
For your comings and your goings

In truth I was
I am and I will be
When all else has long-faded from your memory
I am something which you possess
And something which you seek
I am something which you have
And something which you have not

I am the question and also the answer
I am that which binds and that which sets free
I am Aether.

The time for the questions had come. I took his hands in mine. 'What is your name to be,' I asked. 'You who seek to walk the way which lies between the worlds?'

'Hermes,' he answered.

'You take the name of the Lord of Knowledge. Is it knowledge that you seek?'

'Yes.'

'You take the name of the Lord of Wisdom. Is it wisdom that you seek?'

'Yes.'

'And is there a third thing that you seek; for you have in your power this night to ask of the Gods a gift?' He hesitated, 'I ask for Faith.'

I did not know what to do. It was not what I had expected. More than this, he had not asked for anything I had the power to give. He had asked for faith, the gift of the Priestess of Earth, not the gift of the Priestess of Aether. The answer was wrong.

Had my intuition failed me? In planning the initiation rite, I had foreseen this moment. I would ask him what he sought and he would ask for nothing — no-thing. I had formulated my response:

Only the wise man or the fool
Refuses a gift from the Gods
And only a God can know
Which of these two a man will be
But only the wisest of men
Knows the answer to the third question
Of the Priestess of Aether
For she who dwells in space
Beyond the veil of matter
Is Priestess of No-thing
And has no-thing to give
And so by your wisdom
You have answered the riddle of Aether
And the powers of Aether are your gift
So rightly shall we call you Hermes
For like your namesake

You sought wisdom and knowledge
And gained mastery over Aether the realm of magic
Which is and yet is not
But which contains the root of all.

The doubts I had had about my role in encouraging him to take the plunge of initiation re-surfaced. Had I done the wrong thing? What should I do? My mind reached out with desperate appeal. Dear Goddess, tell me what to do.

The answer came quickly in the form of a picture. I saw Rob kneeling before the altar to take the oath of initiation. It meant I should go on. Then the response to his request for faith came into my mind. As I heard each line I spoke it,

What you have asked in truth shall be granted you
And a second gift I shall give you
And this is the gift of the Goddess
Who takes and gives as She pleases
And is swayed by the vagaries of her heart
And not by the words of women or men
And that is the gift of love.

It was done. Now we could begin the initiation proper. The Priestess came forward to perform Rob's ritual binding. His wrists were placed upright behind his back and then tied with a cord which was taken up and around his neck, back round the wrists and then back again to his neck. A second cord was tied above his left knee like a garter, and a third around his right ankle. His feet were '*neither bond nor free*'. He was committed but not quite, for until the last moment he must be free to draw back.

Rob waited outside the circle, bound like the Hanged Man in the tarot, with one foot tied and one foot free, his hands bound behind his back. The circle was cast by Sarah. Step by step, she was removing us from the realm of earthly time to the place between the worlds. Then, when the sacred space had been made, and the Guardians of the four quarters had been invoked to protect the circle, it was time to draw down the power of the Goddess.

Andy, as High Priest, knelt before me and began the invocation to the Goddess. There was a stillness and silence within me. Then the flow of the power came, down through my crown chakra, down to my feet and out into the circle. She had come. Andy began the Great Mother Charge:

Listen to the words of the Great Mother, who was of old also called amongst men Artemis, Astarte, Dione, Melusine, Aphrodite, Cerridwen, Diana, Arianrhod, Bride, and by many other names.

Then with the power of the Goddess within me, I responded in Her name:

Whenever ye have need of anything, once in the month, and better it be when the moon is full, then ye shall assemble in some secret place and adore the spirit of me who am Queen of all Witcheries. There shall be assemble ye who are fain to learn all sorcery, yet have not won its deepest secrets; to these will I teach things that are yet unknown. And ye shall be free from slavery, and as a sign that ye be really free ye shall be naked in your rites and ye shall dance, sing, feast, make music, and love, all in my praise; for mine is the ecstasy of the spirit; and mine also is joy on earth, for my law is love unto all beings.

Keep pure your highest ideal, strive ever towards it; let naught stop you or turn you aside; for mine is the secret door which opens upon the door of youth and mine is the cup of the wine of life and the cauldron of Cerridwen, which is the Holy Grail of Immortality.

I am the gracious Goddess who gives the gift of joy unto the heart of man; upon earth I give knowledge of the Spirit eternal; and beyond death I give peace and freedom and reunion with those who have gone before; nor do I demand sacrifice, for behold I am the Mother of all living, and my love is poured out upon the earth.

Andy spoke again:

Hear ye the words of the Star Goddess, She in the dust of whose feet are the hosts of Heaven; whose body encircleth the universe.

I was far away, deep into samadhi; that state of consciousness whereby there is no longer any 'I and other', 'this and that', 'far and near', only a sense of oneness with the universe. As though from a long way off, I heard Andy's voice stop. The power of the Goddess flowed through me once more and I made ready to respond; but before I could begin to speak, the silence was shattered by other voices, not mine. Echoing through the window came the sound of male singing. 'Here we go, here we go, here we go. Here we go, here we go, here we go.'

It was pub closing time and the local football supporters were wending their way home after a Saturday night's drinking. Such noises are sometimes the penalty for practising witchcraft in an urban setting, but this was hardly an appropriate time. From communion with the Goddess and samadhi, I returned to my everyday level of consciousness. I looked across the temple to the corner where Rob stood bound. He was grinning.

I laughed. Suddenly I knew the initiation was going to work. The tension had gone out of Rob and at last my mind could reach him. It was as though a barrier had lifted and the way across the border between the worlds, between initiation and non-initiation, between seeker and priesthood, was open. The power of the Goddess came flooding through me, reaching out across the circle to where he stood and bringing in Her wake the words of the remainder of the Charge:

> *I who am the beauty of the green earth and the white moon amongst the stars, the mystery of the waters...*

My consciousness was spinning, diving down through the levels of being to that centre within us where all things are one. Where we are one within ourselves, with one another, and with the One Divine Source who unites all Gods and peoples.

> *...and the desire of the heart of man, call unto thy soul, arise and come unto me...*

I was aware of separateness again. It was as though Rob and I were once again standing on either side of a ditch with steep banks, just as we had done in the village hall those few weeks before; but this time it was not I who reached my hand to draw him across. It was another — it was She. He took Her hand and he leaped — right over the gulf between the human and the divine which only initiation could bridge.

> *...for I am the Soul of Nature who giveth life to the universe.*

From me all things proceed, and unto me all things must return; and before my face beloved of Gods and men, thine inmost divine self shall be enfolded in the rapture of the infinite.

The visual images left me and I merged once more into oneness with the universe, but this time Rob came with me. Down into the depths of being we went and then up again, high into the stars. From far away I could hear my own voice, still speaking:

Let my worship be within the heart that rejoiceth; for behold all acts of love and pleasure are my rituals and therefore let there be beauty and strength; power and compassion; honour and humility; mirth and reverence; within you.

And thou who thinkest to seek for me, know thy seeking and yearning shall avail thee not, unless thou knowest the mystery; that if that which thou seekest thou findest not within thee, thou wilt never find it without thee; for behold I have been with thee from the beginning and I am that which is attained at the end of desire.

It was over. The formal initiation rite could begin, but the moment of crisis had already passed. He had gone beyond the point of no return and entered the circle already a Priest.

Sarah challenged him, pressing the point of the coven sword upon his heart.

O thou who standest on the threshold between the pleasant world of men and the terrible domains of the Lord of the Outer Spaces...

Rob was asked for the passwords which would give him admittance to the circle. 'Perfect Love and Perfect Trust,' was the response. The Perfect Love which loves others because they carry the divinity within them, even though at times they may deviate far from it; the outpouring love of the Goddess which seeks nothing in return. The Perfect Trust which enables us to conquer fear and takes us beyond the barrier of the ego.

The rest of the initiation passed like a dream. I remember that the Priestesses brought Rob across the circle from the West, the quarter of death, to the East, the quarter of the rising sun, the point of birth. The bell rang 11 times, 3. 1. 3. 1. 3; 'the three are one and the one are three', the rhythm of the Triple Goddess, and I stood before him saying:

> *In other religions the postulant kneels while the priest towers above him, but in the Art Magical we are taught to be humble and so we kneel to welcome you and say...*

Then I knelt before him and kissed his feet.

Blessed Be thy feet that have brought thee in these ways.
Blessed Be thy knees that shall kneel at the sacred altar.
Blessed Be thy phallus without which we should not be.
Blessed Be thy breasts formed in strength.
Blessed Be thy lips that shall utter the sacred names.

He in his turn knelt to me to take the oath of allegiance to the Gods. Then came the end and the Priestesses helped Rob to his feet. Three times I consecrated him with the symbol of the first degree, the downward-pointing triangle, the symbol of the element of Water.

I consecrate thee with oil
I consecrate thee with wine
I consecrate thee with my lips
Priest and Witch

It was done. Later, at the feasting I asked him about the initiation.

'It was very strange,' he said. 'At first I didn't think anything was happening, then when you were saying the Charge it was as though you were about 15 feet tall and speaking from a long way off; then I felt myself rising above the circle...'

I smiled. What I had seen had been his vision also. We had entered together that other realm and the way between the worlds had opened for him.

The initiation was done, but not quite. There was one small aftermath. Two days later I had a dream. I went out of my body and found myself making an astral journey to the Temple of Yesod, the realm of the Moon in the qabalistic Tree of Life. Entering the temple and crossing to the altar, I saw something placed on it I had not seen there before. Lying on the smooth surface of the altar was a cord, the magical weapon of Yesod and a symbol also of the element of Aether. The cord began to move. It turned into a snake. The snake twisted and turned and writhed about itself; then its head and tail came together and it seized its tail by its mouth. A voice seemed to be speaking to me.

'It is Rob's faith; "*that which binds and that which sets free*"; for him it was Aether, the cord.'

I laughed and the laughter woke me. As usual the initiate was wiser than the initiator. How was it that Carl Jung had described the world of the unconscious, the world of the circle, '. . .*a boundless expanse full of unprecedented uncertainty*'[1]? In the circle there are no absolutes; no rights and wrongs. Of course Rob's answer was right; for him faith was aether, that which binds together the fabric of our lives. 'A world of uncertainty' — I would not attempt to foresee an initiate's response again. I remembered what I always told those who were to perform initiation for the first time, 'Every time we initiate, we are ourselves initiated. Every time we teach, we learn a little more.'

There I ended the story; though initiation is a journey which never truly ends. Each day we grow and change and learn a little more. We dance another round of the Goddess's Spiral Dance. In some ways it was an ordinary story about ordinary people, but in some ways not, for in the end we are all both ordinary and extraordinary. As Aleister Crowley said:

'Every man and woman is a star.'[2]

[1] Jung, Carl, *Archetypes of the Collective Unconscious*, para 49.
[2] Crowley, Aleister, *Magick in Theory and Practice.*

The Medicine Circle of Turtle Island

Greg Stafford

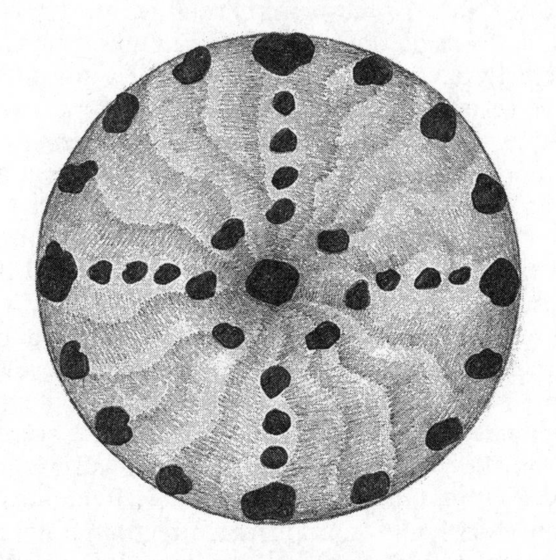

The first time I sat in the sacred circle of Turtle Island was in a sweat-lodge ceremony to prepare for my first vision quest. I was terrified. I had read all the right books but reading about something and doing it are vastly different, especially when you are sitting naked in the dark in a very hot and very small space. The lodge was low and I was sitting on a high spot so that my head scraped the top. Red-hot rocks glowed in the dark, illuminating nothing but themselves. I saw none of the other 12 people squatting in the lodge. It was so hot that the sweat ran down my skin. I tasted the salt on my lips and in my eyes; it made me blink. And the ceremony had not yet begun. I tried to pay attention to Sun Bear's words about staying intent upon the sacred purpose of the ceremony. When he dropped the first water upon the rocks the hot steam filled the small space and I really began to sweat it out.

A sauna can be hot enough to scald your skin and I suppose

that a sweat-lodge could too, but in eight years I have never seen anyone burned in a ceremony. The real heat of the ceremony is a different kind of hotness which can burn away many of the things which separate us from the sacred; it isn't something you understand from books. But at first the spiritual side has nothing to do with it: you must try to accommodate the heat.

I couldn't stand the discomfort of sitting up so I bent forward to the ground, lowering my head to avoid the top, where the heat rose. Now the red-hot rocks toasted the top of my head instead. It still wasn't cool enough. Even now, years later, I am still extremely uncomfortable in a sweat if I am ungrounded. And I was certainly ungrounded in my first sweat.

In between each of the rounds in the sweat ceremony the lodge flap was opened to let in cool air and some light. Sun Bear explained that the first round is to invoke the spirits, the second to receive purification and blessings, the third is the healing round — the time for the deepest moment — and the fourth for thanks.

As the second round began, my initial terror gradually gave way to embarrassment at not being able to sing, and then of being too embarrassed to pray, and then to being angry about that, and finally a desperation in knowing that I wanted to ask for help somehow. After all, circumstances had brought me to this place for this thing, and I sure knew I should not go on a vision quest without some spiritual direction, if not guidance.

One thing to do in the intense heat is to ask the Earth Mother for help, and give her the discomfort. She loves it, for whether it is love or hatred to us the Mother will take it and compost it. I decided to ask, sceptical, but hoping that somehow or other I would earn how to talk back to the voices, to return the messages of the beings which I could sometimes see. I thought to myself, 'If I am crazy then this is the place for it.' I remembered a little boy with antlers from my childhood who was once labelled my 'imaginary friend'. Perhaps I could learn to operate from innocence as I did back then?

The third round is for healing. Often a sweat has a specific objective or patient in mind, and everyone prays for that. There is often a time when you can ask for something for someone else, and it is usually a good time to ask for something about yourself, too. My third round was, at first, insufferable. It was so hot, and I was so tired, I didn't think I could keep in control any more. I didn't. I wept, mortified at first, then relieved. I was not alone in that dark, lonely place. I felt my face in the mud. And I was not hot any more.

Another method of coping with the discomfort is to leave your body and enter into the sacred healing place. The sweat-lodge is a good place to do this because it is safe, as long as certain standards are kept. In a properly led lodge it is possible to experience personal contact with healing, even if you are new at it or don't quite know what it is about. You may not experience it at first, and no one guarantees anything. Maybe you will never touch it, and, frankly, even people who do it often have to work at it too, very hard. But it is worth it.

The fourth round is to give thanks. And thanks I gave, an astonished thanks for the lightness of being which I felt. It was still very hot, but it didn't matter so much.

Afterwards we crawled around the lodge to the door, where each of us bent even lower to thank our relations, then crawled out to the left. I crawled, then sprawled, and felt the hard, dry earth beneath. After a few more minutes I joined the others and leapt into the cold pond nearby. The water was so cold that I could hear my heart thundering in my ears.

The ritual pattern of the sweat-lodge ceremony is the basic form of most of the neo-shamanic ceremony which I have experienced. It is the same for sweat-lodges, medicine pipe ceremonies, singing or chanting circles, and all-night healing circles. This pattern has been popularized by Sun Bear and other teachers.

Shamanism is growing, and its practices are being widely accepted as an integral part of the growing spiritual practices of the New Age. Some people are born into it, like the descendants of the Red Man who lived here before my ancestors did. Sun Bear and H. Storm are among the best-known teachers of this type. Some people seek it out, following the path to the spirit whose call is so plaintive and sorrowful, perhaps inaugurated by intellectual curiosity which opens to something so much greater. Carlos Castaneda, author of the Don Juan books, is one of these. And some of us are dragged, kicking and screaming, to accept what we were told was not, to believe in what we were told cannot be, and to integrate with that which we were told does not exist. But whatever the reason, the movement is growing and defying the lies and half-truths of the decrepit technological civilization which is strangling our world.

Shamanism must be viewed within its current social context.

It is one of many efforts which strives to find new, or ancient, methods of responding to the impending death of our world. The ecology movement, the anti-nuclear movement, the neopagan movement, and even the breakthroughs in subatomic physics are all signs and causes of the impending birth of a new paradigm for existence.

Shamanism is concerned with balance within the microcosm, mesocosm, and macrocosm. It integrates the individual with himself, with his society, and with the cosmos. It is not only a method of mundane healing, though it does do that. It is not just a transcendent experience with the Creator, though it can be that too. It is an experience within living myth, when multiple realities coincide and exercise meaning.

Look at the sweat-lodge as an example of that mythic, multiple reality. The lodge exists in the manifest world as a construction of sticks, rope, and covers. It uses rocks, fire, water, and songs to do the job. Yet it is more. It is shaped like a turtle, with the lodge being the great humped body and the altar which lies before the doorway is its head. To many tribes who performed this ancient rite the continent of North America was called Turtle Island, and using the shape and power of the turtle invokes the power of Turtle Island. The land is our sacred Mother, the Earth. Entering naked into the body of the turtle places us in the primeval state before birth as we sit inside the body of our mother. At the centre of the lodge sits a pit full of red-hot rocks, just like the hottest part of the earth lies in its central core of magma. From it flows the cleansing steam, just like cleansing and nourishing blood flows from our hearts and from the heart of Grandmother Earth. In the darkness we can lose ourselves, meet with the insubstantial, and participate in the unconscious reality which permeates all of creation. In shamanic activity the mythic is experienced, and the impossible can be felt. We must be prepared to feel the impossible.

Spirit communication is never what you think it is. To learn shamanism, one of the first things you should do is try to forget what you think it is like. If you are fortunate enough to have the Earth Mother cradle you to her bosom, or if the Creator lets you glimpse ahead in time, up the road to healing, you should not have a preconception of what it will be. Throw away your astral planes and Trees of Life, because whatever you can think about is not big enough to match what really happens. And you don't want to miss the moment that the cosmic event occurs.

Well, the truth is, yes, most people are going to miss it. No, being in a sweat does not guarantee you anything. Maybe you will just lie there and be miserable like I often have. But even if you are just miserable, try to listen.

The vision quest is another powerful experience, even more than the sweat ceremony. We go into the wilderness, alone with the Creator and whoever He chooses to send to us and who we choose to see.

My first vision quest had many moments even more terrifying than the sweat, and some which were far more ecstatic. I met my first allies who took me through ordeals to view the Black Mountain which lies at the centre of the world. From there I looked out over the world, spying in the distance the spirits of the directions who were waiting for me. I saw, barely at first, the way to my own healing, to the healing of my family, and to the healing of the earth. I determined to begin my journey around the circle of the medicine wheel and upon the path of shamanism. The path has brought me to become a ceremonial leader, a publisher, and a teacher.

Defining modern shamanism is not easy because its practice overlaps so many other psychic practices. The New Age spiritual practices are pluralistic by nature. The cross-cultural merging and synthesis of beliefs and practices obscures the uniqueness which was once so visible when cultures were more distinct from each other. I know no one whose practice is purely shamanic activity. The practising shamans that I know usually incorporate other types of activities into their healing arts. Likewise, many people who exercise other spiritual practices incorporate shamanic actions into their art. Thus in the San Francisco Bay area we are active with several Wiccan groups to incorporate more shamanism into their ceremonies. However, several features distinguish an activity as shamanic. These include the personal nature of the revelation; trance consciousness, often induced by chanting, drumming, and/or dancing; interaction with spirits; certain types of ritual such as vision questing or sweat-lodge ceremonies; mediation and balance to integrate the physical world and the Other Side; and a deep concern for the Earth Mother.

This personal nature of revelation is critical to shamanism. Personal experience is essential to any shamanic reality, and the current movement with which I have had contact centres upon that fact. Take no one's word for it until you have felt it! Do not believe what anyone says until you have done it.

Trance consciousness is one of the keys to shamanic activity. It is impossible to interact with the spirit world and to manipulate the spirit forces with your mind. Shamanic trance consciousness may be deep or shallow, but it is necessary in order to engage parts of the mind, body, and soul into an integrated whole. Thinking is not enough. Feeling is not enough. Being is not enough. All of these things are good and useful, but none of them alone will bring shamanic consciousness.

Rituals are common to all spiritual practices. Certain activities are inherently powerful and contain lessons and processes within themselves, if performed correctly. Shamanism shares many types of ritual with other practices. Initiation into adulthood, for instance, seems to be universal in pretechnological societies. Other ceremonies are unique to shamanism. The sweat-lodge ceremony, for instance, is one. This is a ritual held in common by many tribes of Turtle Island which is used as purification for itself, or as preparation for other rites. Another is the vision quest, wherein an individual goes out into the wilderness to pray, communicate with the spirits, and cry for a vision from the Creator. Another is the sacred pipe ceremony, given to us by White Buffalo Woman as a method of communicating with the Creator and his children.

Another characteristic of shamanism is that it interacts with spirits. Spirits is a vague word which includes almost any living, non-corporeal being, whether a ghost of something once living, the intelligent life force of a place, a manifestation of a natural force like fire, a major vehicle for life force such as the Earth Mother, or the ultimate Supreme Being. Because of the magnitude of these latter forces some people prefer the term transpersonal forces.

Mediation and balance are integral to shamanism. The world has reached the limits of its imbalance within the current cycle and has begun the purification to reintegrate its lessons with the ancient wisdom. People are going crazy from it and personal transformation is an important part of the current shamanic healing to bring individuals into harmony with the world. As individuals grow stronger and more harmonious the social milieu is changing in a slow, but permanent, way. Society is learning to deal with its needs and desires in a holistic manner to preserve the world for the future.

The Earth Mother is central to shamanism, and the Creator is at the centre of her heart. Care and love for her is critical to care and love for ourselves and for the universe. It is as important to a shaman to pick up litter as to lead a ceremony.

However, not everyone who drums or uses the trance state is being shamanic. Many psychologists use skills which are shamanic in nature, or which are shamanic in origin, but are essentially devoid of the spiritual context which is critical to shamanism. Those non-spiritual activities are *shamanistic*, not shamanic. Shamanism deals with entities, shamanistic practices deal with *things* like archetypal forces.

Shamanism can be a blissful and beautiful activity, but it is not without its inherent dangers. Each of its unique characteristics has a potential danger. Ceremonies can be abused; a vision quest which is not prepared for correctly can result in significant kidney damage, for instance, as the participant deprives himself of needed water. Healing can be dangerous to the healer if he depletes his own energy instead of tapping into the universal current. Indiscriminately opening oneself to spirits is downright foolish if the channel is incapable of distinguishing between a hungry ghost and a benevolent spirit of nature. The use of psychedelic agents can be deadly or incapacitating if done without clarity, protection, external support and respect. In general, growth and transformation comes from *use* of a power, while danger stems from *abuse*. An obvious example is the use of tobacco, a sacred herb placed here by the Earth Mother for the carrying of prayers to the Other Side but whose abuse has grown to epidemic proportions.

Another danger is the inherent danger of dealing with real power. I have yet to discover a spiritual activity which does not have both a dark and a light side, and shamanism is no exception. Every activity which deals with real power has its lure towards abuse, often to serve selfish ends. A little power is a dangerous thing, especially where it leads to action based upon judgemental thinking. I do not support unthinking activity, nor do I propose a lack of discrimination, but every action must be carefully weighed to find whether or not the motivation is based upon the public good or upon a private desire.

The best way to deal with the uncertainty is to question everything. In fact, *always* question everything. Don't take anyone's word for it. Do it yourself. Sometimes I never feel whatever exercise we practise, whether is is sweats, journeying, healing circles, or simple singing. Instead I try to just perceive what I do actually experience, especially during sacred ceremonies and times. This is not to say that you ought to disbelieve everything a teacher tells you, and it is certainly not giving permission to be rude or ridiculous in your actions. Respect is a tool of life, and we must respect each other, our teachers, and those who seem to be less than we are. Arrogance, anger, and aloofness are the signs of a stunted spirit which has denied a part of itself. Remember that even the worst fool can be a teacher, but there is no need to subject yourself to ridicule and pain, and the greatest teacher lies within yourself.

I often heard that the path of shamanism is the path of the heart. I did not understand at first. I could not, for my own heart was blocked and painful. The thought of love embarrassed me, the idea of feelings frightened me, and the practice of compassion amazed me. But over the years of work and study, of suffering and understanding, I finally learned to trust my heart. Your heart is your centre of the universe, and it is your connection with the Great Spirit. You must learn to trust it.

The sacred circle of Turtle Island provides the guidelines for all of our journeys. My path to power followed it, repeating and clarifying the lessons which I learned in my first sweat.

I began in the South. In the South lie the powers of the heart — innocence, love, and family. I had spent many months tending to my dying father, watching him grow smaller and smaller and more and more silent as he lay wasting away in my home. When I was an adolescent, 10 years earlier, we had expressed hatred towards each other, a bitter poison which nearly killed me. Over the final months we spent the time healing old wounds, expressing the tremendous love which exists naturally between father and son, healing the things which I once thought could never be fixed. Now I felt his love, saw into the generous heart, understood his own terrible pain which had caused the fierce rift between us. Shortly afterwards I was given the gift of a workshop to Huichol land for the price of a $5 raffle ticket. There, among the Indians of Mexico where my teachers had studied, I delved even deeper into the realms of my ancestors and was blessed with the meeting of my southern spirit. I was not surprised to find it was the deer spirit, the sacred dancer who had amused and protected me as a child. No 'imaginary friend' any more, he taught me the dance of the heart.

The West is the land of introspection, death, fear, and healing. A sensitive child, I was ridiculed and disbelieved when I spoke of the thoughts and feelings which rose up from within me at the sight of a jewelled flower or a laughing black dog. Denied the truth of my self, I invested instead in the suffering of madness which was the only excuse I could understand. My life became haunted like the land of the dead. It was a place I had visited many times, growing to surround me during the darkness of my adolescence when my own blindness drove me to hate my parents, my country, and myself. Steeped in disbelief and denial I surrounded myself with the dark dance of death and drug addiction, trying to block out the voices which I heard and the beings which I saw. At last, subject to the fatal illness brought on by my own addiction, I met the Lord of Monsters who opened my weeping eyes and turned my vision inward. After many years I found the magic place again, and from deep within the darkness I learned how the Black Monster is the White Healer. Since then she has sung to me, and sometimes I can sing her songs in this world too.

The North is the land of elder wisdom, of mature strength, and the power of the giveaway. Once I sat upon a mountain, leader in a ceremony, when the person who I respected most turned upon me with anger and righteousness. I saw the world split before me, two paths whose outcome depended entirely upon my choice. I chose the hard one, stood up for the correct outcome instead of the easy one, and felt the crystal mountain move into my heart.

The East is the realm of beginnings, of insight and vision, and of the golden powers of light. Once I was blessed with a free journey to England, and took the time to visit Glastonbury. Suffering from the wrongness of my marriage and the pain of denial, I walked the magical world of the labyrinth. There, in the centre of the world, I met my spirit of the East, another childhood image which I had carried throughout life. I was liberated from the dark, and at last I understood the call and challenge of the Holy Grail, of the knights who seek it, and of the responsibility of those who take the call.

Now I can sit in the centre of the world. Now, sometimes, the sweat-lodge is neither terrifying nor unbearable. Now I have a dozen stories of power and of love to relate, holding out the hope to others that their dreams are not madness, that their hopes are not foolish, that their desires are not in vain, and that their darkness need not be death.

But remember, there is a world of difference between reading and doing. Do not fool yourself with words and thoughts. Follow your heart, and find the path which is yours.

Pictish and Keltic Shamanism

Kaledon Naddair

I come not from this Land cried I,
I come from the Land where the Secrets lie.

My People are not your People cried I,
for they are the People of Forest, Mountain and Sky.

Your Races migrate, change and die,
My People are Immortal and never die.

You lost your way, pronounced us dead,
We wonder why, for we know that is a lie,
For we have never left these
Mountains, Forests, Rivers, Sea and Sky.

I come not from this Land cried I,
I come from the World where the Secrets lie.

'Through Another's Eyes'

Just like a traditional Shaman I acted as a channel for the above message, and whilst I allowed a mighty Keltic God to speak through my body, my own higher consciousness was instantaneously teleported to a far-off steep hillside.[1] Even after years of preparatory training, I found that experience (and others like it) quite extra-ordinary! Many 'ordinary' people may reasonably ask what is desirable about undergoing such strange happenings. I shall present, I hope, quite a few desirable reasons shortly; for the present one could perhaps appreciate the importance of the above poem representing as it does a viewpoint other than human.

Pictish and Keltic Shamanism is the native initiatory system practised by the ancient Druids (not to be confused with the white-robed genteel claimants to such titles today). On the whole, it is a nature-based *Pagan* spiritual system in that the Otherworld Beings plus Gods and Goddesses that it deals with were worshipped long before the Incarnation of the Christ.

It was formulated by wise men and women of a people who lived within a close symbiotic interplay with Mother Earth, it thus embodies thousands of accumulated insights into the subtle cycles and resonances within Nature. That such European Ancestral wisdom is now increasingly precious, should be obvious from the fact that modern humanity has become dangerously out of harmony with the environment. Apart from general pollution of the air, land and water, we have the chemical manipulation of the soil, its crops and livestock; large-scale climatic disturbances; acidification of the rain, snow, rivers and lochs causing, in turn, decimation of fish stocks, and the blighting of much of the Black Forest and similar old woods. In the last decade we have been given many warnings, to recall just a few:

1. the death of millions of elms (including the demise of many rookeries) with yews, oaks, beech and other species shaping up to follow.

2. a million dead eels in the Rhine after a discharge of toxic effluent by just one factory.

3. the weakening of natural defence and immune systems by seaborne pollution such that thousands of seals are now dying from a disease akin to canine distemper.

4. the continual extinction of plant, bird and animal species as well as their habitats.

5. freak storms and droughts.

6. Post-Viral-Syndrome, AIDS and many other anomalies.

In the face of all this, governments continue to fail in their responsibilities and drag their heels, whilst industrialists only promise us more technological pseudo-solutions. As yet, it only seems to be ecological environmentalists, green pagans and certain rock groups that are displaying the required urgent concern. The immediacy of the problem for Shamanistic Pagans cannot be overstressed, for I have sadly monitored how our totem-channels to power, such as trees, birds and animals are increasingly diseased or disappearing, whilst the ancient sacred sites are being destroyed or proscribed as 'out of bounds'. In the face of such a depressing situation (which does *not* go away if one closes one's eyes to the worsening problems), I believe only a major re-educative 'green philosophy' can save our ailing environment. By relating some more of my personal involvement with Pictish and Keltic Shamanism, I hope to share a few of its main characteristics and how to reuse it in modern life.

Well, after about 10 years spent giving myself a thorough grasp of the Western Traditions (Qabalah; Gnosticism; Keltic, Scandinavian and other Indo-European Mythologies) I became ever more drawn to my present incarnational roots in Keltic and especially Pictish Shamanism. One of the special things about the ferocious Picts was that they were the only mainland British people to consistently fight off the Roman legions, hence ensuring that their Pagan system of beliefs survived unclassicized down into at least the sixth, seventh and eighth centuries. Much of this wisdom was encoded into the class I and II Pictish symbol tones.[2] Other elements were retained within Highland folklore as to the correct ritual actions to be done at Cup and Ring mark sites. At the time when the Cup and Ring mark carvings were being pecked into the sedimentary bedrock (c. 3,500- 1,000 BC) the Picts inhabited the whole of Alban as well as much of the North of Albion (those portions that later became the Brythonic kingdoms of Elmet, Rheged and Brigantia). At this early period they were probably known as the Pretanoi, Qretanoi or Kruithny (hence Prydain, the Prettanic Isles) their other name of Picti (or Ffichti as the Kymry denominated them) likewise focuses on the 'Kruiths' ('shapes, animal forms and designs') that they painted or tattooed (peik) upon their bodies.

Starting from the position of post-industrial, mid-technological age urbanities, I believe it is still possible for us to draw close to ancient Pictish Shamanism but to bridge the cultural gulf successfully requires strenuous and major reconditioning. Whilst

imagination and creative visualization have a role to play on this reclamation process, they must be guided so as not to err, by:
1. an in-depth intellectual study of most of what was written about the ancient Kelts covering all aspects of their culture, language and spirituality.
2. a practical experiential contact with Nature to acquire some firsthand tactile knowledge of what our Ancestors would have been steeped in as their everyday reality.

To aid people in these aims, I founded The College of Druidism in 1982. Some of the teaching material that we supply is designed to lead students' minds right to the heart of lore on Native Shamanism.[3]

To balance such copious intellectual re-education I encourage people to emulate the training processes that my Druidical group has undergone. A very elementary step is to learn to identify all the types of Keltic trees and shrubs at all times of the year (and at night also if possible). Now, whilst you are trying to recognize the various tree clans, don't just stand there looking and reading your 'Field Guide to Trees' book (for that is much too cerebral an approach), also touch and feel the leaves, for some are rough, hairy, sticky, silky-smooth, moist, dry or waxy. This will help you tell them apart (a real Druid could, for example, easily tell alder and hazel leaves apart in misty pitch-darkness, for, although both are roundish and similar sized, the hazel leaves are distinctly hairy). Another method is to smell or even taste leaves (a useful check at night especially). Aim to learn the 20 main Ogham trees first, then the 'five extra trees', thereafter the 10 alternative native substitutes. Please, when identifying, try and go beyond their usual English/Latin names and link them with their Ogham-Gaelic/Koelbren-Welsh Keltic names. Apart from hand dowsing, another energy-attunement is to meditate up in trees (asking the permission of the tree first of course). If you intend a long meditative trance, or period of dream-sleep, then please tie yourself onto a thick branch safely first (note that an hour or more up in a tree cleanses the human aura, lightens it and alters our sense of balance and orientation — doing is believing, I speak from experience).

Another channel to work upon the senses is to employ the blossoms, leaves, fruits and bark from certain native trees, shrubs and herbs to formulate Keltic incenses. My Tree Wildman Guide overshadowed me last year to create a range of two dozen Shamanistically-matched purely native incenses. Whilst most are pleasantly uplifting and gently healing, some are magically much more serious and powerful. For example, one type called 'Dark Evergreens' affects the left brain control circuits of the motor- nerve system, encouraging you to learn how to work consciously through the will-centre and thence to the right-brain circuits. (The first couple of times my ritual group used this incense in our temple, some of the more cerebral men constantly fell over whilst dancing, whilst the women fared well and I had the strongest and clearest contemplations ever!) Another of our incense range called 'Dream-Maker' always does great things (for myself especially, as it contains a totem herb, Valerian root) but in our woodland grove this Samhain, it was truly magical. So the power-smoke of the Shamans is back at work in Keltia, and as none of our mixes contain hallucinogens, that is doubly impressive.

One avenue for Shamanistic exploration that is of great importance (especially with the British and Irish climate) is water. Most of the year (except perhaps summer) rivers and the like, all tend to be pretty cold places to swim in. This fact gives most people (especially city dwellers) enough of an excuse to never go in them. Such physical cowardice renders urbanites far less hardy than our ancestors and far more prone to 'catching colds'; it also deprives such people of many invigorating and profound experiences. In magic, it is often a case of the more you give, the more you are likely to get; thus, if you were intending to become a real Shaman(ess) you would have to attempt much that ordinary 'comfortable' folk would leave well alone. For example, members of my own Shamanistic group regularly, at all times in the year, swim in rivers, lochs and waterfall pools. Whilst being brave, trainee Shamans should also be wisely prudent and know their own limits, thus, I caution against swimming in rivers in spate; going under waterfalls during the thaw; or exploring dangerous tidal caves. One can start from a pleasant midsummer paddle in a clean river and progressively tackle more demanding options. The rewards can be fantastic, for as Viktor Schauberger[4] indicated, each healthy river *is* an alive river-serpent spirit; thus I know of techniques of how to meditate in rivers, wade through them to gain power, and how to achieve a consciousness-exchange with them. I will never forget the 'out of body' psychic sight I briefly obtained through the shock of swimming naked underwater in a river of which I had broken the border of ice to enter (it was midnight on the winter solstice). Less extreme Shamanistic attunements involve silent contemplation of water sounds, or conversely to use an appropriate Keltic invocatory chant whilst striding through the Linn-Uisge (water serpent).

As the boulders that protrude out of rivers are often slippy, I'd advise the following exercise to be tried mainly in rocky coves at the sea-shore — it is simply to jump from rock to rock, thereby recultivating a better sense of balance and agility. If sea waves are washing in-between, this will give one added incentive to 'make it' (and not get wet), or deter some others from even trying. Remember that to properly redevelop Shamanistic powers, one has to do more than 'in the head' attunements; in traditional cultures the Shaman(ess) was often physically dynamic and supple, unlike most modern stiffies. Storing psycho-physical power to make a physical/metaphysical 'leap' is a cardinal tenet of Keltic or other Shamanisms.

Without ascending in a hang-glider or basket balloon, one can yet experience a fair bit about air currents and wind characteristics by, for example, dancing with totemistically-emblazoned Keltic pennants on a windy hillside; or flying a Keltic kite! This can be accompanied with chants in the Old Tongues, suitable Keltic tunes backed by flutes, tin whistles and even bull-horns.

Whilst not immediately romantically appealing, bleak moorland (like Dartmoor, Ilkley, Bodmin, Doddington and Rannoch) can make a profound impact on the soul (they also host a particular type of faerie wildman and some Cup and Ring marked stones). Long walks in the wilder hills and mountains enrich the spirit with far more energy than is physically expended (as Calum McDonald of Runrig[5] says, Mountains are Holy Places). The ancient Druids well knew this and did mountain-top rituals to the rock spirits and relevant Gods and Goddesses. Although often found within such environs, caves (especially if deep) demand a radically different magical approach. The structure and acoustics will dictate what is suitable or permissible in the line of chanting. drumming, bell-playing, as well as silent contemplations. They can sometimes produce truly remarkable psychic and spiritual contact such as I and friends recently experienced in a quarter-mile deep Limestone cave, in Germany (for a fuller description see my forthcoming book on *Druidism: Ancient and Modern*[6]). This magical- spiritual dimension to deep caves is of course why the primeval medicine -men used them for their superb rock art (easier to reach, but less 'potent' surfaces were available but not utilized).

As I have mentioned 'Spirits' and 'Faerie Wildfolk' a few times already so far, perhaps this would be a suitable juncture to explore the subject more fully. During the several thousand years of Keltic history, and within the various Keltic tongues, several hundred names for nature spirits have been noted. Their names (analysed via root words) show them to have been described according to (i) their appearance or mode of manifestation, (ii) their role within functioning Nature, (iii) their habitat or Shamanistic station.

Although I'm cautious about employing generalizations, it is perhaps allowable to group the Faerie Clans into two main types: (i) The Light Elves (Alp-Luachra, Leuchairpins, Lios Alfar, White Boggarts), Shamanistic East through South to Shamanistic West in station; (ii) The Dark or Swarthy Elves (Am Fear Glas Mor, Bukka- Dhu, Black Boggarts, Swart Alfar), from Shamanistic West through North to Shamanistic East in station. On the whole, the Light Elves are of a gentler, friendly, more tolerant disposition, though they are harder to see, even psychically, during daylight (due to their extreme speed and high rate of vibration). The Dark Elves tend to be much more reserved, harsher, sultry, intolerant and even ferocious in disposition. Due to their heavier, slower rate of vibration, it is somewhat easier to see them in the dusk or darkness, though still far from easy. None of these beings are anti-human in temperament, but from their essential nature which is un-human they act according to far different laws and modes of action. Before the age of church-fostered superstition, these beings were known to be generally beneficent, occasionally ambivalent, rarely actively hostile, and never 'evil' (a completely inappropriate concept). Our Ancestors had more finely- tuned physical senses (not eating chemicalized junk food, and not living in a polluted world) thus they more often perceived these Otherworldly beings, and in a truer appearance. Nowadays, many urban people suffer from bad conditioning, and clouded or twisted psychic vision, thus distortion can occur in the visual tunnel.

Whilst I feel it is vital for humanity to re-experience a dialogue with the hidden forces of nature, I always advise some cleansing deconditioning first, plus personal atonement for the devastation homo-sapiens have caused within the delicate web of life. To be convinced of your integrity and commitment to healing the poisoned wounds in Nature, the Wildfolk and Gods may nowadays require more than mere verbal platitudes (for 'words are cheap'), thus my group and I have planted several hundred native oaks, ash, willow, rowan, beech and pine as well as grappling with mud to dig out a whole new woodland pond. After such thoughtful caring in action even some of the taciturn Svart Alfar may warm to your human company; but as mankind's debt is massive never presume to familiarity, always just seek contact with those Otherworldly beings with whom your own 'Shamanistic station' can harmonize.

Although genuine sightings are rare, if one gathers the traditional accounts and more recent encounters together, then it is possible to delineate some of the main forms that the Faerie Wildfolk archetypally manifest through. Perhaps the commonest form of appearance is roughly hominid (upright stance and about six – eight feet tall), possessing a thick, shaggy, overall hair-covering, otherwise being naked. Such Faerie Wildmen (occasionally also the Wildwomen) are extremely thick-set and give the psychological impression of being immensely strong. Notable un-human characteristics are that they (i) sometimes have red glowing eyes; or eyes that glitter and sparkle extraordinarily; or eyes of swirling mist-light; or eyes like deep, black, calm pools — rarely human-like eyes, (ii) their mouths are sometimes broader, as a gaping slit, (iii) where one would expect a nose they sometimes have but two holes, (iv) their forehead or ears can slope back markedly, (v) they sometimes possess a short or long tail.

These features have been perceived not only in the hairy Faerie Wildfolk of Keltia, but also in the original Greek and Carthaginian descriptions of Hairy Saytors; in Chinese, Tibetan and Siberian illustrations of the Yeh-teh; Almas; Tungu; Mi-Go; Leskii (Wood-Spirit); Kiltanya ('Goggle Eyes'); Teryk ('Dawn-Man'); Dzhulin ('Peaked-Head'); Mirygdy ('Broad-Shoulders'); and lest Christians forget them — the Hairy Angels of the Sinai or other desert mountain wildernesses (akin to the Being Yaqov (Jacob) wrestled with all night until the dawn, a true Djinn).

Back in Keltia, some of the Faerie Wildfolk from the bleak, wet bogs such as 'the Brown Man of the Muirs' (of Northumberland) are a stocky four – five feet in height (a friend has given me a similar eye-witness account from Dartmoor). Some cave and underground Spirits can materialize as a squat, heavy four foot tall Being. Other graceful and slim beings have been observed in sunny meadows and birch-scrub field surrounds.

The more noble hill and mountain spirits like Am Fear Glas Mor (The Big Grey Man of Ben Mac Dhui) have been seen as standing nine – eighteen feet tall by several respectable witnesses. If genuinely encountered, such mighty beings make an awesome impression on the viewer's psyche. (Whereas the mainly derogatory tales about the 'little folk' I put down to, (i) imperfect human consciousness like when your TV malfunctions to give only a narrow band across the screen, (ii) confusion with tiny flower-elementals/spirits which are completely different in rank from the mighty Faerie-Wildfolk, (iii) adverse Christian or Victorian conditioning.

Apart from the roughly hairy humanoid form of the Wildfolk (well depicted as British Woodwoses, or in Rhineland Wildfolk tapestries) others are more animal, bird or tree-like. Indeed, they can appear as an 'Owl-Man'; a spectral black dog with red glaring eyes; a wolf, bear, fox, goat, horse, seal or stag-man. Some are twice as large as the ordinary creatures could be, others are uncannily elongated (thin eight – ten foot characters are depicted on some Pictish symbol stones and Anglo-Saxon illuminated manuscripts).

Also, as associates and I have at times witnessed (and perhaps even photographed) the Wildfolk Spirits can draw near to us in pillars of light; luminous bobbing spheres of misty white light; glittering shimmerings on cave walls; a hollow cylindrical larger-than-human column of coloured light; a shining, serpentine, very fast energy flow (about as quick as a speeding arrow), and yet other modes near impossible to put into words, such as 'abstract' shapes, flowing patterns, spinning fiery wheels etc.

As varied as these modes of manifestation are (once we filter out distortions in perceptions and 'fear-induced human imaginings') there still remains certain regularly recurring forms that the different orders of these Beings choose to appear in. If one surveys these archetypal forms (Kruiths) carefully, then I feel it is possible to discern the 'station' of the Being of the Shamanistic Wheel, as well as its rank (i.e. does it operate on the subatomic, etheric, astral or truly spiritual plane predominantly). Your reaction can then be adapted in the light of such an insight.

Some of these Beings can act as guides into the subtler workings of nature; some of them are messengers from the Gods, Goddesses and even the almighty Godhead; some are Pagan deities (for the upper echelon of the Faerie Wildfolk merge into the Gods of various parallel mythologies); they are thus the rungs in the ladder of existence.

By contacting such Beings, one can learn about the super-sensible richness behind the world and kosmos. Although these Beings (especially the more mobile higher entities) can come into our urban dwellings, this rarely happens without first of all contacting them within their retreats in the unspoilt wild places, such as Cup and Ring mark sites

Being little better than most moderns at first, I found it hard to relate to these cup-shaped hollows with their enclosing grooves and tailing-off runnels, for initially they all look pretty similar and give the casual observer little else to go on. However, as I realized that they obviously were of major importance to my Ancestors' spirituality, I repeatedly visited dozens of sites and patiently let them subliminally go to work upon the deeper levels of my psyche. Whilst being unaware of all the wheeling and dealing going on behind the scenes, I slowly came to realize that Cup and Ring mark sites had 'claimed me' at a profounder level than affection or intellectual fascination. It was some months later that I had my first, conscious communication with a Rock Spirit; since then I have contacted, experienced and received telepathic instruction, from several different types of Rock Spirits and Wildman Allies.

One of the first, and most important, forcefully emphatic insights I was given was what constituted the essential purpose of these Cup and Ring mark sites; namely to be used as places of ritual offerings of milk, lustral water, cereal grains, etc to the rock and land spirits. Through a complex chain of energy exchanges (which I can but hint at here) the telluric currents were fertilely galvanized and linked through the luminous liquid-light (milk) to the Wildfolk-guarded herds of deer, goats, sheep and kine and through reflection to interact with the sun, moon and starlight. (Other more steeply sloping Cup and Ring marked sites were used for 'dry-contact' solar energizing; some were used to summon the wind from a particular airt of the compass, whilst the reused Cup and Ring slabs or upright stones functioned as Gruagach/Bodach contact stones (e.g. in Fogous) or as geomantic regulators within megalithic circles.) Most of these revelatory insights were later confirmed by research into historical folk-customs in the Highlands and Scandinavia.[7]

As I have become a sort of Shamanistic pioneer in this field, perhaps it would be instructive if I partially recount one such Rock Spirit encounter. In this case it was with a species of energy being that inhabits a sacred site of volcanic rock near to Edinburgh (that makes this type of spirit rather different from the kind that prefers to manifest themselves through the water- based sedimentary rocks and their Cup and Ring marks). I went to the site with a few members of my Kaer Eidyn Druidical group, after we had chanted a Highland Gaelic invocation to the rock spirits (Frideach na Kreag). I then settled into a receptive contemplation. The energy beings in this instance entered my body through my feet, up my legs and thus permeated my chest, head, arms and hands. Next they took my breathing through two or three abnormal rhythms (this quite often happens in such experiences, but in a variety of different ways). In the process of this, I became suffused with a most extraordinary internal 'heat' and a very different 'rate of vibration' (both these effects were noticed and commented upon by my lady friend Linda, who was sitting above and slightly behind me). The glowing heat was worthy of remark for it was a cool, breezy, high rocky escarpment, especially in the eveningtime.

The changed 'rate of vibration' (and with it a slightly altered perception of the world, especially stones and metals) stayed within me for three days, slowly leaking back to earth, thereby returning me to human 'normality'. If the experience be credited, many average readers may reasonably enquire what is the worth of being so strangely, if pleasantly, possessed. Well, one long-term benefit I have noticed is that my dowsing abilities through my bare hands have greatly improved, and whilst they were initially tutored by energies in stone, I can now hand-dowse temples, churches, trees, wooden tools and human auric fields (allowing me a better diagnostic and healing potential). This obviously broadens and deepens one's understanding of the material world and the humans functioning in it. Another contact with an earth spirit, in the form of a toad elemental, was a directly healing experience. And, as some of the other rock, mountain or river Spirits can sometimes be thousands of years old, one may occasionally be entrusted with an insight or vision into the wisdom of times long past (I have had one such vision, the knowledge content of which would be impossible to obtain via archaeology or by any other normal means). One spin-off benefit from my guidance by rock spirits and the knowledge that they have taught me, is that I have what to others must appear as an 'uncanny knack' of discovering new Cup and Ring mark sites long- buried under the turf and moss of Argyll, Dumfries, Galloway and Northumberland (over a dozen sites, two of them quite major, so far).

Whilst Cup and Ring marks are found in many far-flung corners of the planet, one unique development that happened in Kaledonia was that much of the knowledge previously experienced at Cup and Ring mark sites was encoded upon the later Pictish symbol stones. The Pictish Druids consciously made the transition, not only reusing some of the Cup and Ring mark sites, but even certain Cup and Ring stones became symbol stones (e.g. Meigle No. 1, Ardblair etc). The earliest 'sketched' representations significantly appear on initiation cave walls (e.g. at East Wyeems). After the Roman threat to Native continuity, it was thought prudent to enshrine more of the arcane tradition into petroglyphs. Thus there arose the unique* Pictish system of between 150-200 Shamanistic symbol glyphs.

In the Pagan class I stones, the symbols are mainly of the naturalistic totem animals and birds, some depict Faerie creatures, some composite symbolic beasts, as well as 'abstract glyphs' (most notably the superb 'arch and v-line' — a sophisticated calendrical device). These Pagan symbols continued to be used alongside a knotwork cross (in class II stones) for Pictish Christianity happily retained much of the Elder Wisdom.

It was only as the more narrow-minded, Pagan-hating missionaries from the Church of Rome and Scotic Church forcibly took over in Alban do we see the demise of the Pagan Pictish symbols (c. ninth- tenth centuries in class III stones). It is thus sad to relate that dozens, possibly hundreds, of the priceless type I & II Pictish symbol stones were broken up by the Orthodox Church in its bigoted zeal (both in its early 'conquering' phase as well as in post-Reformation Scotland). To grasp the immense cultural & spiritual loss that such vandalism has wreaked one has to fully appreciate what these symbols conveyed; thus I suggest you read my *PICTISH ART : Its Shamanistic Symbolism, Aesthetics and Sacred Geometry*, Keltia Publications, 1989.

Between the Church and callous farmers such destructions have left gaps in what would have otherwise been an even more impressive heritage of Pictish Shamanistic art. Apart from the

*Unique in Europe because although a few of the symbols have Indo-European parallels, and although Lappish Shamans painted symbols on their drums and costumes, the Pictish symbols were standardized and used for centuries by the Pagan Druids throughout Pictland.

fruits of long, exhaustive research, I have also been given the 'lost' meaning to certain Pictish symbols through my Wildman-Teacher. Being one of the guardians of such spiritual knowledge he can impart it, but first of all you have to come up to his very stringent tests; then you have to achieve the difficult technique of 'lining-up' inside, so as to become a suitably trustworthy channel. The process of one such encounter I have partially described as follows:

'The Dark Man of the Forest Door'

by Kaledon Naddair (12.30 p.m.-3.30 a.m. 26-27 December 1984)

The Visitor from the Otherside
has returned again
bringing that old familiar restlessness
which no sop to true satisfaction can shake;
I feel a discontented churning of my psychic waters
as the wing-beat of my Spirit descends to draw near.
It comes to prepare my lower self
for another encounter with my Gruagach Guide.

Though my ego seeks a release from this meeting
in each and every passing option.
the great brooding continues to grow
until nothing but its intended fulfillment
will cause it to abate.

I have thus been claimed for another trial.

So be rough with me o' Dark Man,
Mighty Giant of the Hidden Door.
turn me, push me, guide me,
as you have often done before.
For your hard manner is dearer to me
than any soft life of comfort and security.

Under your gaze, that wracks my Soul,
my thoughts are stripped down to their seed-cores,
my emotions are traced to their deep sources,
and my beliefs are taken back to their roots in truth.

What remains to me is always only Pictland:-
its Mountains for my Aspiration,

its Rivers & Lochs for my Purification,
its Forests for my Magical Initiation.
its Carved Rocks as Doors to Power and Communion
And it is from there you've come to test me

All my work-a-day interests drop away,
the chatter of pressing concerns
a rough hand sweeps aside.
I am left to still my Centre
and wait.......
wait.......
to know if he will cross to my World
or I be drawn over to his.

I wait to see his eyes of dark fire,
which sparkle with an agile cunning.
I wait to hear his gutteral, deep-throated laughter,
which pours scorn upon superficial city-humour.
I wait to draw near his Mighty shaggy form
which radiates power all around.

He is my Teacher
my heart leaps, the Salmon-leap,
to follow at his leading.

I cry tears but seldom these days
only those young children of my yearning
and of my caring heart.
Self-pity I have long-since transmuted
in the Alchemy of the will.
For my time is too precious to squander
on whatever lies outside of the Quest.

So be rough with me o' Dark Man,
shake me free
from any remaining foolishness,
slap me Awake.
For still I grope my way over the Thresholds
and stumble half-blind through the dimensions.

Teach me your shape-shifting Artistry,
Teach me protection as I carry my light aloft,
Teach me swift-travel along the Inner Pathways,
Teach me how to enter my beloved Koed Kaledon at will.

These you know to be the longings of my stilled centre,
O'Dark Man of Kaledonia's Wild Places,
lead me home.

Notes

1. The author's spellings of 'K' for 'C' have been retained throughout, in accordance with his wishes. The 'C's' are only an imposition of the Latin (and later Anglo-Saxon) alphabets, thus Kaledon wishes to reuse the more authentic Keltic and Indo- European spellings of 'K', 'Kh', 'Ch', & 'Q', (e.g. the Latinized 'Hercules' is more properly 'Herakles' in Ancient Greek). This article retains the author's idiosyncratic capitalization.

2. Slightly differently from Allen and Anderson the author uses class I Pictish symbol stones to denote those essentially pre- Christian stones featuring solely Pagan zoomorphic and calendrical symbols pecked/engraved onto the rough stone. (The late dating academics give to this type the author rejects as it is based on not a scrap of evidence.) Class II the author defines as those exemplars of the art of the Pictish Church — a harmonious blend of the Elder Pagan symbolism with a rich knotwork cross (dated sixth-eighth- ninth century AD), often executed in high relief. Class III cross-slabs are those showing signs of the encroachment of the Church of Rome & Anglo-Scotic missionaries e.g. all Pagan symbols have been dropped, only a few Angels & Evangelists remain, all the knotwork is cruder in execution and inferior in design (eighth-eleventh century AD).

3. During the first two-three degrees in The College of Druidism course students are required to buy and learn from Kaledon Naddair's books *Keltic Tree Lore* (due 1989); *Keltic Bird Lore; Keltic Animal Lore* (2 Vols); *The Keltic Shamanistic Calendar* (2 Vols); *Names For Trees (& what they mean)* and other pertinent titles. Also various Keltia publications 'Wall-Chart Calendars' on the Keltic divinities, Faerie-Wildfolk & Ogham & Koelbren alphabets are deemed most useful. Students are also given 'further reading lists' recommending excellent books written by fine Keltic scholars last century, as well as by contemporary authors.

4. ref. Olof Alexandersson *Living Water (On the Discoveries of Viktor Schauberger)* Turnstone, 1982.

5. Runrig a truly great Gaelic Rock Group, albums to date are: *Highland Connection, Recovery, Heartland, The Cutter and the Clan* (all on Ridge Records), and *Once in a Lifetime* (Live) on Chrysalis.

6. *Druidism : Ancient and Modern* a major book by Kaledon Naddair in preparation at present and due out late 1989 or early 1990.

7. Some of the evidence for traditional practices at cup and ring mark sites has already been presented in a chapter in my book *Keltic Folk and Faerie Tales*, Century, 1987, more will appear in a forthcoming book on *Cup and Ring Marks and Other Sacred Rock Art*.

She of Many Names

Beth Neilson and Imogen Cavanagh

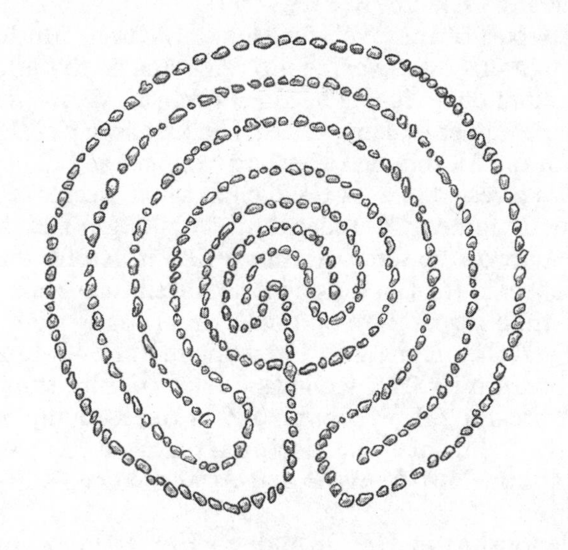

The all-encompassing Goddess has, over time, been seen in various forms in different cultures. In some, She has been seen as one, in others two, three, four or more aspects. Within European Pagan traditions the Goddess has most commonly been understood as having three faces or aspects. In the literature, and within Pagan groups, these aspects are most often characterized as Maiden, Mother and Crone. This way of seeing the Goddess has been written about at length in many publications, for example in the works of Starhawk and Janet and Stewart Farrar. There is a lesser-known tradition in which the Goddess is seen in triple aspect, but these aspects are significantly different from Maiden, Mother and Crone. The aspect, which stands at the centre and is symbolized by the full moon, is not for us the Mother and bears little resemblance to most other Pagan conceptions of Her.

As the wheel of the festivals turns, we see the Goddess changing and transforming through the year, the seasonal cycle reflecting the transitions She undergoes. For us She reflects not just the changes in the lifespan of women but also our individual relationship to Her. It is helpful to our understanding of the Goddess to consider the sets of triple colours, symbols and qualities we associate with Her — the colours of white, red and black; blue, green and purple; waxing, full and waning moon; the hearth, maze and cross-ways; heaven, earth and underworld; life, power and wisdom.

The early part of the year sees Her as Creatrix, Mother and Virgin Daughter — the Waxing Moon, giving birth both to the universe and to the twin Gods, sun and storm, complementary mirror images rather than opposites. The first aspect of the Goddess is both the Mother and Her own younger self. The younger aspect is revealed to us at Candlemas as the Bearer of Light, the Virgin Daughter. To understand why Virgin and Mother should be part of the same aspect we find it helpful to reflect that this aspect of the Goddess does not bleed. Her main colour of white symbolizes both the pre-menstrual young woman (the daughter) and the pregnant and lactating mother — white is the colour of breast milk. Her secondary colour of blue symbolizes the sky, the realm over which this aspect rules. Mythologically Artemis, the Venus of Willendorf, the pregnant Maltese Goddesses, Hat-hor, Nut, Yemaya[1] and Arianrhod can all be seen as this aspect.

Our relationship to Her is both as Her children and, for women, She is a reflection of our young selves. During those periods of time in women's lives when we are pregnant and mothers, She is the aspect of the Goddess who watches over us, Her pregnancy and childbirth reflecting our own. There is a long tradition in pagan groups of starting new projects, and planting seeds in our gardens during the waxing moon. This aspect watches over all new enterprise and over all young growing things, plants, animals and children.

As the year moves through spring and summer she grows from young girl to full womanhood. From the first stirrings of sexuality with the budding of the leaves, to full autonomous sexual glory shown by the open red rose, She reflects our own growth. This aspect of the Goddess, the Full Moon, stands at the centre of life for us. For women, she rules over our lives from menarche to menopause; She is the Goddess who bleeds. Fire, raw sexual power, and the creative tension of contradiction are all combined.

She is the Goddess whom we have almost lost under patriarchy. Her rediscovery is paramount for women. It is as autonomous, sexual, powerful women that we relate to Her. No gentle Goddess this, she is dangerous and forces us to make difficult choices. Often depicted as wielding a double-bladed axe, which cuts both ways, it comes as no surprise that independent women have chosen this axe as an emblem. What is most important about this aspect for us is the way She cuts through the conjunction under patriarchy of sexual activity and reproduction. This aspect of the Goddess rules over sex but She is not the Mother, She does not give birth.

The queen bee, lions and hawks are all associated with Her. Mythologically, Ishtar (Lady of Love and Power), Inanna, Neith of Egypt, Oshun of Nigeria[2] and Maeve of Ireland can all be seen strongly embodying this aspect. The colours of red and green are most obvious in images of the Faery Queen. For men this aspect is the most difficult to meet because She demands total independence, She must be approached on Her own terms, and like fire, She can burn. She is the aspect who as the muse is the inspiration and tormentor of poets.

The wheel turns again, from autumn to winter and the Goddess transforms again, from Priestess to Disintegrator. Symbolized by the waning moon, She rules the third part of the year. Magic, vision, healing and death, are all parts of Her realm. Her Medusa/Hag faces hide her beautiful face as the Queen of the Underworld. She is the Goddess who rules our old age but who also reflects our magical, healing, visionary, witchy selves. She is both stillness and movement combined — the darkest night and the destroying hurricane; the cauldron of rebirth is Hers. Mythologically Morgan le Fay, Kali, Oya, Hecate and Persephone can be seen as this aspect.

The wheel has turned full circle and the Goddess has transformed, aspect through aspect. For women and men all three of Her aspects reflect our lives from birth to death, to rebirth, and also reflect the parts of our lives as they unfold. Waxing, full and waning moon, all blend one into another, overlapping and circling — the three aspects of the Goddess are not divisions, but a symbolic metaphor, a way for us to approach Her.

We see the Goddess, as waxing moon, giving birth to Yule (Winter Solstice) to twin sons, sun and storm. They too grow and transform through the turning year. Symbolized by oak and holly, their relationship to Her as sons, lovers and dying gods reflects our relationship with Her. All of us, both women and men, are born of Her, passionately relate to Her and will die one day. As rulers of equal halves of the year and also as their own mirror images the Gods are both twins and rivals, lovers and destroyers. For men, the Gods present a way of understanding their outer and inner being, as well as a route to approaching the Goddess, Under patriarchy, just as we have almost lost the powerful autonomous and sexual aspect of the Goddess, so too we feel that the aspect of the God symbolized by storm and holly has barely survived. The sun God has remained and in many pagan systems He combines both the qualities we associate with the sun/oak God and some, though not all, of the qualities of the storm/holly God.

For the men who celebrate the festivals with us, working with both aspects of the God is the means to rediscovering their own role as priests and as men in the outer world. The Gods enable them to develop their relationship both with/to the Goddess, with/to women and, perhaps most importantly in this society, with/to each other. The twin Gods offer a means of developing their love and understanding of their own sex, whether as heterosexual or gay men.

For us the three aspects of the Goddess and the two aspects of the God turn the wheel of the year, their interrelationship creates the movement of the festivals of an ever turning spiral, the dance of the universe.

Beth Neilson

The cycle of the seasons gives me something new every year; it is a spiral process in which present understanding resonates with the echoes of the past festivals we have celebrated. The marking of the seasons brings me great joy, a sense of mystery, and a heightened perception of the changes in nature around me. The reflections I see of the Goddess and the Gods in the seasonal dance of nature help me, too, in very practical ways.

Like many who work as healers and counsellors, I have a continuing need to accommodate and transform my emotional reactions to the painful experiences that are shared with me. My work with others cannot be done coldly and objectively, and I am always aware of the parallels between my own experience and theirs.

Though we do not celebrate the Goddess and the Gods as a form of therapy for ourselves, working a seasonal cycle offers us insights about our own lives that are renewed and deepened each year. The best way I know to share some of my experience of the Goddess is through the heart rather than the mind, by offering very personal recollections of the seasonal festivals of the year that we celebrate.

Candlemas Eve

The light is really increasing now, daylight will linger till almost five o'clock. I hang new crystals in my South-facing window to catch the growing light, and check that I have many candles for tonight. It is St Bride's Day and the feast of the Goddess Brighde. Last night I hung my rush-plaited St Bride's cross over the doorway.

I think of the Goddess as Snow Mother piling delicate coverlets of white lace over the countryside. The image is interrupted by the phone ringing. It is my own mother who tells me she will go to church on the next day for the Purification of the Virgin. Immediately I am pleased that she and I will both celebrate the feast in our own ways. Yet I wonder why women have to be purified because they have performed that great act of magic, childbirth, that holy act that seems to have inspired humankind's early instincts to religious awe. I think of the pregnant Goddesses carved on rock faces and hewn from stone — surely they did not need purification from the mystery of blood and pain?

At our feast of Candlemas we imagine the Goddess going down to the sea, sick at heart and exhausted, a sorrowing mother who has been parted from her child born at Winter Solstice. For us it is in part a festival of loss, of the separation of mother and child because of society's constraints. I see the woman in wartime who parts with the child whose hair, skin and eyes are the 'wrong' colour (not her husband's), and wonder again that humankind has dealt so badly with the discovery of paternity. A wave of longing passes through me for a place outside time where children are the greatest wealth of the community, and no one questions how they arrive in the womb of the Great Mother and into the wombs of the women who are her image.

The phone rings again. It is my friend Helen — a new bout of depression and self-hatred has come upon her. She feels self-destructive, and though she knows intellectually that her self-hatred comes from years of sexual abuse by her father, she cannot heal herself overnight. There is no single miracle of healing and self-renewal that can be sought as an instant answer for years of abuse, but I think of Brighde and tell Helen that today is Brighde's day, Brighde who extends her protection particularly to women and children. I tell her that tonight we will visualize the Goddess going down to the sea-shore to renew her virginity in the gentle waves, a Mediterranean legend that we have adopted for Candlemas. I tell Helen that we will see the Goddess return as a young girl, untouched by intrusive lusts. I talk of the snowdrops that push through the snowy mantle to bring hope and renewal of innocence each year. This night of Candlemas we will send healing energy to all children, both female and male, who have been sexually abused. I feel there is little I have to offer Helen, but I give her what I have, the faces of the Goddess that have been shown to me. And amazingly, it seems to help, for this moment at least.

Jane is coming to tea with me. Our friendship has been confused by emotional muddle between us — we need some of the simple clarity of the snowdrop and of the tiny pink hazel flowers I have seen on the heath. When she arrives we are careful and quiet with each other, hopeful of a springtime to come, but forcing nothing. This is still winter, and we are far from the vibrant unfurling of April. Our friendship cannot be pushed into a clearer mode, we must wait for its season to return. I shake out a lacy white table-cloth and lay the table with my grandmother's tea service. Before I can light my white candles in the fading light Jane says 'Look!' She points to the window. Snowflakes are fluttering out of the sky like goosedown. 'They began when you shook the table- cloth,' she says, laughing.

Yes, I am Brighde, too, and so is Jane, and Helen; and She is more than we can imagine or encompass together or separately. The snow starts to spread its protective layer over the garden. Brighde's plants survive the cold touch of death and quietly promise spring.

Spring Equinox

The blossom is spreading urgently now over the sloe bushes, and catkins swing from the alder and goat willow. The sap is rising in trunk and stem and the day and night are of equal length.

I shall walk the maze this Vernal Equinox, making each of its sevenfold turnings a moment of choice. This walking of the Cretan maze that we make with silver sand on the bare earth is an important and very personal meditation for me, the final part of a long process of self-healing. The Goddess has grown from young girl to young woman, She is ready to make the rite of passage towards sexuality, towards the dance of Her power as a mature woman. I think of my own adolescence and of my first sexual relationship in the confusing sixties. I did not know then that you could call forced sex 'rape' even if the man was your boy-friend. It took me 14 years to recognize and name it for what it was.

There is a healing here that I need before I can walk the maze and be open to new love in my life — a healing that has waited for 18 years now. I think of the polarities we were offered in our adolescence: the repression of our young sexual urgency that was advised by parents, school and church, and on the other hand the message of our own youth culture — 'have sex or be forever condemned as an uptight virgin.' The spiral of the Equinox maze speaks to me of a way that is not a choice between stark polarities, that allows transition into sexual maturity by gradual unfolding, by deliberate and meditational choice, a maze in which you cannot become lost, and which you enter only when the time is right for you.

My friends walk the maze where the young Goddess meets the beloved young God, a meditation on openness to the new growing energy in our lives. We can imagine the young Goddess taking off Her white cloak and revealing Herself in scarlet splendour, copper discs tinkling around Her hem and ankles. She is glorious in Her sexuality, but still young and shy. The ambivalence in the image is reflected by the plants around us — some buds are unfolded joyously while others wait, tightly closed, the leaves of the ash tree still darkly encased in their wrappings.

I feel as though I am 16. I realize that I can move slowly towards sexual relationships in my own time, with my own deliberate choices. I am a woman in middle life but this adolescent shyness is still part of me and is in every new meeting in which the possibility exists of the Scarlet Lady's joyous dance.

I open my eyes. Now it is my turn to walk the maze. . . but what has happened? The silver sand is scuffed by the feet of those who have walked before me, I cannot see the path under the moonlight, the sevenfold turnings are lost. My heart sinks. Someone whispers to me 'You'll just have to walk straight into the middle.'

My grief is huge the next day. Somehow the muddle of my own young womanhood has been recreated for me, it seems I have to re-enact it symbolically before my healing can be effected.

My beloved friend (an inspired priestess) has a suggestion. Why don't we go together to Saffron Walden and walk the maze this Sunday? It seems perfect. We arrive at Audley End station and start a pilgrimage to Saffron Walden. I am carrying a wreath of red roses. The turf maze on the green hardly shows from the distance, but when we reach it I see how large it is. We take our shoes off and start to walk slowly. I am wearing the red rose crown on my head. When I reach the centre I feel that I have truly changed a pattern in my life, healed a very old wound. I lay my rose crown in the centre, and give thanks to Her who is the maze.

As we leave the green I look back towards the maze. A child is lifting the rose crown, his mother is watching. 'Good,' I think, 'my offering will find a home rather than be dragged away and wantonly destroyed.' Yet the child must have left it there, for two of my friends visited the maze a week later, and rang to say that my red rose petals were scattered in the middle of the maze. Drops of blood, shed this time without pain.

May Eve

The apple blossom in my back garden shivers voluptuously in the faint breeze. It is May Eve. This festival is hard to write about, it is like finding words to describe a taste or smell.

I catch glimpses of the Lady of May in many guises — as Maid Marian in the May games, as the Queen of Elfland who appeared to Thomas the Rhymer in grass-green silk with 59 silver bells on Her horse's mane. The Victorian revivals of May Day celebrations gave us visions of dimpling May Queens in white and pastel colours surrounded by maidens and flowers. She is there too, but Her power is held back and made safe for the village green. In Her true domain of wildwood and moorland She is far less predictable. She comes between the worlds, on the path She pointed out to True Thomas, the path that is neither the narrow thorny road to heaven, nor the broad and lily-bordered road that leads to hell, but the bonny road that winds about the ferny moor and which leads to Elfland. Neither is Her Elfland the picture-book world of the Flower Fairies, but a land approached through dark starless night where there is neither sun nor moon, where you can hear the roaring of the sea, and you must wade through rivers of blood shed in our world.

This is the Lady who bewitched Tam Lin and took him to live inside the green hill, this is the mysterious visitor with a silver apple branch who came from the Land of Women and sang to Bran, this is the beautiful Niamh who came from the Land of the Ever Young to take the poet Oisin away with her across the the waves.

The apple blossom shivers again in the fading light, petals fall around me. The bees fly lazily home, leaving the blossom to ripen into the Queen of Elphame's rosy apples.

I see Her in scarlet as well as in green, the Lady of Coming Summer, the wild rose and strawberry that decorate Her gown are hidden as yet beneath Her sepal green cloak. She is made of flowers as Blodeuwedd was by the magician Gwydion to be Llew Llaw Gyffes' bride, and She is just as dangerous if we try to hold Her in our world.

I have fallen in love in May, but as folklore tells of all May marriages, this passionate love only lasted the summer. She pulled me between the worlds, the Queen of May, but she scoffs at settled partnership. They say hawthorn branches should not be brought into the house, for it is not the marital bed and table that they bless. May is the time for the love that has no place in society, which hides in the greenwood. This is its natural setting, in the newly luxuriant foliage — the fourteenth-century Welsh poet describes 'a place for two in spite of the Cuckold's wrath; a concealing veil for a girl and her lover.'

I have been faery-led on May Eve and I understand some of the enchantment worked then; I know why Irish villagers made sure to keep safe at home and not to wander near the faery forts. We tried to find our own familiar clearing in wildwood on May Eve in 1986 while radioactive fall out settled across Europe. Perhaps the wildwood was angry with humankind, for we were lost for hours, wandering in circles and retracing our steps.

For me May Eve is not so much a time of license, as some see it. The orgiastic Maying parties described by Puritan writers seem to have been more the product of their repressed and pornographic imagination than a true tradition. It is the time for the beating of the bounds, for protecting all that needs to be protected. If you step between the worlds you must know the risk that you are taking, that you enter a world where the rules are all quite different. The faery folk seldom seem to be deliberately cruel, the Lady of May is not quite Keats' Belle Dame Sans Merci. Rather, they are capricious and there is no saying where you will end up if you go abroad on May Eve, or if you fall in love under the apple blossom.

It is dark now under my tree, the blossom looms whitely above me. I shall go now to meet the Queen of May, to look into the mirror of Her still pool by candlelight. There I shall see my own face, and perhaps Hers.

Midsummer

The wild flowers' abundance and variety has intoxicated me for weeks. I have saved the last flowers of the oak, gathered cloudy meadowsweet and plucked yellow spikes of broom. Am I to see Her tonight, the Queen of High Midsummer conjured from the flowers as Blodeuwedd was conjured?

I sit in the garden eating strawberries at noon, the high solstice sun lingering above me. I wonder if I am ready to meet this Lady and accept the choices She offers me. All my life I have feared to venture too courageously, to ask for too much, to fight too valiantly for what I want. Yet Midsummer has called the sun to his flaming height, and pulls on me like full moon on the spring tide. This year I cannot refuse Her promise, the whisper in my ear murmuring with the bees of glory for those who dare. Am I prepared to risk overreaching myself, to fall like the sun from the zenith and reel towards destruction in the dark of the year? I know that it is the Midsummer Queen who turns the wheel of fortune in the leaping firelight's glare, and that she who rises falls, and she who falls must rise.

It is far safer, surely, to risk nothing, to stay safe and obscure and hope that Lady Fortune will consider me beneath Her attention. I understand the instinct that leads parents in some cultures to disparage their children, so that jealous Fate will not choose to take them. I am not really very clever, no, not inspired at all, not eloquent, certainly not beautiful, even by firelight. It is difficult to accept praise or compliments, however sincerely given, to hold your head high and dance life's glory when you know that death and failure exist, and will come again, however high your reach or firm your grasp.

I move from bright sunlight into the shade of the apple tree, glancing up at the small swelling apples, roundly displayed like the breasts of Cretan goddesses. I have left my scarlet china bowl of strawberries behind in the sunshine but I feel too lazy to move to retrieve them. I sit in the shade and watch the insects moving around the garden, thinking of my beloved project that would expose me to publicity's glare, the risk of defeat. I wonder too about love's declaration, my vulnerability spread out nakedly for someone else to see and scorn. She asks too much, the Queen of Midsummer, though She gives passion, the fire in the blood, the chance to succeed or fail in one glorious attempt. I know well that Her terms include the necessity of sacrifice, that I will have to give up something of myself to dance Her dance, or to ride in Her chariot flanked by proud lions. I think of Icarus and King Bladud of the Britons flying too high, too near the sun; they answered Her call, how can I?

Yet it is chilly here beneath the apple tree, I wish that I were back in full sunlight against the fence where the roses trail. The scarlet bowl of strawberries is insistent as I gaze at the garden. My mouth is parched in spite of the shady coolness and I am restless in spite of summer's languor. I imagine the crimson sweetness of the largest and most perfect strawberry that I have saved. Saliva floods into my mouth.

Yes, She has given us desire, desire that makes the most cowardly courageous. Deliberately I stand up and return into the heat of noon. I sit down, leaning against the warm wooden fence, its roughness delicious against my back. I reach slowly into the scarlet bowl. One deep red rose is hanging over my head. I pause and look into Her secret golden heart. 'I am with you now,' She says, 'but I shall not always be with you.' I note the thorns, accept Her terms and raise the soft lush fruit to my mouth.

Lammas

The grass has been cut now and the first corn is yet to be harvested, the abundance of delicate flowers in the hedgerows has been replaced by the coarser plants, the pushiness of hogweed; thistles dominate the meadows.

Memories of the hay harvest are still with me, of cutting hay with sickles in the Pyrenees, riding home on the wagon drunk with sun and poppies, grass-seed and cornflowers in my hair. There was a hay fever upon me then — not (mercifully) running from my nose, but coursing through my blood. It kept me awake until dawn making love in the new cut hay beneath the moon.

They say in Kent that the corn ripens after Lammas as much by night as by day,. The heads are becoming heavy and crave harvesting. Cutting the corn down seems far more like a sacrifice than making the hay, though all harvest has undertones of death in it. I am making paper cranes in memory of the dead and maimed of Hiroshima and Nagasaki — next week on Hiroshima Day we will take our cranes to the peace Pagoda in Battersea Park and mourn the death that is no harvest, which brings no richness to the land.

The Goddess is weeping for the Sun God who was vanquished at Midsummer by his rival, the God of the Waning Year. I shall go to weep again this Lammas Eve and to see the miracle happen once again. I imagine the Harvest Queen turning Her grief into mystery and making bread to feed us, sustenance out of despair. For an agricultural people the imagery is strong, the cold iron of the sickle harvests the warm life of the corn and golden sunshine can be stored to keep us alive all winter. For most of us this imagery is lost, we do not watch harvest or bake our own bread, we do not feel the sunlit life of the corn under our hands as we knead the dough. We have not experienced Hungry July, the time of dearth and deprivation before the harvest: the bread in our shops never runs out. We have another kind of famine, for we call bread with all the golden life bleached from it: 'Mother's Pride'.

Country people hearing the words of the funeral service 'he cometh up and is cut down like a flower' may keep a stronger awareness of the annual cycle of harvest and replanting, echoes of a sacred agricultural cycle that offers, if not consolation in grief, at least the promise of new life in the future, as the wheel turns onward.

Lammas is a hard festival for us to understand, I was told by a wise friend who has celebrated the annual seasonal cycle for many years that if there is distrust or suspicion within a group it will flower after Lammas with the thistles. He had seen this often, and I have seen it too.

Perhaps this is because the Harvest Queen must turn from the sunlight towards the dark Underworld where the grain will germinate for the next year. I shiver and think of my August of betrayal, when I could no longer conjure magic with my lover, and saw myself replaced by another woman. The harvest was theirs, not mine; yet I knew that the wheel must turn.

I have completed my paper cranes now. I shall go to the gathering tonight to mourn the God of the Corn and all beauty cut down, I shall dance for the harvest, leaping high with exultation and triumph, and a small part of me will die, as it does each year at Lammas.

Autumn Equinox

Though the leaves are still green the mists are damp and heavy. Blackberries hang in the hedgerows as deep and purple as the grapes and aubergines sent to our shops from warmer lands.

The twilight comes early and I turn eagerly to the darkness. Fear of the dark runs through our thought patterns and our language, yet how many people cannot sleep unless the curtains are closed and the mothernight of the womb recreated? The newborn child must fear light more than the familiar dark, and learn to fear the night as she grows older and separates from the mother. It is understandable for a Northern people to long for light in winter, yet caves and night call sweetly to people who live further South, offering healing and rest.

It is the Healing Goddess that I seek now this autumn, at this time of balance when the year turns towards the dark, when the seed falls from the fruits to rest and wait. She is dark and beautiful, blackberries stain Her lips and Her feet are luscious magenta-purple from treading the grapes. She is all richness and fullness, and She rules fermentation and decay. Intoxicated by Her, we fall into drunken sleep at Her feet, and She heals us before we wake.

I touch the bloom on the grapes in my black glazed bowl, it is musky and mysterious, I will drink dark-red wine tonight for the Equinox and go hunting mushrooms tomorrow in the woods and fields. We shall take great care what we pick for She also rules poisons, all plants that can take life, or heal if used wisely as medicine.

She calls us to darkness, to go down into the Underworld with

Her, to give something up at each of the seven gates to the Great Below. I wonder what I have to give and my glance falls upon my golden ring set with a red stone. I love this ring, it has the power of summer in it for me, it is the symbol of my power and my sexuality, of my dance around midnight fires under the full moon. I know I must change with Her who turns scarlet through purple into black, I must wear rings of amethyst and jet this autumn in Her honour. I take off the ring and put it aside. I will give it as an offering.

I do understand why we fear Her, as well as long for Her, this Autumn Goddess. In reclaiming the Goddess from patriarchal myth I was once too eager to dismiss Her destroying power as mere propaganda of Her enemies, or to claim it too quickly as merely showing my own righteous anger. Yet even in the most perfect world I can imagine She is there as Destroyer, and death will come not only to those who have opposed Her but also to Her faithful servants. She is in me, too, and to deny Her and to honour only a more comfortable Goddess makes me both ill and crazy.

We see Her not only as wise Crone but as Hag surrounded by creatures of the Underworld, the bats and toads who live in the caves that are Her domain. Her face is twisted and has the green pallor of disease. I think of the Indian goddesses of leprosy and smallpox, of every disease that can kill and maim.

She is indeed terrifying, and worst of all horrors, She wants something of us, not merely our awe and obeisance. She asks us to make place for Her in our lives, to embrace Her, as courteous King Henry of the ballad embraced the monstrous and hungry woman who appeared in his hall. Having eaten up the bones and flesh of his favourite horse, his hounds and his goshawks, having drunk wine from his horse's bloody hide, she tests his courtesy and generosity to the limit by demanding that he lies down naked beside her and shares her bed.

Like King Henry I find that if I 'give Her all Her will' She turns into the 'fairest lady that ever was seen'. The Autumn Goddess tells us of inner beauty, of the mystery that cannot be found by those who look only at the surface, who will not enter Her cave, who flee from the reality that one day they too will die and return to the earth.

I pack grapes and wine into a basket, I will go to meet Her tonight, the Destroying Healer; the loss of my red and gold ring is a small price for one fleeting glimpse of Her mystery.

Samhain

The leaves are blazing orange and red and falling from the trees. The last blackberries must be gathered in today, for tonight on Samhain Eve the fairies are said to spit on them and blast all goodness from the hedgerow fruits.

Sensible folk stay in their homes this night as they do on May Eve, for the fairies and the spirits of the dead are abroad. Yet it is a time for generosity, for honouring the dead and the Otherworld. I am preparing a plate of especially beautiful food for the dead, an offering to memory. In Mexico they picnic on their family graves on All Soul's Day, to share food and company with their dead, but this might raise eyebrows in the London suburbs. It is a night for divination too, for seeing the shape of your future partner, for discovering the fate of the company who gather to pass this dangerous night together.

Terror is there for me at Samhain too, but it is not fear of the ghostly dead or of the borrowed shapes of the living. I sympathize with the old Irish story teller on the subject of ghosts: 'In dread, is it? What would I be in dread of, and the souls of my own dead as thick as bees around me?'[3] No, the terror comes from the crack between the worlds that opens at Samhain. Every year it takes me days to recover a semblance of balanced normality.

I know why it is so for me, the lesson that I am taking years to learn. My relationship with the beloved dead is too intense. I have still not completely given them the freedom implored by the ghost in the ballad 'The Unquiet Grave'. My silent weeping interferes with their sleep. There is still much for me to learn from the glimpses I have of the Goddess at Samhain.

For me She is not entirely Celtic, though Samhain is a Celtic festival. I have inherited many cultures. When I scraped away the more superficial layers of Christianity and freed myself from the hell-fire and damnation I had feared when I was seven, I found a mixture of Anglo-Saxon, Celtic and Graeco-Roman beliefs that resonated equally for me. My Goddess of Samhain is as much Persephone, Queen of the Underworld, as She is Ceridwen or Morgan le Faye. Within the Greek mask She wears there are lines that remind me of Egyptian Sekhmet, Sumerian Ereshkigal and Indian Kali. She dances the dance of death, yet She can be as gentle as the white hind that came to fetch Thomas the Rhymer in his old age. I cannot look Her in the face, yet

I know She journeyed to the Underworld to succour the dead. The blankness of Her gaze freezes me, yet She is also the bawdy old woman Baubo who tricked the sorrowing Mother Demeter into laughter by the sudden display of her genitals. When Demeter laughs famine retreats a little and the people find that a few winter greens will grow in the frost-bitten earth.

I know Her. She stood over me remote and implacable and asked me to see the appalling waste of young life by suicide. Grief had opened my heart so completely it was hard indeed to separate from the dead. It was the so-called 'lower chakra energy' that saved me, not my heart. I did not feel sexual, rather I was numb and in deep shock, but at my friend's wake I danced my sexuality into life and found I was not ready to die too. No wonder the Sheila-na-Gig is found protecting churches, her vulva displayed below a skeletal head and trunk.

I walk the path between the worlds to West Kennet Long Barrow on Samhain Eve. The path is veiled in mists, only the barrow and Silbury Hill rise from the grey-white twilight. I stand in the barrow where people were buried, in the rounded pockets beneath the skirts of the old Earth Mother, a meditation with the ancestors and Old Ones. By the time we reach the road on the way back I have a new insight, an inspiration given to me in that place. It is an inner knowing, deep and mysterious. It will take weeks, months, years to understand, and as yet I cannot speak of it. When I can let go of my attachment to the dead it is She who waits for me, veiled and unnameable. When all the Hallowe'en masks of terror drop away She is there. This is the real terror, long-desired and holy, to know Her and accept Her gift.

Yule

The nights are so long they eat up daytime, the trees bare and stark. In the years that I lived without electricity I knew midwinter well, out on the hills without the tinsel and multi-colours of the December shops. The red of the holly berry draws the eye in a midwinter landscape, flashing like a jewel against a white cold sky. This is the landscape from the tale of Deirdre, who saw a raven pecking the blood of a slaughtered calf on the snow, and wished she could meet a man with lips so red, with cheek so white and hair as black. It is in this midwinter landscape that the God of the Waning Year will die, it is the time of standstill, the longest night, darkness depth.

The Celts did not seem to celebrate Midwinter, but many other cultures have observed it. New Grange is aligned to the mid-winter sun, so the solstice may have been celebrated long before the height of Celtic culture. The Roman Saturnalia and the Babylonian tale of the hero and the dragon came to Britain and mixed with native traditions to give us mumming plays at this time.

The long night cries out for fire and light so that we may survive it, and work sympathetic magic to help the sun to be reborn. Yet Christmas lights are lit too early in the consumer culture. Before I make a blaze of light I need to witness the dissolution of the waning cycle. I am listing the things I want to lose, my old year dissolutions — fear of isolation and poverty in sickness and old age, fruitless worry, joyless work. The flurry of consumerism has tempted me in these last weeks, the urge to spend money, to build a huge fire of generosity and feasting, to laugh in the long nights. First I must pay attention to the old year that I am casting off. She is still implacable, this Crone Goddess of Midwinter. She cuts away all that is dead within us, and the universe dissolves into chaos as She stirs her cauldron.

No wonder that I have feared cancer, a long but early death, in these past few weeks, for this is Her time and I see the skull beneath the skin even when I am surrounded by plastic robins and holly in the shops. This was the shortest day when my sweet friend came back from hospital with the news that her death would come very soon. We shared wine and chocolates together, wrapped her Christmas presents and discussed the changes to her will, we talked about dying. I shall keep vigil again tonight, see the universe dissolve, hear the howling of wolves and enter into a place outside time where the universe is recreated. At the still centre of the longest night the Crone becomes Creatrix and danced the world into being like the dancer on the World card in the Tarot. I shall be reborn myself with all creation. The miracle will become personal for me, for this year, as every year, my thoughts of death and dissolution will leave me as I meditate on the mystery of birth. Sun and storm will be recreated, rival children of the Goddess who come from the same substance. I shall see the Goddess as the bird who broods on the waters, as Mother who is solid as rock, who catches me at the bottom of every abyss. Each year I experience this clear and pure joy, so simple and immediate that it cannot be explained; it lies in the part of my experience before I had words. I shall remember that when I was born I felt this enormous joy and appetite for life, and I shall watch daylight return after the longest night.

Imogen Cavanagh

Notes

1,2. These two Yoruba goddesses, though they represent comparable archetypes to the other goddesses listed, are in fact attributed to different phases of the moon than we have listed here.
3. Danaher, Kevin, *The Year in Ireland*, p228, Mercier Press, 1972.

Breaking the Circle

John Matthews

Introduction

I have chosen to write part of this account as though it were fiction — which it is not — because the border line between what is true and what is not, especially in matters relating to the occult, is slim; and because writing in this way enables both writer and, it is hoped, reader, to put a certain distance between them and the subject under discussion.

The account is much as it happened — those who know to *whom* it happened will know its truth; those who do not will perhaps allow the deeper meaning to flow into them in an abstract manner. It was possibly the most difficult piece of work that the writer has ever attempted, and it was not written without a great deal of heart-searching. It is hoped that what is *not* said herein will sound as loudly as what is.

Of the Tradition

Of all the different kinds of Craft, 'Traditional' is the hardest to substantiate, the least clearly defined, the most intractable of understanding. Trying to explain, to those trained in Hereditary, Gardnerian or Alexandrian groups, what is different about Traditionals is the hardest task of all, since most answers to questions consist of negatives: 'No, we didn't do that', 'No, we never used those', and so on.

In part this stems from a totally different outlook, intent and purpose. Traditional groups meet in a rural setting which they have probably used for generations, and which is their own native space; their members are drawn from local, rural communities (with occasional exceptions); they are concerned with the seasons, with the right relationship of mankind to the earth. They are not interested in power, either personal or general; nor do they work needlessly or from habit. What they practise is neither exactly a religion, nor is it exactly magic; yet both labels, if applied in their broadest sense, describe something of the way Traditionals function.

Their observance of the seasons is as precise as their ancestors', whom they remember, fondly, as links in a chain stretching back into the distant past. They are thus, in as much as they are like anyone, closest to the Hereditary families of wise people, who like them seem to have no roots but to gravitate to a particular place and lock onto its energy centre. They themselves scorn labels, seeing what they do, and are, as so much a part of life that it needs no categorizing.

Many are Christians, who attend local church services and honour a god who is younger than theirs but who nevertheless stands for many of the same principles. They see nothing strange in this, being, above all, supremely adaptive and knowing that all gods are one god. Nor are they to be confused with the medieval idea of 'Witches', who were burned in their thousands by zealous Christians. Most of these, they well know, were harmless old women with nothing to fuel them but the horrific images conjured up every day in the local church. The Traditionals were always there, following a path that is at least as old as the bones of the earth Herself.

It is no longer possible to say with any certainty how much their practices have changed with the centuries. Sometimes, one might say, hardly at all. Yet they have ever been adaptive, tak-

reading (a method of foretelling future events which is astoundingly accurate; a single image implanted before the sleeper begins to dream, expands to fill the whole dreamscape) are all based on extremely ancient methods — simple, direct, drugless, ultimately safe. Above all there is always a sense of a job to do. Members turn up at the meeting place, do what they are there to do, and then depart again. There is almost none of the cheerful back-slapping and general horseplay experienced in many neo-pagan circles; though this is not to say that all meetings are dead pan affairs. Celebrations do take place, stories are told, thoughts exchanged, jokes cracked. Yet it remains still harder to describe what is done than what is not.

The lack of definition is perhaps summed up best by saying that the Traditionals follow the laws and customs of the land, dressing, speaking and behaving like everyone else in their locality. They blend into the landscape and, though their fellow villagers probably know that they follow old ways, they are neither offended nor scandalized by this; it is considered as much like a public duty as jury service or sitting on the district council.

All in all, there is nothing special about being a Traditional. Witches in the revival may demand to know about the glamorous rituals and the strange, antique practices; the only problem being that there are none. It is not even a matter of being unwilling to share the old wisdom; the sheer impossibility of communicating a sense of belonging to the land and its subtle, ordinary rhythms creates its own barrier. Finally, and most importantly perhaps, there is really no need for dialogue between the revivalists and the traditionalists. Despite having almost no common words with which to do so, they are both still speaking the same language. The distance between the one and the other is indeed vast, but the unifying principles, in whatever form they may be worshipped, are still the same. It is to a better understanding of this that the work which follows is dedicated.

More than this it is difficult to say. What follows is an attempt to record the incommunicable in a manner that will yet be understood by all. It is also a deeply personal response to a network of images, dreams and memories stretching back some 25 years. Sometimes, indeed, the edges are blurred — but the essence of deep joy and primal energy experienced remains as clear now as then. The Traditionals, who are unimpressed by such labels, remain because there has always been a need for them, a function for them to fulfil. If ever that need ceases to be, they will

ing what they needed from each successive influx of peopl
these islands, so that one may hear more than one archai
guage in their chants.

The place of the Traditional in the contemporary Craft r
is, without doubt, invidious. Among many covens formed
the repeal of the Witchcraft Act of 1951, there has come
felt a great need to get to the roots of their tradition. But
the revived sections of the Craft doubtless feel that Traditi
should make themselves, their material and their wo
methods freely available to everyone, in order to set the re
straight, this is really unnecessary, since both ways of wor
are, in their own right, perfectly valid. The more recent rev
are simply an urban reaction to a still deeply-felt need to k
and understand the relationship of mankind with the ea

But what really are the differences between Traditionals
other members of the Craft? Is the discrepancy so vast th
cannot be breached?

For a start, Traditional groups (which are not called cov
vary greatly from place to place, so that what may be tru
one may not be true of another. They were often establis
and worked in isolation from each other, so that certain l
practices and usages were employed. Some groups had 'mast
some had 'ladies' (never high priest or high priestess.) S
had no leaders at all, but shared the guiding inspiration in r
tion. For the most part, they work robed, not naked, exc
for initiations or certain rituals. Because they do not derive t
working methods from books, nor commit their work to w
ing, there are no records, no 'Book of Shadows'. In the s
way there are no 'weapons', the thought being that one
fingers, and therefore required nothing else. The work
methods tend to be inspired by the need of the moment, or
tated from long custom.

Traditional Craft is thus perhaps one of the last bastion
'tribal consciousness' — that unspoken, unwritten sense of c
munication with the ancestral land. Its wisdom, native ind
but common to all peoples, is part of the very fabric of C
tion. As such, it is not surprising that the most unique wa
working among Traditional groups consists of their use of so
The chants which resonate throughout their workings are ec
of the first sounds made by our ancestors in ritualized resp
to their environment. Similarly, methods of working which
clude a wide use of trance states, out-of-body travel and dre

quickly follow suit. When, if ever, that happens, the earth will be lessened, in some way made poorer, by their going.

Breaking the Circle

They used always to meet on hilltops — to be between the earth and the sky — and because of the numen of the place, whose influence was to be felt in all that they did. There was no sense of worship, simply of respect. Higher devotions were kept for the principles of earth and sky, usually referred to as 'she' and 'he', or more often 'Her' and 'Him', said not with disrespect, but with a jerk of the head or a lifted hand in acknowledgement of the shaping powers.

Meetings were regular, moving with the seasons. The changing moods of the land dictated the mood of the celebrations — to call them rites would be wrong. There was, though, an underlying savagery about them, something itself born of the impervious earth, which knew nothing of the sufferings of humanity, but which yet knew everything, was mother to them all. Thus they always wore some scrap of green about them 'in token that the Mother keep her fair face'; and this memory brought others, that 'wearing the green' meant something else, but also the same thing.

The green door was for the Otherworld, the red door for Paradise; and it was through the green door that he went, over and over again, to meet in a place that was part of a far greater landscape, where there was a 'version' of the hill itself.

There, they did many things to 'help the flow', to 'set the seasons in their places', to 'spin the wheel and turn the weaving until the pattern is complete'. That was how he remembered it, afterwards; the healing and the putting of things in their natural place. For within their own universe they were supreme, kept to the laws that ruled there, tried never to offend those who shared it with them, who were, by definition, other...

The red door was less often used, a more private entry point into another kind of Otherworld. Here, Paradise was the home of the dwellers' own soul, where he or she fought personal battles, won or lost, honours or dishonours, in the place of the Gods. There were no hierarchies within the group, no 'higher' or 'lower' powers — Paradise, through the red door, was in no way superior; it simply was. There, he saw and understood the meaning of his own visions, heard the song of the ineffable spheres, and joined with them in a song of his own devising.

He came upon them by chance as it seemed, cycling through deepening dusk to come at length to the foot of the hill. Looking up through clustering branches, leaning outwards into the air like crones at a well-side, he almost turned away. But something, curiosity perhaps, or a stubborn streak that refused to relent after the long ride, pushed him on. Somewhere, at the top, was an ancient temple of Roman gods — his purpose for coming. There would be little enough to see, even by day, but still. . . he pushed the bike into the shelter of some bushes and began to climb.

There, near the summit, was the circle; a random grouping of trees and bushes that made a place set apart. There he saw figures move, silhouetted in firelight; there he heard them chanting, the rise and fall of sound, the calls and the answers, male voices pitched against female, then joining.

Hesitating, he almost turned away, until one came through the circle towards him, arms outstretched, welcoming. 'You are awaited. Enter.' Four words only to change a life. Yet from that moment his was never again the same.

Two years of training followed, often at a distance because he 'lived away'. Books were distrusted, some that he showed them laughed at. Sometimes, a dream would come, and he would walk again through the green door, and learn what he could and strive to retain it aftwards, in the cold light of day. He learned to fly, in these dreams, not on some besom, but on his own wings of thought, fleeting across the green land, seeing it — the same, yet different — with new eyes. And he learned the chants. Some of them wordless, ancient, springing from the deepest roots of the earth herself; others, a strange mixture, some Greek words that he knew, some Latin, others unknown — 'We take what we find and make it to ourselves.'

These chants could do many things; conjure rivers from dry rock, split boulders or raise a storm — all of this in the green world where its effects were like the merest shadows on the surfaces of the world outside, but where the people met and talked and discussed the way of things, as they had always done, in awesome timelessness.

Regularly, in those two years, a summons would come, an envelope containing a single sheet of paper on which was written in fine copper plate handwriting, his name, the new name they had given him: 'A passing name, until you be ready for another.' Then he would go, and be permitted to watch, as he had done that first time, apart and yet part of, sometimes asked, suddenly, for a comment, a pronouncement. 'Shall we call upon the Swift Steed or on the Slow?', 'Is it time yet to show the Dream to those who know it not?'

He learned the words he was taught. There were few since 'spells and stuff of that sort are for the late comers' by which they seemed to mean anything from the Romans to more recent walkers of the Old Way. Only once did he dare ask for knowledge of their history, to be told: 'Not taught. Not remembered. We were drovers' wives once, that came together to do what men forgot. But the way is older — no names, no times. We are what we are and nothing more.'

But they were something more: dreamers who never dreamed, teachers who never taught, thinkers who never thought. And yes, there was a kind of unconscious cruelty about them — they were impersonal and did what they did, not only because they had always done it, but because it was always meant so to be done. Thus the 'initiation', a foreign concept they found hard to accept until he told them more, at which it was said: 'Ah, the key in the lock; the opening of the door', the initiation he underwent, which he afterwards thought of as re-learning the things he had been born knowing but had forgotten, had its own share of savagery. . .

(He paused in his memorizing of these things and fingered the green man head that hung on a thong at his neck. They had no images of their god, nor of their goddess. These were two impersonal polarities that held the whole of life in balance.)

The initiation then — the only time for nakedness, 'because it's only right that you enter as you were made', entering this time between the sturdy legs of one of them, into the bright and burning circle.

Then the words, murmured in his ears though none stood close: 'Be that you be, see that you see; shine, and in the shining, show what you be.' Ancient words? Perhaps an echo. But by whoever or whenever first spoken, potent now as then. He felt enclosed, safe, yet at the same time set free, poised on the breath of a great beginning.

Other words, forgotten now, that spoke of the year's turning, of the part each must play in its continued restoration, its endless making.

Then, the touch of hands, seven pairs, on his back and arms and thighs, and more words, whispered now, that he could not catch. Then the thonged punisher 'To remind you always, what you are.' The seven strokes and the three, and then the five, and with the last, released from the hand that had held it in check, a thong on which was tied an arrow head of long-past time.

Brief, burning pain. Some blood, soon cleansed, salve applied that brought swift relief and healing. Gentleness now in the hands that touched brow and shoulder and foot. Last words, half remembered: 'Shallow is the shadow world. . .deep the world of earth and stone, where the Seasons turn. . .'

Like a waking he hears them again, remembers the thoughts they conjured, that between the two worlds lay very little space, and often they overlapped. That was only a part. Other truths followed: that to be part of life was to feel the flow of the earth's own blood, through the feet, mounting to the body, until the head was filled with its fire; that to be one with Creation was the greatest gift, though little known and rarely understood. They had always known, had always sung or chanted, its rhythm, celebrating the round of the year in all its patterns, below ground and above.

Thus there could be no set initiations in the understood sense; the coming in was merely the open hand, the word 'welcome', which had its own magical volition. Beyond this, he was considered ready, ready to have the key turned in the lock, so that his understanding flowered within him and he was attuned to the inner harmony of the group, where no one, man nor woman, spoke of having greater authority, the seal of man-strength or woman-power. He saw again, more clearly now, the balance within the group, the polarized strengths that worked for one direction and that all theirs, the 'will' of Creation.

Thus, they each 'acted out' that will, singly and in chorus, as the laws governing chant allowed for one voice or two, three or many, according to the song of the hour. Earth sang, the Mother sang, in answer, and the stars fell into alignment, those above reflected by those below.

He reflected, briefly, that there was greater similarity between the concepts of 'High Magic' and the work of the family, than most would acknowledge; the working in harmony with the inner realms was at the heart of all their work.

The last night, remembered still with difficulty and some pain. A big night, season-changer, a night of song and story. Then, a summoning, all of them, and he, drawn close and tight in the circle, chanting the end note and the dawn note in changing harmonies, drunk with the sounds, drawing ragged breaths full of the night. And he, focused, no longer aware of anything but the circle of light before him and the power he sought to fill it with...

But, what came there, what filled the circle, overflowed across the hill, drove back the rest, overwhelmed them, was something other. A man-shape cut out of the night, a vast-seeming darkness that shut out the moon and the stars, a great voice roaring in his head: COME!

Just as violent was his response, his silent-shouted NO!, and then the reverberation, the tearing aside of the curtain, and the circle of faces, some shocked, some bewildered, two at least, angry. He remembered the anger for a long while after, the shouted words: 'Be darkness and be fear and be not of us'...

After, long after, when he could think again of these things, could seek interpretation and meaning, he wondered at what had really occurred. Was it his own psychism which had acted as a catalyst to some waiting energy, releasing it like a volcano from within the hill? Or were they to blame, as someone had suggested; had they sought him as a gift to the numen of the hill? But would they not, at the least, have asked this of him? To go unwillingly was not to go at all — or so he believed.

Was it then, simply the unexpectedness of the thing, for none had foreseen it, least of all he. For many years he was to wonder, following another course that yet brought him back to that broken circle, to that hill top night. Often, he was asked the question 'come, give up yourself, be part of the circle again (meaning other circles, never the first which was forever closed). But always he refused, until she came, who knew all the ways by intuition, who smiled and was gentle and taught him again the meaning of the way, until he was able, in part, to teach her.

But all was fragmentary, forcibly suppressed through the years of being dark, of being fearful and 'not of us'. Only now, writing this, he remembers the deepest joy of all, the quickening of the earth beneath him, the answering heartbeat when his hands, their hands, struck it in rhythm; or when their voices, rising and falling, seemed to snare the moon.

And he remembered the trees, that seemed more than trees, and that beyond the green door were more than trees. Best of all he remembered the meetings on the inner hill, beneath a moon that was always full and yellow, where he saw and understood the blurring of many tracks into one, and saw that he and his were truly appointed guardians of the earth, to see that it always held true to them and they to it. Right relationship with the living earth was their true calling; his also now.

Then he remembered, too, something else. That theirs was a religion of love and of light, just as much as the Christian God's; that they celebrated the natural world, its greenness and its brightness, because these were sacred things. That knowledge brought its own release, and he recalled some words from a book supposedly meant for children, which yet said all that he would wish said of these things:

> *Long ago, when the world started there was magic everywhere; every race and country, every tribe and tributary had its magic-handlers, its wise witch-people. Magic is another word for Creation, for the creation of the world was the biggest magic of all.*

The Witches and the Grinnygog by Dorothy Edwards

Of the Voices of Animals

Gwen Blythe

Can you see the stone I stand by? Lit by the flickering fire you can just make out carved lines worn by time, difficult to see. Come nearer, trace them, wondering, with a finger. Carved long ago, in low-relief, swirling inter-woven lines that, though abstract, suggest living forms. Here is the leaping hare, the soaring kite, the running wolf, leading to the centre. Here a face; part animal, part plant, part human. Is it truly a face, or just part of the pattern? Around it, leaf-like forms turn outward into stag, salmon, boar. Forms intertwine, embodying the spirit of eagle and raven, bull and stallion, owl and otter.

What can we learn from this stone? The animals are a direct link between ourselves and the earth we live on, if we are open to the altered modes of consciousness necessary for such awareness. They may act as guides and guardians on the many paths that may lead us to and fro in this and in other worlds. We may also gain wisdom from observing them simply as they are; but such singleness of eye is harder to gain, for most adults, than entrance to other worlds. Let us not forget this world in our travels.

The face, like that of the flower-owl-woman of the old tales, is a symbolic representation of the interdependence of all things. The plant-animal-human triad encompasses all earthly life. Behind the symbol of this head lives a reality one will meet sooner or later if one follows the lore of the animals. Should you choose to accept the guidance of the beast that waits to show you the way between the worlds, to establish a relationship of mutual trust with it, the animal will act as guardian and guide. You will be shown a hidden door into another world.

There should be no hint of atavism or of a 'descent into bestialism' on this path if it is followed in truth. Animals cannot lie. But during this experience you may be tested in every faculty; it is not an easy path to follow.

Look beyond the safety of the stones, into the gathering night. Eyes, green and lambent, reflecting with cool light the firelight behind you. Can you tell which creature of the night waits here by the dolmen arch? Is it a disguised god or a tribal totem? A shape-changer or simply what it seems, a night-travelling animal?

Can you make these distinctions in everyday life and in meditation; in dreams and in dream-time? Your choices of action, and more, depend on your discrimination. How good are you? Will you retreat or follow, proffer hand of welcome or weapon of defence?

Perhaps you look into those eyes, and sense a quizzical friendliness, not quite human. You avert your gaze, sensing that eye contact may be seen as a threatening gesture in the animal world. Perhaps the animal retreats a little, the angle of the eyes changing so that you know it is holding its head on one side; pleading, playful. Hoping you will follow.

Perhaps you will take a brand from the central fire, or bring light from a source you see as holy, blessed. You hold the light aloft to see what kind of creature awaits you. It stands there revealed, still and unafraid. If you feel any kind of interest or affinity with what you see, you may decide to greet it.

It will have greeted you like an old friend; recognition flaring momentarily in you both. Then the creature will have turned swiftly and leapt, or flown, away. You will have admired the strength and speed of its going, the beauty of the beast in motion. And you will have followed in your own form, or changed shape to mimic that of your guide or, if feasible, have been privileged to ride on its back. Smooth and swift your journeying, over strange and familiar landscapes, time held in abeyance, until you have reached the Door.

Mark well the symbol upon it, for although it is simple, this device held in your imagination will bring you safely home at any time. Now you must choose to enter or not to enter.

For those who choose not to enter, return will be swift and exhilarating, leaving the memory of an old friendship rekindled. For those who choose to enter, some will find themselves alone, others will see their animal friend rapidly outdistancing them, so that they too stand alone, surrounded by trees.

You will have wandered through the trees, seeing them sending their roots deep into the earth, their branches towards the sun and stars. Some will see the leaves and the flowers of the forest with new eyes; will have watched woodland creatures going about their own lives, apparently unaware of you. And eventually you will come to a clearing, where there is a spring, and a stone. On that immense stone is seated a great and savage figure, dark-visaged, huge, and more animal than human.

He is dressed in the rank skins of beast and bird and fish, trophies of needless slaughter on the earth. Yet he is shepherd of the wild creatures, not slaughterer. He takes unto himself these symbols of waste and pain, pain which shudders about him like a palpable cloud, and is absorbed. Here fear is transformed into peace, understanding. The swift killings for food and for shelter do not add to this burden, for they are part of the pattern of the worlds, only the result of wantonness. His task is not easy, and he is grim-visaged and weary.

He is of human form, and in this form he partakes of every element of creation, from single-celled animals of the primeval slime, through all evolution, plant and animal, branching out like a great tree through the ages of the earth; through the ages of beast and man and tree and flower. There is nothing created that he has not been.

He is a master of trickery and tales and riddles, although like the animals he cannot lie. He will try your strengths and skills and wisdom, but is generous with praise. He is a music maker and a poet, plucking sounds from the stars and the sea and the song of birds. He will stir your blood with the sound of the hooves of horses, the music of whales, of running rivers, of the dry winds of autumn in the trees. He can drive men mad, and make them saner than they ever were, with the sound of his voice. He is a wild thing, and yet you are not in danger if your heart is true. And he will find a true heart in everyone, though the finding may be painful.

You have met the Lord of the Animals and endured, perhaps, the withering sarcasm of his tongue as he tries your mettle. You will have realized that, locked inside this tree-like man-beast, is a man of culture, a truly civilized being. His face is familiar. You have seen it carved in great cathedrals and you have seen it formed in the loops and whorls of great trees. His the pumpkin head and the guardian of the portal, twin-visaged, the faces of fear and laughter, drama and comedy, night and day. His the ancient terror of the woodlands, the leader of the pack. He has been called by many names, Herne, Arawn, Gabriel. His name is at once more and less familiar. Look into his eyes and know his name; eyes kind with true wisdom. There is nothing to fear here except that he knows you as you truly are, and loves you as he loves all living.

It is not easy to be seen without cover or defence. One feels momentarily trapped in that gaze like a hunted animal, with nowhere to hide. Perhaps this is why he is linked with the wild hunt, but the poem 'The Hounds of Heaven' comes nearest to the truth of it.

How has this paradox arisen? How has this child of light become imprisoned in the tower of this body? Why the fearsome aspect? Why this eternal imprisonment?

To understand this one must speak with him directly; it is not a secret, but each should learn the mystery for himself. Suffice it to say that he entered his prison willingly, to serve the land he loves, and the people of the land. As we are all people of the earth, he is our protector rather than the predator he appears to be.

Walk awhile with him, and listen to the tales he tells. He will show you the many-coloured creatures of the world, the forest dwellers, the desert creatures. He will reveal the secret lives of the Lords of the Oceans, and of the great white bears and the silver wolves who sing under the Northern Lights. He will show you life above and beneath the earth, and then the tiny lives that are born and die in a drop of dew, and the great creatures of the aeons that swim between the stars.

Perhaps he will call a deer from the forest or a hare from the fields, and call you brothers, or sisters, that you will have a special friend in that world, should you venture there again; an animal whose form and name are known to you alone, with whom to explore the natural world more deeply.

Maybe he will show you beasts out of legend and memory; a white hart running, the unicorn, or perhaps the great white horse forever running the dragon paths of the land. She is in our blood; the mother-maiden who is the kind he loves. She who is both night-mare and bringer of the rich fermented milk, most ancient of the mothers of the son of the Sun.

And what is he doing all this time? Perching in a tree like a moulting buzzard, his eye single, ravens at his shoulder? Sitting cross-legged in a cave beneath the ground with wolves and serpents at his feet? Playing harp or lyre to the forest beasts in an oak grove? Once more fearsome, surrounded by the animals that love to be near him. Some have called him Odin or Orpheus, Cernunnos or Apollo, because he partakes of their nature, and he has been all that is. Yet his true name is simpler because he is as old as time, time wherein names cease to be important as they change as the world changes.

He is as abiding as sea and stone, and as ever-changing. His is the life of river and wood, his the strength of sap and sinew, his the force of light and fire. He will remain as long as the land remains.

Now you have briefly entered another world, in your imagination, and you have met a great being who is apparently half-human, half-animal. Most of us coming here for the first time are seized by a sudden panic, because a thousand years of folklore, not to mention one's local vicar, warn us to avoid confrontations like this. Are you being trapped into consorting with evil?

Remember another world, created in imagination by a conventional Christian, where a young girl goes through a wardrobe door to the land of Narnia. On entering her otherworld, the first creature Lucy speaks with is a horned man with hooves and a tail, in this case a faun. Many of us who are older, less innocent, less wise, might have run screaming for the safety of our armchair. But the guardian is no demon. True, Lucy's faun was in the pay of an old, dark power but, transformed by the child's trust and friendship, he redeemed himself by sacrificing his life for her.

The guardian has a terrifying aspect for good reason, best shown perhaps in the three guises familiar to us from folklore, by which I mean tales and songs. The first guise is that of Riddler on the Road; the second is that of Guardian of the Gate, and the third is that of Leader of the Wild Hunt. The first, like Jacob's angel, is an adversary whose purpose is to test your strengths and weaknesses. This is usually, but not always, a test of wits rather than physical strength. If you can outwit him, the adversary becomes a trusty ally. In folk-tales, the innocent often overcome the adversary by their innate kindness, not even recognizing that they are being tested; youngest sons who help old hags across streams, lost princesses who help the birds and beasts upon the path.

The second guise is a more extreme form of testing because the Guardian of the Gate is your own dark twin, and the struggle to come to terms with a personification of your least acceptable aspects is always painful and can be downright terrifying. However, you are being helped to help yourself. If you cannot face these things, there is retreat with honour. Only your own pride will have suffered. Each of us must handle this meeting in their own way, there are no magic formulae to help you here. The only advice I would proffer is that the key does not lie in domination.

The Leader of the Wild Hunt is working on a more general level. In the folklore of Northern Europe the Wild Hunt is something to be avoided, fearsome beasts led by a demon in pursuit of Christian souls. However, the real purpose of the hunt is once more to bring confrontation with the self, but this time to those who have, by some physical action, so outraged the group consciousness of their community or even of their nation, so upset the harmony of the land, that the Hunt is joined. The Hounds are called from their sleep, and they direct the quarry to the place where the quarry is brought face to face with what he or she has done. There is no judgement here, the hounds have acted more like dogs bringing in stray sheep to the shepherd, yet to the sheep, or the quarry, this is a terrifying experience. Their apprehension by police or others in the 'real' world often coincides with their acceptance of what they have done, although this is not a conscious process and they would retain no memory of it. Unfortunately to my mind, the Hunt cannot respond directly to the rape of a planet.

Who, then, does the Guardian serve, he who is not a god? Whose are the animals that wander behind the doorway of the Green and Burning Tree? Why do they appear in our myths and dreams, poems and songs? Animals as symbols play such a huge part in our everyday life. Even banking, surely the most materially-minded of modern institutions, used the signs of the Eagle, the Griffin, the Black Horse in their advertising. The familiar forms of heraldry displayed on public buildings, the names of public houses, are all redolent of animal lore.

Part of the answer lies in their relationship to the circle of the year. Animal symbolism relates to the turning of the seasons and the festivals and holidays. These symbols encapsulate and extend meaning and memory. Take any calendar or almanac. Almost every saint, goddess, god or national hero is represented by or related to an animal of some kind. Seasonal lore relates to animals, the March hare, Dog Days, the Halcyon days. These are some of the totem beasts of racial consciousness. There are the Lion, Eagle, Bull and Man who represent among other things the writers of the synoptic gospels. The Celts used the bear, the stag, the horse and the cow to make similar representation. Look at Amerindian medicine wheels, at the Zodiac creatures of occident and orient.

We see a cyclic pattern, a cycle of animals that often change their form from one to another, both describing and illuminating the changing year and all that relates to these changes. Here are cycles of life, of death and rebirth.

The Druids supposedly divided their year into 36 10-degree sectors represented by animals; Robert Graves tells of a calendar of birds used in Ancient Ireland, and even I have compiled my own year circle of totem beasts. The reason why these are not reproduced here are that I believe that the only valid way of obtaining and using such a calendar is to compile it oneself. There are many traditions, but no fixed list of correspondences; each person's wheel would be made up of different correspondences that have particular resonance and meaning within the psyche of that individual. Groups could evolve group Wheels if they wished, using symbols of common relevance. One wheel I have used only uses horses, and was originally inspired by a vision of Black Elk, yet through it I was able to hear the voice of these islands. One need not be limited by history or culture, although it may be helpful to stick to the native beasts of your own tradition, and I am working in Britain. It may be useful to mention that in my experience the animals appear in pairs; pairs that at first sight suggest the relationship of hunter and hunted, although this is not necessarily so. In my calendar hare and hound run together, as do otter and salmon.

A lot of nonsense has been talked about totem beasts, as though they can be assigned as simply and inexorably as Zodiacal sun signs. Misunderstanding may arise because distinctions are not made between universal, racial and personal symbols. Any particular totem animal may act in any or all of these roles.

Universal totems are meaningful to most cultures through most of history on this planet. 'Global' might be a better term than 'universal'. These exist within the collective mind, conscious and unconscious, beasts such as the Lion, the Spider, the Dragon. Next come the animals with resonances to particular land masses and races of people. Although more particularly relevant to these lands and races, they may still cross cultural and continental barriers. These are beasts like the Feathered Serpent and the Unicorn.

Then there are tribal totems linked with particular groups of people and with specific bloodlines. These still operate in cultures where tribal consciousness has apparently ceased to exist; and include animals like bear, wolf, boar, stag. Often these animals occur in heraldry and all matters referring to lineage, breeding, relationships and bloodlines.

Lastly there are personal totems, which can be found by an initiatory process, or may be met with during the course of one's life. Such initiations have nothing to do with the joining of groups or societies; they are journeys made alone and untutored, the necessary education takes place upon the way. The animal or animals one meets on such a journey, like those met with in song and story, act as the voice of the land and of our ancestors, distilled and concentrated into a voice that speaks to you alone. The initiatory journey is described in many cultures; in our own, nowadays, it would usually be undertaken in meditation, although there really is no substitute for putting one's feet firmly upon the land, one's head firmly in the clouds, and walking.

You may wonder how one might meet and recognize one's personal totem without any such reaching out, during the ordinary course of life. A special kind of awareness must develop so that one can distinguish between truly numinous events and 'mere' coincidence; discrimination being the necessary virtue one must develop, as in all walks of life, if one wishes to take an active role in one's personal development. Women have an inbuilt advantage here, in that they are naturally active, creative, in the inner worlds whereas men tend to be more passive within these realms. A generalization of course, but one which may prove helpful.

However, without the use of discrimination it is easy to fall into a kind of lazy superstitiousness, when one will see every coincidence as a Coincidence. Then the shining network of orderly intersections becomes merely a tangled web.

Let's take a fictitious example. Anna is a small girl, nervous at school, who dreams at night of a huge golden bear who frightens away the playground bullies and lets her ride on its back safely home. These dreams comfort her, dreams she forgets as she grows older and has children of her own.

Alone one day, cross (as a bear with a sore head) and tired (of licking her children into shape) she sees herself as lumpish, clumsy and aggressive, and does not like what she sees. Switching on the radio, she gives a mental groan because it is half-way through the Daily Service. She makes herself coffee, half listening to the droning cleric who is reading something about a prophet calling a she-bear to devour some irritating children. She smiles over her coffee, telling herself she knows just how he felt; then sits up with a jolt as the meaning of what she has just heard sears into her brain. She must have misheard! Holy men don't set wild animals on little children. Wasn't there a Bible somewhere where she could look it up? And the phone rings, and she is distracted, and it is maybe weeks later before time and inclination combine so that she checks the reference out.

Perhaps the message would be hard to find, and Anna would be tired and worried, and finally, disturbed by the story. A primitive tale, the unpleasant servant of a nasty little tribal god who behaves badly, held up as an example to an alien culture in an alien time. The image, however, of a great wise man behind whom stands a golden she-bear holding a dripping honeycomb, lingers in her mind. Anna does not like it; she finds it profoundly disturbing, especially when she remembers that her unused middle name, Ursula, means 'She-bear'.

Her boys are mad about Arthurian stories, they must be doing them at school. She recalls Malory and Tennyson from her own school-days, years ago now in her late girlhood; she recalls dust motes rising and falling in late summer sunlight as the English teacher read aloud, pupils drowsed or giggled, images of Elaine, Morgan, Launcelot, floated before her.

And had there not been a television programme once, full of Druids and barbarians, she had fancied one of the actors. Memories. They had called him Artos, the Great Bear. That was the only constellation she knew by sight in the night sky. Wasn't there a Little Bear as well? Why not three bears, or perhaps there were, she knew nothing about astronomy. Anna saw in her mind's eye the seven stars of the Bear, Arthur's Wain and then she remembered the bear-guardian of her childhood dreams, who had looked so terrifying, but had made her feel so warm and safe.

This may be how it begins, the recognition of a set of stresses with an inner relevance particular to you. Once you recognize such resonances you will start to look out for meaning every time a new reference turns up. Now you need to tread carefully and use your discrimination, and a certain amount of will.

Anna will begin to see significance in all kinds of things. It may strike her that it is significant that a woman 'bears' children, for instance. This might seem silly to most of us, especially to etymologists, yet the links between 'bear' an animal and 'bear' to carry, to present, to take on burdens, are of deep meaning to Anna in her personal life. She must be able to distinguish whether this linkage of words has meaning on a general level as well. Perhaps she may seek to strengthen her identification by using Ursula as her forename, though she could prefer to forget the whole thing.

She could relate her temper to the idea of 'going berserk'. Does this mean 'bear-shirted' or 'naked'? Does it matter? Can she accept the irate Grizzly as easily as Paddington or Pooh?

Her dreams may lead her into deep caves full of old bones, to necklaces of teeth and claws, to a tall man with a bear's skin covering him, to a woman who is the Bear-goddess, Callisto, most fair, bringer of honey. She may meet with Beorn in Middle Earth as she reads aloud to her sons. Or Beowulf, slayer of Grendel.

She may meet other people at work with whom she feels an unspoken affinity, sensing that they too are bear-people, People of the Bear. What she does about it, if anything, is up to her. Her interest could range from a mild academic curiosity to downright obsession; a state which should be resisted in any sphere of activity mainly because one's obsessions are so boring for everyone else.

If Ursula is wise she will keep her thoughts to herself. Work with totems involves deeper exploration of such themes, perhaps rescuing hitherto unconscious material, which can be a slow and painful process. Perhaps she will find herself working with global archetypes, becoming aware of what is happening to their living representatives on earth. Much work on a practical level may be involved with ecological issues and the greening of the planet; one should be aware of the plight — and sadly it is almost always a plight — of the remaining members of the species one feels linked with.

Through contact with one's totem one reaches a greater understanding of, and contact with, the earth we live on as a living entity. We may see ourselves in proportion as one of the many beings living within her protective mantle. We may, painfully, see ourselves as we really are.

I must stress once more the first role of the totem beast, that of communicator. It is dialogue between you and your totem that ultimately provides gifts of lasting value, and this dialogue must work both ways. The totem should not be followed blindly, much less revered. It is not a god and wants a friend, not a slave. It is a different order of being, certainly, but may be treated as you would treat a true friend with different but complementary strengths. Listen, argue, learn from each other, explore, have fun. As with any positive relationship you should both grow and be transformed in your different ways through your contact. It will present an ever-present help in time of trouble, too. Remember, a totem beast is the voice of the land and of your ancestors.

One will also discover, sooner or later, by work done with the totems that the animals served by the Lord of the Animals will ultimately lead, spiral-wise, to godhead.

The voice of a tribal totem would speak to the tribe through its shaman. The voice of a national or a universal totem may speak through a national hero, but as these days true heroes are hard to find, the voice of the land emerges into the group mind through images in the mass media. Isn't technology wonderful? Needless to say this is not a conscious process in the minds of media people.

These classifications are both arbitrary and flexible, as any given totem animal can be active on any of these levels or even active on all levels at once. As an example, take the horse, a totem animal of great antiquity and world-wide relevance, as may be seen in any study of comparative mythology. The horse also has particular significance within the Islands of Great Britain. I will end with a brief meditation on the nature of the White Horse.

Look up into the skies and see the seven stars of the great

mare, whose milk streams in a many-coloured path of splendour across the heavens. She is first among gods, beasts and men; she was before time was, and will be when the universe returns to the dust from which she wove it, turner of the great wheel, hauler of the great wain. She who dwelt in the sea of becoming, she who turned its tides, the great mare, earth-shaper; she who so loved the world that she gave her only begotten son, Care, for the world of men. She who so loved the world that she rode through the portals of her own so swift that none could see her coming, so slow that none could approach her. She who was stayed in the name of love.

Her son became man, suffering at the hands of those for whom he was brought forth, the Sun Stallion whose blood made a dead planet blossom. She became a beast of burden, reviled and slandered, because she loved much.

And when in a time beyond the time of dreaming, One came to live out in reality what the Son of the Mother had foreshadowed, and the Son of Man had no place to lay his head; the White Horse gave up her stable and walked forth into the dark, to make way for the Dayspring from on high whose time had come in the eternal Now.

So she became a shadow in the memory of our ancestors, for some the grey nightmare, the bare bones of winter, but for others the Great White Horse running forever in our blood. Her symbol is stretched out on the land and in the stars.

She has many faces; the skull on the spear that guards the gate; the queen of battle with her dark birds; the eight-legged one who takes the warrior dead to their reward; the mother of twin foals, whose sweet-singing birds lull the living to rest and the dead to memberance. She is the guardian of the sacred head who is a bridge, she is the seven-skinned dancer. Loving wife, mother, sister of mortal man, oldest symbol of the islands of Britain. Mari Llwyd, Mari Wen, Lady of the Great Sea from which all life springs, we honour you.

The Woman of the Birds

R.J. Stewart

Introduction

In 1980 I was snowed into my apartment in Bath for three days (unlikely as this may sound) and a sheet of ice effectively sealed the door to the street. Under such primal conditions, I found myself writing the basis of a multifold novel, which I was to develop over the following six months, in which five themes interlinked in a very devious and complicated manner. Needless to say my agent at that time (long since gone the way of most agents) shrank back in terror at the thought of placing such a monstrosity with a publisher. Such are the vagaries of a writer's life. . . but superficially simple situations hide complex subterranean rumblings. I was particularly pleased when Caitlín Matthews, who had read the bulky manuscript in 1982, asked me to contribute a section of my own choice to this anthology.

The original novel consists of five visions or worlds inextricably woven together. During my work on the manuscript I saw these worlds, entered into them in inner vision, and interpreted what I saw in my own language. One such world, that of 'The Woman of the Birds', seems to be in the prehistoric past... readers with a good knowledge of British geography and prehistory may recognize the locations, though it took me several weeks to do so myself.

The two scenes which I have chosen are part of a coherent tale, which makes a full novel in its own right, though I would prefer it not to be separated from its four companion stories. For the present anthology, however, these scenes are offered as insights into primal or tribal magical arts, retold from my vision. I would stress that this appeared to me in every way as a real world, with real people, and that their plight moved me very deeply, for they were dying out. The scenes, however, deal with two magical themes or aspects of oral tradition and initiatory knowledge. The first is concerned with what would nowadays be called genetics, but genetics for magical or spiritual ends. I have been told by a geneticist that the 'code' described in the communal chant of the birds is perfectly viable in modern scientific terms, but I merely take his word for this.

The second scene is a tale within a tale, and deals with the much vaunted, little understood subject of relationship between matriarchal and patriarchal cultures in the distant past. The story develops as a myth told to a group of children, but it includes an account of the deadly art of cursing, a number of highly energized visionary symbols, such as were later to be formalized in tarot, and a version of one of the most famous myths found world-wide in so many forms, the 'Massacre of the Innocents'. Many of the elements of this second scene, such as the Spider and Weaver Goddess, were to appear some years later in my *Merlin Tarot* (1988) as emblems or symbols in the cards, drawn primarily from Merlin texts and traditions written out and adapted by Geoffrey of Monmouth during the twelfth century. But in 1980, shivering in my winter woollens, I had not yet read the *Life and Prophecies of Merlin* and had not yet written my books on these curious texts.

The Woman of the Birds

The Woman of the Birds sat uneasily upon her High Chair. This chair was large, made of many animal horns twisted and tied together with thongs; it was crowned with two immense curving long-horns rising in a crescent far above her tiny head. The creature that once wore those horns no longer walked in the land. Perched upon a mound of skins and furs, the Woman of the Birds shifted uncomfortably from side to side. She was the smallest of a long line of small women, and old and wizened. Most of her people towered over her, yet her word was absolute law. In the Wooden House, smoke and shadows danced from flames that burnt pungent herbs; in that shifting light the women who gathered for the evening chant loomed as silent wavering giants against the reed-lined walls.

Within the smoky warmth there was security of hearth and home, but outside winter gripped tight upon the marshland. That very morning she had stood upon the wooden roof platform, newly cleared of snow, to peer out over the flat white land into the grey wall of mist and cloud that hid the sea. The log causeway to the West was covered with thick, hard ice, and snow upon that ice, so even the lightest runners could not travel between her settlement and the hilltop fort that guarded the route inland from the sea. On clear days, when the fort was in full sight, mirror and fire signals could travel back and forth in their own languages; mirror for women in tongue of mirror, and fire and smoke for men. Today. . .nothing. Dull grey snowlight hid the road, the edges of the marsh, and the distant fort.

As the Woman of the Birds relived her look-out of that morning, the last of her women entered the chamber, drawing the doors tightly shut against the bitter wind. There were rustlings, soft breathings, the sound of bare feet in rushes as they put their wrappings into a small side-room. No one spoke. All waited for the little creature on the High Chair to signal a beginning. Still she moved restlessly, lost for a moment in an inward dialogue, in memory pictures. Why was she so uneasy? No warriors would seek to travel in such foul weather. . .no raiders could sail; so why be concerned about the guardian fort? She told herself that there was a strangeness about, a strangeness that prickled upon her innermost thoughts, remaining withdrawn and unclear, as if she had seen something in the morning mist yet forgotten its importance. That family vision, inherited from her mother and mother's mother, which came often in time of need, was strangely silent. When she used her Sight upon this mystery that troubled her, she saw nothing. The disturbance came from a different source, from a place where Sight could not reach; it made itself felt as an awareness that whistled and twittered during the most quiet moments, withdrawing instantly whenever she looked directly for its source. Recollecting herself and her time and place, the Woman of the Birds raised her chin slightly and nodded into the smoky light of the hall.

Instantly the great bronze gongs boomed and rumbled, and the high voices of her women opened out into song. They uttered a wandering air, each word elided into the next until any part of the chant seemed to offer many simultaneous word patterns. For the listener the effect was entrancing, confusing, for it relaxed the normal lines of verbal logic and opened the mind directly for waking dream images... and for subtle power-words that held multifold meanings. In certain men this chant produced a fit, with frothing at the mouth, jerking of the arms and legs, and then a huge energetic flinging backwards of the body. Such men, it was rumoured around the evening fire when women told quiet stories of the past, had been used physically in bygone days. No one knew the truth of this tradition, first whispered in girlhood training, at bath time or in the sweat chamber, then repeated in old age with other fragments of the past. But in the present men prone to falling fits were rare, and all men were excluded at all times from the chanting, so there seemed little ground for the suggestive tale.

Herbs and resins were added to the central fire, which was kept burning day and night all year round, save for one night in which it was allowed to die prior to the Mystery of its rekindling. Though the hall grew dark with smoke, no one coughed or paused in the chant. Of those who sat and sang, each knew her own level of chant, according to her age and skill. Some had been singing for as long as 30 years or more, while a few of the youngest girls merely hummed parts of the melody, being just old enough to begin speaking.

On the Horn Chair, she who led the people, men and women both in all aspects and patterns of life, was silent. Silence was her right; she alone was exempt from the rule of chanting, whereby all women must learn the sacred songs as soon as they begin to speak. Her silence stemmed from total knowledge of all chants in the world, all words possessed by the people since the first opening of the eye of the Moon. It was said, by those who told the tales of men and their ritual use in times gone by, that if a girl could not sing and learn the words of power, she should be impaled (as was the rule once long ago). But a woman who could not sing was impossible, unthinkable, so no such rule could be enforced, even if it did truly exist.

The Woman was old, and had both led and listened to this evening chant, the most powerful and secret of all, for more than 50 winters. This was long indeed for one of her people to live; she knew each word, each doubled and seemingly accidental syllable and musical inflexion, each phase of inspiration and interacting resonance. She knew every image that arose within the chant, always the same images forever. Sometimes, alone at night, and greatly daring, she had speculated upon this chant, seeking out its mystery which none had fathomed . . . for no one understood its meaning and purpose now. Faint echoes of meaning sometimes came to her, preserved within the dream of the tradition, but whatever sacred knowledge those perfect words and tones contained was lost to her, and certainly lost to her people.

Not first there is man. . . of the seed.
There is also woman. . . of the blood.
Man of seed, woman of blood.

Man of seed comes from blood and blood:
There is also man of blood.
Man of blood is from woman-blood
Once joined with not-blood.
Woman-blood and not-blood.

Woman of blood comes from blood and blood:
There is always woman of blood.
Woman of blood also comes from blood and not-blood:
There is always woman of blood.

Not last comes one of seed-blood
From woman of blood and man of seed:
In right time of turning
Comes one of seed-blood.

Woman has the line of blood
Woman has the mystery of blood
Woman ends the exile by her blood
By mystery of blood and seed:
Woman has the line of blood.

Man has one chance of blood
Man has one chance of seed
Man has one given chance.

Woman has the line of blood
The line of blood all ways:
Woman gives the blood to man
Woman is the branch forever:
Woman ends exile by her blood
By mystery of blood and seed.

Not first there is man. . .of the seed.
There is also woman. . .of the blood.
Man of seed, woman of blood:
In right time of turning
Comes one of seed-blood. . .

As the chant repeated, her mind relaxed into that half-sleep that comes with great age, resting yet in part alert. She knew many chants, yes. . .chants for the growing of corn and of nut trees; chants for the homing of bees to their hives; chants for the summoning of black birds in autumn; chants for the rising of shoals of fish in the river pools; chants for the making and birthing of babes. They all had clear meaning but for one, this first chant learned before speech, this last chant she would hear one evening soon.

In her dreaming memory the chant led her back upon her childhood journey, a tradition that had long since ceased with the lessening of the people and the closing of the sea-ways. She had travelled with a small party of other girls of her age, led by an aged woman who had also commanded the sailors. They had rowed and then sailed to the South and West, to a group of islands far away in the racing sea. There lived the furthest families and rulers of her race, not led by Bird Women as in her homeland, but by Man Kings. These curious male Bird Women had spirals pricked out painfully around their eye sockets, dyed in rich blue-black and purple. Some were patterned around one eye, some around both, some even had balancing spirals upon their cheeks; they met the girls and immediately pointed to the patterns upon their wind-brown faces. . .this is the Pattern of the Eye.

In strange lilting accents they claimed to see into anyone's most secret heart through this pattern, and although her cousins were doubtful, she knew this to be true. For a thin brown man (they were all kings, each and every one of them), had sat her upon his knee, given her a fruit to eat, told her wonderful stories, and sung the secret evening chant of the women to her. Then he predicted her entire life. He told her of the Horned Chair, leadership, responsibility, pain, joy and great age. Before he finished the tale she had fallen asleep.

On returning home she had told this wonder to her elder cousin, the senior woman of the group who was destined to be Woman of the Birds when her mother's mother's sister, the current Woman, died. The older woman, already preparing to rule, had been surprised and offended.

Those weird Island Men . . . know more than a man should. In our settlement any man even listening to the great chant has his globes cut off and is cast out into the marsh! This had puzzled the little Bird girl for a long time, she not knowing what a man's globes might be. Even when she found out all about men, their globes, and the uses that men might be put to over and above being herders, runners, sailors and musicians, she never saw one castrated and cast out to die. During her time the community was so small that no one would have wasted a man, no, not even the most conservative and easily offended Bird Woman, such as her elder cousin had never become. Ah! That slim young runner from the fortress men; what endurance and sweet breath. Ah! That fine man who had made the voice within the wood speak out, the song of the hollow tree branch and the fine beaten wires of red metal. Her head nodded, and the evening chant washed over and through her dream.

If any woman noticed that she slept within the shadows, none dared to comment. Besides, none could stop the chant with its numbered repetitions, until all variants were completed. Each woman was enwrapped utterly in the flow, the resonance, the rhythm, sometimes breaking into high subtle ululation. This call marked the bloodline of the Bird Woman, even to the lightest degree. Occasionally the bronze gongs roared, cutting through the flow of the chant and creating complex counter resonances with the voices. And still she slept beneath the powerful high spreading Horns.

The Woman of the Birds tells a Tale

The upturned faces were attentive, the gathering was quiet. Once in each year, when the Seven Stars were seen to mark the onset of fine weather and sailing time, the children were taught by the Woman herself. This was a great event. Each solemn small face was scrubbed clean; best woollen clothes had been patched and whitened with clay or bleached in the sun. Sitting in a wide semicircle at a respectful distance from the High Chair of Horns, the children hardly dared to breathe; any that wriggled or coughed were instantly jabbed by the hard elbows of their neighbours, or smothered in restraining affectionate grips. No adult was present other than the Woman herself.

Sunlight radiated through the open vents in the steep roof, and the sound of birds singing was clear. Already the swallows were beginning to build their nests; the Woman of the Birds could sense them flitting in and out of the swallow-gates at either end of the Hall, even though they could not be seen. The tiny ornately carved archways would not be closed until the last birds were seen to fly off into the unknown at the end of summer, when the ships came home and the Seven Stars began to move towards the place of winter.

Looking at the little ones she realized with no surprise that there were less this year than last. It had been so for several years. But one time, one fine year long ago, this Hall had been filled with children, and many of them male! Why, she had been young and healthy then, and three (or was it four?) of them had been of her own blood and body. Today there were 30 or 40, perhaps a few more, and it was unlucky to count them lest such daring brought further losses and misfortunes. Her chairwomen counted sacks, counted sheaves and jars, stones, even single beans . . . but nobody counted people, not even the Woman of the Birds herself sitting upon the Horn Chair.

As she considered these waiting children, she realized that they must think her very fierce and stern, glaring at them in silence from her immense throne. She smiled to soften their judgement of her, to relax them ready for her lesson. What should she teach them upon this day of days? It would set the tone for all the lessons that followed until winter, for the children would retell it to their teachers, who would draw upon their vast sources of tradition to elaborate endlessly and introduce skills and examples into the telling and the learning. Her mind moved back to her own childhood, in this same Hall, listening hard to a very stern Mother give her annual lesson at springtime. There had been the story of the cow that never ran dry; the meaning of the heron's call; the naming of the trees which told of how they gathered on the highest hilltop to catch their names as the moon emptied out her travelling sack, and each had to catch a name before the sun rose or be nameless forever. But she had told the tree story only last year, and now the children knew the name and function of every tree to be found in the land. . .though these were few enough.

It was required that the Woman of the Birds tell a different wisdom tale every year for each of the eight years that any one child would appear before her. Musing upon this, she knew that although there were many stories, each child would only be able to hear eight, and that it was difficult to remember which tales had been told in any mixed age-group of children, and to ensure that no child heard any tale twice. Her mind trembled upon the edge of most daring calculation. . .until a small movement caught her attention, directly in front of her left eye.

Shining in the sunlight, descending from a high beam, a small spider busily spun her way to earth. Her long lifeline glistened, and the warm light made her waving legs and bright body glow like crystal. Just below the Woman's nose, she paused and turned slowly, slowly, in a full circle as her line was caressed by an unfelt wind. Grasping tight for an instant, the spider waited, then released her grip to continue spinning her journey to the hard-packed earthen floor. There, thought the Woman, am I; a long frail line from the unseen to the final earth.

'Today you will hear of the truth. Hear and remember, that the truth will never fade away.'

'We hear and remember, Mother of All.'

'Today, under the blessing of our roof, under the shining of the Sun, upon the foundation of the earth, you will hear of. . .The Spider.'

'We will hear and remember, Mother of All.'

'So let the story and its telling now begin.'

This ritual opening over, she leaned forward smiling, and summoned them close with her hands. For a moment they hesitated, unsure, surprised, but the first few jumped up and boldly ran right to the foot of the Chair, and the rest soon followed. With the sound of bare feet upon earth she heard little laughs and mutterings, for the sudden release from that respectful sitting had given them the chance to make a sound . . . to risk that which was usually forbidden in her presence.

So few! She wanted them close. Close so that her voice could be easily heard by all, close so that they felt warm and crowded together, brothers and sisters all, as it had been in the better years long gone when children packed the Hall from the Chair to the Door. But most of all she wanted them close for their own sake, and for her own, almost forgotten, long-dead loved ones. Waiting while they settled, she watched the older children hold the hands of the little ones who could hardly speak, or who might wander off, fall asleep, or lose full attention to the story. She saw those nearest to her feet look carefully for the travelling spider before sitting down. Very few of her people, young or old, failed to see and mark the path of a spider. And then she began . . .

'A very long time past, when the world was smaller and stronger than it is today, this land was sister to another land. The other land was really a group of islands, which are little lands that stand upon the surface of great heaving waters, far over the seas from here, in the direction of the sun at evening, where he goes to sleep. At the time of this story, a great ruler had arisen who strove mightily to unite all lands under one strong arm; this arm was, of course, his own. Such ruling of lands by one person, and a man at that, was not a good thing. With his loud booming voice and his black curly beard, he rode upon a horse, something which was unknown before his time. The horse carried him to many distant places, with his male guards and male weapon-people running and leaping and stumbling along behind.

'When this man upon the horse reached the sea, and could not ride or run or swim, he caused a great wooden ship to be built. This ship was held together by thick twisted hide ropes and hard wooden and copper pins, and it had many oars, so many that no one could count them, even if they had been allowed to by the vigilant male guards with their bull-whips and clubs. So great in size was this ship that even the horse could ride upon it, standing in the prow just as boldly as he might stand upon the grassy earth.

'This mighty male ruler, with his hard hands and leather armour over his thick skin, forced all the wise women and seeing men to obey him and him only. Those who did not obey he killed, as easily as if they were marsh chickens. There was no end to his ruling, his power, his name and his glory. The Sun shone down upon him and into him, making him glow hot. Soon he would rule all beneath the wide summer sky.

'But take heed, for power is never given without the seed of its own destruction hidden in its heart. Through each season of riding, ship travel and conquest, this man of sinewy arms and broad shoulders knew little rest or sleep. No, not even in the gentle dark night with women close by, not even at the right and proper times for resting could he rest. And it was not the passion or the fire of his power that kept him wide awake, even though his eyes hurt and his mouth tasted of sand, even though his shoulders sagged and his muscles twitched with fatigue. No. . .it was the power of a curse!

'Now a curse is no small thing to make, and no small thing to be the victim of. As soon as it is made it grows and feeds; first upon air, until it begins to seek. As it seeks it travels with the wind for company, and so feeds deeply until it finds. With every spiteful thought and evil deed seen by the wind, a curse will feed, growing strong and heavy, tough and tangled. Until, at last, it finds the one for whom it was made! Some curses find their man or woman quickly, others take many years. A really well-made curse will take a long, long time to hit its mark, for the maker knows that it has grown slowly to become a curse of immense power and cunning, not easily endured or shaken off or destroyed. Such was the kind of curse put upon this bold and mighty self-appointed king, and this was why he could not sleep, for he feared it drawing close upon him.

'Listen now to the story of how he earned that terrible curse, and what came to pass after the curse had been made.

'One hot summer day, while sailing from island to island, with his horse standing proud in the prow of the great ship, just as if it stood on dry land, the ruler of men espied a little mark upon the surface of the sea. As they travelled on, he soon saw that it was a small boat of skins bobbing over the bright wave-tops without oars or sails. In this round frail coracle was a wise man from an island, who had the Seeing Eye in deepest blue upon his own eye and upon his face. This wise man, a type of male Bird Woman now long gone and almost forgotten in the world, was not, as you might think, running away.

'No, for just as a traveller in our straight marsh roads sees first the tree-top then the whole tree as she draws closer and closer to the woods, so had this wise island-man seen the ears of the horse sticking up over the wave crests. As soon as he had seen those ears pricking out over the watery hills, he knew that he must set foot within his skin boat. Even as he pushed his way out into the sea-road, he could see the horse's eyes peeping over the weed-strewn waters, and then the gleaming top of its proud head. He knew that if he was to make a good strong curse, he must be off his own island and out into the open ocean before he could see that horse's nose!

'And this he did, for when his round leather basket, held tight across by one rough wooden sapling pole, floated up to the great ship, his homeland was far, far behind. The great self-appointed king looked down upon his visitor, who looked back up at the king with deeply-spiralling eyes, right at the broad hairy face of the invader.

"There's some who spend their time in laughing!" said the man in the little boat.

"There's some who spend their time in play!" said the king in the great ship.

"I will bring the time of passing" said the one with spiralling eyes, and even the horse laughed at this unlikely threat.

"And I will take *your* time away!" yelled the invader as he hurled a great studded and spiked club right at the island man's head. But as is often the way with the sea, his great ship rising up and the little leather boat bobbing down, the club missed its mark, and tore through the skins of the bottom of the boat. As it began to fill and sink, the island Bird Man stood upon the sapling that spread the leather tight. He perched upon one foot, with one eye shut, and one hand raised.

"Cursed are they that would ruin a fair land" he said out of the left side of his mouth, "And as this boat is filling up with sea faster than the sea fills up with boat, I'll leave out the rest. But I will tell you this much. . .exactly nine moons from the day that you dare to set foot upon my island, one will be born who will be the death of you and all your works in years to come. Goodbye."

'And with these words his mouth was filled with sea, then his nose, and his eyes, until the salt waters closed over the top of his head. Not once did he struggle, or flap his arms, or shout, or even sneeze; Nor did he try to swim away below the water. And this sort of death is the strongest way of birthing a curse that a man or woman may ever contrive.

'So the great invader, enraged by the challenge, took all the islands. He ruined and burned the island of the Drowned Man, and set foot and feet all over it until nothing was left. He then returned home to the mainland, to a certain place not far from where we are sitting today. But as he sat idle, he began to fear that curse, and so he had all the men who had rowed his ship put to death, lest they spread the tale of it far and wide. Still he could not sleep, for after their needless deaths those dead men rushed upon the wind and on the backs of flying geese to feed the curse, and join with it in revenge. Oh sorry man to have dared what even a woman would not dare! The only living witness left of that cursing was the horse, who never spoke a word, and who enjoyed riding around upon a ship and cloppering over the hard roads with a great warrior king upon his back. So the horse was not likely to tell anyone of the curse, and he lived on.

'As each Moon came up from out of the earth and grew, as each Moon faded and closed her eye upon the acts of women, this false king grew to dread the fruit of that sea-made curse. It was indeed a great curse greatly shaped; a curse of curses. He knew that it would last for many generations, working its way through the bloodlines of the first-born carrier, always seeking to destroy his works, his hollow-reed empire that was to last forever. And he wished that he had never seen the sky over that island man's head.

'By the eighth Moon, the false king had concluded that there was only one answer, one way to steal sleep. This answer was so simple, so daring, and so horrible that none but a great leader such as himself, so he thought, would dare to carry it out. His solution was this. . .all children born around the period of that ninth Moon would be carried off and executed, which means killed.

'He laid his plans well and set spies through all the corners of his realm to watch. When the ninth Moon opened her all-seeing eye and walked upon the sky-ways to illuminate the land, he sent out his warrior men, with hair standing up straight in hard clay-stiffened spikes. Each new-born child, they announced, was to be taken for counting by the great king's Chair Women. But the secret plan was not counting at all, but killing. When all those tiny babes were gathered into one place, the warrior men whipped out their sharp brown knives and cut them to pieces! The blood flowed into the earth at that place until the earth could take no more, and even to this day there is not a tree, a bush, or a blade of grass that will grow there.

'But this awful deed was that false king's undoing, and was in itself the first effect of the powerful curse against him. It turned all the women of the land into his enemies, and they spat upon the floors where he had walked and ground sharp points upon the ends of their distaffs. No man dared eat food prepared by a woman, and all the secret herbs that breed death were gathered in until no more could be found, for they were all making their way into the food of the great false king and his spike-haired warrior men. Yet this was only the merest beginning of the power of that curse. Listen again and you shall hear who defeated the strongest of men, and she only small and weak!

'In one village there lived a quiet, peaceful woman who had just given birth. Her own story is one that you shall hear upon another telling, but at this time she lived in an old hut, with heavy wooden doorposts; as is the sensible custom the animals lived in with her through the cold winter nights, and they all roamed free in summer. Every morning this woman would take a nutshell and draw pure water from a holy well that rose in a cleft rock just behind her house. She would place the nutshell full of water deep within a large crack in the left-hand door pillar. And who was it for? It was for her who lived within that left-hand pillar, she who loved fresh spring water to drink, and who spun her thread and wove her web in peace to guard that simple woman's home.

'From her dark abode within the crack in the doorpost, she felt the ground begin to tremble with the arrogant tramping of men. Peeping out she saw bold warriors hunting, and guessed that some trickery was soon to pass. Quick as the wind itself this wise weaver ran across the roof and took her secret way into the backwards room where the baby slept. She flexed her delicate legs and spun and spun and spun, working until the entire cradle was covered in a thick grey web. Just as she scuttled into the roof timbers to hide, the inner door was flung wide open.

"Any babies in here? Any babes new-born? They must be counted! We have come to take them to the place of counting!" And whether it was virtue in the web or whether it was that men have always been afraid of spiders, no one knows, but they looked at the place where the cradle stood and saw nothing.

"Ha! No babies here brother, she doesn't even *clean* this room!. Let's be gone!" And they stamped off shouting and rattling their clubs against their shields, as such men do. Of course the child in that cradle was a special child who did many wonderful deeds when she grew up, but those are in stories for other years to come. You may have guessed by now that one of her deeds, though it was a lesser one, was to carry that curse to the false king and destroy him and his line forever.

'So listen my children and remember. Three things that are never to be done: to kill the spider, to count the people, to wake the babe new-born.'

Her voice was dry as she leaned over to strike the gong beside the Horn Chair. In a chorus the children replied to the Woman of the Birds, looking up at her:

'We listen and remember, Mother of All.' And the solemn crowd dissolved into chattering children; the smallest of all, who were asleep, were carefully carried out into the sun by their brothers and sisters. As soon as the door to the Hall closed, whooping and shouting began, and the sound of games being played. Only one small girl remained. She bit her knuckles and bowed her head, then looked up at the tiny withered old woman upon the High Chair.

'Well daughter, what question must you ask me?' croaked the Woman of the Birds. The girl stood up, first upon one foot, then upon the other, not daring to speak. The sound of laughing and playing outside made her turn her head, drawing her back to the lovely day. Almost she ran off to join the others, but at last she pulled her fingers from her mouth and said...

'Mother of All, what happened to the horse?'

(Two further episodes of this title can be found in R.J. Stewart's *Magical Tales*, also published by The Aquarian Press.)

The Weaving Goddess

Felicity Wombwell

A Journey in Poetic Prose to my Inner Circle

To me life is one continuously moving spiral. Around and around it goes, as my life passes through the cycles of the seasons, the cycles of my life, the cycles of my body. In order to give this abstract concept form, I call it the Weaving Goddess. To me the process of spinning, weaving and cutting, encompasses the energy that I feel this deity and life has for me. To me, she is the ultimate form of life, the spark that starts all things moving. I see her energy most clearly in the cycle of the seasons. As a child, I lived in the countryside and from this I gained a strong connection to these spiralling changes.

I put a name to this Goddess when I was at college doing textiles. I studied the history of textile production and found the Weaving Goddess when looking into ancient history. At the time I was not interested in any form of religion but the idea of the

Fates fascinated me. The Fates are the Greek version of the Weaving Goddess, Clotho, Lachesis and Atropos: the spinner, the weaver, the cutter. They are responsible for spinning, weaving and cutting the thread of life; they are responsible for our destinies. In the Norse myths, a similar set of goddesses were present above the battlefields and were thought to direct the way the battle went. This was why carpets and other kinds of weaving were thought to be magical, because they were thought to contain the spirit of these deities. To enhance their magical power the goddesses themselves were also represented in the abstract designs. A mistake was also incorporated into the weaving on these carpets so the spirits may enter and leave; hence the term 'magic carpet'.

These investigations started me on the path to the Goddess and towards finding my own strength. The first step on this path was learning about the Goddess and meditating on these ideas. At first this was very strange but I developed the technique while hand-weaving at college. I was surprised at the difference, when I concentrated on a subject like the Weaving Goddess, how intense the images could be, and how I could do much more weaving and feel so good afterwards. I found this technique of visualizing the Goddess while I was doing mundane tasks very centering and energizing, taking the tedium out of the task.

From these beginnings my journey took me to tarot and astrology. I arrived here through studying the symbols on the textiles and finding how they were very often those of the stars, or astrology, or the Goddess in one of her forms, or like the archetypes on tarot trumps. It was about this time that I made the connection between the Weaving Goddess and the universe. Since then, astrology has always been a great passion of mine.

My interest in the Spinning and Weaving Goddess was taken up again with great enthusiasm when I joined a women's group interested in the Goddess religion. Things then really fell into place and the Spinning and Weaving Goddess was suddenly everywhere. There she was in the patterns of the old textiles; she was in the sky; she was Spider Woman; she was the creatrix of all. I thought while I was at college that she was an obscure Goddess; now studing women's spiritual history, she was coming up everywhere. Somehow this was making me feel better and better all the time. It was like discovering a new part of myself that I did not know existed before. I found other aspects of her in characters from mythology like Ariadne and Arianrhod. As I studied her more and more she began to take form for me as the Goddess with four faces: princess, queen, enchantress and wise woman. More often these aspects of the Goddess are called Virgin Mother and Crone. I found that these titles did not speak to me as they were too sexually based and although I visualize and experience the Goddess as a sexual being, she is many other things besides.

Through the women's group I discovered more about her aspects, especially the dark or hidden side. In the group, we mainly used ritual and pathworking to try to understand the Goddess as there was so little reliable material in books — most of them having been written by non-initiates of the Goddess religions. I found that relating the aspects of the Goddess to myself very useful and this worked most successfully when I coupled her to the moon and to my menstrual cycle:

Princess; crescent moon; post-menstruation; spinner.
Queen; full moon; ovulation; weaver.
Enchantress; waning moon; post-ovulation; cutter.
Wise woman; dark moon; menstruation; hidden aspect.

By following the aspects of the Goddess in my own cycle I learnt a lot about myself and Her, especially about my energy levels, how my energy changes. For instance I found the hidden aspect of the Goddess by seeing that during the enchantress period I was very tired and needed sleep, so giving myself this I found the Goddess of my dreams who usually appeared veiled. All this was a real revelation to me as I lost the need to be consistent in my life and I allowed myself to change as my emotions changed. The dark, hidden Goddess, to me, is the Goddess of the abyss, because she is the energy that starts creation going, that forms something out of nothing. She is the Goddess of Creation and for me the Goddess of my creativity.

Discovering this aspect of myself gave me great confidence as a woman. This is the part of me that society ignores, that is not spoken about. It is the part of me that menstruates. It is my hidden self — the side that likes to be alone. Finding this was a high in my life which is still giving me energy and support. I see this part of me like a compost heap. It is the source of my ideas and it contains the fertilizer from which my creative seeds are going to grow. It was from this source that I found the strength to be myself and not what others wanted me to be. Here in the darkness and the hidden places I find all the parts of myself that I had forgotton or rejected. It is like my own treasure trove.

After I left college I had drifted into accountancy and was not happy as this only fulfilled the survival aspect of myself. The more I worked with the Dark Goddess, the more the creative and artistic sides were beginning to push strongly for attention, and the more I realized that I needed more balance in my life. Up until now I had symbolized the idea of the Goddess on a circle like a compass. The idea arose from the phases of my menstrual cycle and the phases that the moon takes each month, displayed in a circular form, with the princess aspect at the East and the others going around clockwise, ending with the hidden wise woman aspect in the North. I did not see this as a closed circle but as a spiral slowly turning.

The Spiralling Energy of the Weaving Goddess

I then began to put the various parts of my life onto the wheel or spiral so that I could begin to see if I could see them in balance. In doing this I found that certain aspects of my life, in particular accounts, did not fit in anywhere on its own. What I could fit in was textile design, art, art therapy, the mysteries and organizing events. Because I wanted to do so many things, I decided that I was best starting up my own business. This was when I began to see that all these things were connected. Aspects of my life that now interest me began to look like threads that I was spinning together. I realized that these threads had been spinning for many years and I had not seen that they were all spinning together.

This made me feel that the influence of the Goddess was stronger than I realized and that I was now coming to the end of her first phase and moving towards the second, or queen phase. At about this time I did a long series of meditations to the Goddess Astraea which at the time was the name I was giving to the Weaving Goddess. I give her different names at different times according to what has come up during my meditations. This involved a daily devotion to Astraea which lasted six months, and I was to make a direct contact with the Goddess during my meditations in a type of controlled setting. Previous to this my experiences of contacting the Goddess had been when I was not expecting them. After a very intensive workshop, the Goddess appeared to me in my room when I got back. I was so surprised I just stood there and so missed the moment when I could have spoken to her.

In the meditations to the Goddess I worked towards forming the image of her temple, then finding my way around in the temple, then finding her, and then the communication and the receiving of her teachings. When I got to the Goddess's temple I found that it was a four-cornered castle. This fitted with my Goddess circle — one tower for each of the cardinal points. There was also a basement and a fountain in the courtyard.

To start my meditations I concentrated on my altar on which I had put objects to Astraea, like a spindle, a pair of scissors, a piece of weaving, a star map and some incense. I found that this altar needed to change as my meditations changed and slowly this became a very important focus for me as I could feel my connection to the altar when I was away from the house. The altar was underneath the window so that I could see the stars when I was meditating. Crystal balls then became the next focus for the altar as to me they are like the stars. Altars are now a very important part of my life and I think much can be learnt about ourselves and the Goddess from them. Flat altars on the floor can also be used in a circular or mandala form, like the Goddess circle I have been using.

Slowly, I put more and more aspects of my life onto this circle. One of the most useful was putting the inner landscapes from my meditations onto the circle. This was a little difficult at first because I could not decide in what direction the landscapes should go. As usual I got the answer from my meditations. The landscapes were always in the same direction from my centre when I thought of them. In the North I have a cave which is behind a hawthorn tree; in the East is the sea-shore; in the South are the plains and mountains, and in the West the jungle. Doing this I found that I could easily find which aspect of myself was out of balance. The West or the jungle was the weakest of them all; and I found that by strengthening this, I strengthened all the others.

While working on this I was introduced to the Native American teachings. Finding that they worked in a similar way was very affirming. Again I got this feeling that the several threads that I had been following in the mysteries were beginning to weave together. A form was beginning to appear and now I was getting stronger and stronger feelings that it was time to leave my job and this event was what started the weaving process. The threads that I had been weaving were my interest in art and design, the use of the voice, my interest in ritual and my love of dancing. The catalyst for starting this process was beginning a Creative Arts in Therapy course. Doing this made me realize how connected these otherwise separate things were. Creative art therapy involves establishing a therapeutic situation where the client has the choice of doing any one of the creative arts: music, dance, drama, dance, play, puppets or simply talking. The idea is that the client and the therapist can choose the most appropriate medium for the expression of the emotion and also change mediums as the session progresses. While working with these ideas I realized that all these were componants of ritual or magical ceremonies. This connection was a major breakthrough.

As a result of this, my ideas about magic and therapy have changed; instead of them being separate I now see them as part of each other. For instance, we can see this in the healing that occurs in a sand painting when the artist paints a picture around the patient for healing; the healing that can be achieved with sounds and tones. A hearty laugh is healing because it massages the heart; the healing that drama achieves is the expression of the emotions that we individually and collectively feel in both theatre and ritual. This was the weaving really coming together. I then added all the other parts of my life and started to look at mystical, spiritual painting which was very rewarding, especially the work of Cecil Collins. I followed his techniques of using the colour in triads, having night and day colours and trying to paint with my body and spirit rather than my mind. This has totally changed my way of working and I now look forward to each new development with bated breath.

When doing my devotion to Astraea I drew pictures of her after the meditations and I have continued this process since then. This has been very helpful. It is very similar to doing meditation reports and has a very similar function of giving a fix to the image. (A meditation report is a written report usually done straight after a meditation, which is kept to see how the meditation or devotion is moving or changing.)

I have also found that if I am mediating on one aspect of the Goddess it is very useful to paint using those colours and images I have assigned to that aspect. I use the tones of the seasons around the circle, so for the princess I have spring colours, light and clear golden tones; for the queen I use the colours of summer flowers, pale tones with white; for autumn the bright golden colours of autumn leaves, and for winter the strong, bright reds, blacks and whites of the snowy landscapes.

I use the circle that I described earlier and I have found that practically anything can be put onto it, even the housework which I do in phases according to which aspect I'm working with. When I am mediating on the hidden phase I don't do any! As a textile designer I paint mainly flowers and I have developed a list of correspondences from these flowers so that I can continue the meditation sequence while I am working, as I did when I first discovered the Goddess while I was weaving. Each meditation sequence lasts about nine weeks. Within this I try to go through each of the Goddess's four phases within the meditation so that a balance is maintained. I feel that each day has her four phases as well as each month.

When I left my job, I did not feel very special or different, so when I was ready to start my own business I felt the need to acknowledge this feeling formally and to recognize this as a new phase in my life. The form of acknowledgement I used was to do a ritual for the start of my business. This was very successful on a personal level as after the ritual I felt a lot more self-confident.

The ritual was very simple. I began by setting up a special astrological chart for the best day to begin and then I wrote a simple ceremony to which I invited all my friends. The ceremony consisted of a dedication of my business to the Goddess using sound, symbol and celebration. As I live in Ravenstone Road I called my business Ravenstone Designs. A ravenstone is the Scottish equivalent of a crystal ball. It is found in raven's nests and when discovered it gives the gift of prophecy to the finder. It can also be used for healing by placing the ravenstone on the patient's body. A raven is sacred to the Goddess in her dark aspect, so it felt very appropriate as, to me, the dark aspect is the creative spark. This connection feels very special to me now as it showed that I had been on the right road if only I'd known it.

I was surprised how effective the ritual was as afterwards I really felt that I had moved from one level to another, or from one spiral to the next. At this time I began to see the career path that I was following clearly for the first time and I could also feel that for the first time I could actually achieve what I wanted in life, both materially and spiritually. As things wove closer together I began to know exactly what I wanted and so I did not have to waste time trying things out to see if they were right. This was especially so with my meditations. At first I tried various things, either because they sounded good or because they might fit but as things wove together more strongly I knew what to do next.

The next step on the path was for me to start doing workshops and teaching. I really enjoy this as I find that the questions I am asked really make me think hard about what I've said and what I'm doing. With the workshops came another way of seeing the Goddess; the four aspects from around the circle became different levels of knowing the Goddess: the princess being the first, and the hidden the fourth. They became like layers through which I could ascend. Doing this I found out many new things about the Goddess, especially ideas to do with Her as a force for transformation and change in one's life. I try to incorporate these teachings into my workshops. I also like to show how all the aspects of the Goddess are within each phase, that within the queen phase there are also the princess, wise and hidden aspect. Each part of the Goddess contains within herself the essence of the others. They all spin, weave and rest. I found that to teach this I had to have experienced all the different levels before I could even teach the first.

Since I experience the Goddess primarily as an energy vortex spinning in space, I find the easiest way to explain Her and Her energy is by sound as the universe was created by sound, and sound forms spiral energy-cones which I think are very like the Goddess, always moving always changing.

To teach sound and chanting, I don't need to mention the Goddess but I have to know it is Her that I'm aiming for — a sound creation of the Goddess. When I have achieved this with a group, we then dance to these sounds and experience the Goddess within our moving bodies. For me this never fails to find the Goddess within and the experience stays for several days afterwards. I find that all my work culminates in a ceremony like this so that after every one of my workshops, everyone leaves with an experience of the Goddess and some understanding of Her mysteries.

The Goddess and Her mysteries have been ignored for many years and when individuals find Her again the experience can be very strong because that side of their natures has been ignored for so long. They are then desperate for more, but more only comes with studying the Goddess within the self. To me, starting to teach was a recognition of the queen aspect of myself, the role of giver and nurturer to others, but with this is also I suppose what could be called the king role — the business person, the keeper of the rules and laws. This came as a bit of a shock as I was not expecting it and I have never felt really comfortable with these aspects of myself.

Following the path of the Weaving Goddess has not always been wonderful — I have often regretted starting the process, especially when things are difficult or take a lot of effort to get finished. It all sounds so easy till it actually comes to doing it. I remember how my body used to ache when I was meditating, how the breathing exercises used to make me feel sick, all the times in groups when every one else got wonderful meditations and I got nothing, and so on. But all this is more than made up for when something works well. At one of my workshops, we made an image of the Goddess from the rubbish that we could find in the local street of Acton. We all went out for a walk after lunch and collected objects that appealed to us. When we came back we put all the objects on the floor and started building, and instead of the three-foot figure that I expected, we built a seven-foot Goddess to mark the coming spring. She was made of last year's rubbish which will be the next year's fertilizer. Another really amazing experience was when I took part in an outside ritual and we all danced and danced to the energy of the Goddess of the Forest.

I have been walking the Goddess path now for seven years and feel that seven is the length of a cycle. With the start of my business I felt that I moved onto the next spiral. When I started on this path I was looking to change my life as I felt I had become stuck and that my life was not moving in the direction I wanted it to. I feel the changes that I have made in both myself and my life have been easier and worked better for me by following the Goddess and using Her as a role model. The area where She has been of greatest help is when things have not changed as quickly as I would have liked; by meditating on Her changing aspects, I have realized that changes happen when they are ready and that I have to trust. I have to trust myself that I will allow these things to occur and to have that belief in myself. I have also had to learn patience and not to push things too quickly.

The Goddess, when I saw Her, was not really solid but a mass of energy, like moving light in a spiral form. This was sometimes stronger, sometimes lighter in intensity. At first I tried to visualize her as being more solid and tangible but this did not seem to work for any length of time. Again I meditated on this problem and the answer that came to me was to try to see myself in a similar way. I did not understand this at first but with thought realized that by my becoming less solid and not so insistent on having everything, including the Goddess, in tangible form, I could attract the things to me that I wanted. Also the other things that were coming towards me that I did not require would pass by, or through, or at least not attach themselves to me.

This is where I feel at present, trying to perfect this feeling within myself. This is part of the trust. Things don't have to be solid or tangible for me to know that they are there and are giving me support and advice. I want to learn to be more transparent, so that things pass by and through me rather than sticking to me. This is especially so in the case of worries which seem to attach themselves rather too heavily. I have found that this is like becoming a net or web which is yet another aspect of the Weaving Goddess. Her net is the network of stars which make the heavens and guide travellers towards Her with their mystery. I am working towards becoming a star net, the stars being the good experiences that I have and will have in my life, and the lights that guide me, as the planets do in astrology.

The magic of the Goddess for me is how She works in my life. I have always been dreamy and find being present and concentrated very difficult, so at first I found it very difficult that when I saw and used the Goddess She helped me with my mundane life, with my work, my job, my home, my garden. She was not this mystical apparition that appeared in front of me and gave me mystical teachings. She gave practical teachings; then as these became stronger and stronger, I saw that she helped most in the area of my greatest weakness. Help with dreams and visions would have taken me even more away from myself and my centre. With her help in the outer part of my life this has also helped the inner part, as my imagination has became stronger and more connected to the centre of my being, what I was and who I am. It became integrated with what I am, instead of being a little disconnected. When I had fantasies, they were things that I could now make into part of what was happening, like the landscapes. If I had a battle in one of these, say on the sea-shore, I would know that I was fighting with the East, the princess part of the self, and I was probably wrestling with an idea rather than an emotion, which would very often have a jungle background. I now have dreams that help me with what's happening around me, far more often than I did before. I have also had dreams where I met the Goddess. These were very common when I was doing the devotion to Astraea.

The Weaving Goddess has given me a greatly improved self-image and confidence. By coming to know Her aspects I have found and come to know myself much better. The changes this has brought are only good and I recommend this path to all. To start on the path, carefully study your life and find how and what the themes are that you have been working with until now. If this is difficult, you could try drawing a road map of your life and see if there are any common roads that you travel more often than others. Are these a thread? When you find the common thread you can try to find the Goddess or the God that is closest to your path and then work with the themes that you both have in common, just as I started with the textiles and the Weaving Goddess. The meditations you do will show you the rest of the path. Happy travelling!

In a Circle of Stone

Caitlín Matthews

To the Circle

If I close my eyes I can see the circle. It stands on a level place surrounded by sky, sea and hills. The time is twilight. The stones are etched against the ebbing stain of sunset. If I come closer I can see how the stones are weathered, veined with lichens, split by the harsh winds, smashed by lazy farmers who needed a new wall but were unequal to the task of dragging away such heavy stones.

The stones bear a family resemblance to each other; it is known that they were all quarried from one mother lode. They were raised by our ancestors, the people before our earliest documented forbears. They raised it for a purpose; each stone, like members of a community, served a distinct function which was yet integral to the whole.

If I stand very still, in this time that is between the worlds, in this place which is a gateway to another place, I can catch the drift of song, the scent of wood burning. And the stones lean together, huddling over the acrid warmth of the heather snarls and the sparking driftwood.

This is a good time to gather here for then, as now, it is festival time when the tribes come together as a family to sing and celebrate; to share news and to seek the known, loved faces; to barter and receive judgement.

Then the curlew's solitary cry reminds me that this land, once populous, is deserted. Few but the hardy hiker or the archaeologist come here now. But I have remembrance of this gateway between the worlds and know it as a place to envision an eternal truth: in this land there is no death, in this circle there is no ending. I know that if I stand in its very centre and turn, sunwise to each stone, I can trace the echoes of the wisdom that was encoded here in the foretime, and that those who once stood, hereditary guardians of each stone's power, will stand beside me now.

At the Hearth Stone

Mother, I am kindling your fire,
Mother, I am feeding your flame.
In the name of your peace,
In the name of your love,
In the name of your compassion,
May all who come here feel your indwelling presence.

If I start from the ground beneath my feet, it is because that is the place I started from. It has been a long journey to this circle for me. But this hearth, the circle's heart, must be kindled by all who would call it home, in the ways they know best. My steps have been led by a quest which is both search and service — to find a face to fit the body which has never ceased to nourish me.

The icon: hieratic, Byzantine madonna with her dark face fits, as does the horse-headed Black Demeter whose daughter, Despoina, conducts the dead to places of refreshment. The Mother's face is furrowed by care and concentration, for she is a bearer of burdens and a walker of roads, like many an exiled mother, fleeing across boundaries and mountain passes to give her children a new existence. Her face is dark, because hidden from the world. The diamond radiance of a transcendant goddess appears dull carbon to us, but it is a cloaking device, ready to surprise us by changing her careworn features into the utterly beautiful. She is the Mistress of Freedom through service. That hard road is the one I've tried to walk also, led by the knowledge that she had gone before me.

Perhaps, because she has so many unacceptable faces which strike resonating chords in many of us, many disassociate themselves from her. But who will embrace the hag to become the true sovereign? Who will disenchant the monstrous maiden who is but one feature of the wasted land? Who dares tackle the running sores of poverty, disease and violence?

The mother I serve has a well-defined cult in the East, as Kali. Indian mothers are distressed when their sons or daughters vouchsafe a devotion to the transformative Mother, because they say she demands sacrifice, and if it is not given, she will take one.

In the West, the Dark Woman of Knowledge has many appearances. She is sometimes called the Cailleach, the Old Woman, the Hag or the Loathly Lady — a euphemism which puts me in mind of the Eumenides. Black Annis stalks atavistic Lincolnshire and the Gyre Carlin propels her washing basket through the Scottish cloudscape with all the energy of Baba Yaga. She was certainly known to the tribes who gathered here, as she is to anyone who would seek to work with the earth's energies, for she is the Giver and the Taker, whose katabolic function is to break down in order to clear the way.

Is this my Mother? What kind of people serve her? She certainly does not suffer fools gladly. She scours souls, but she heals them too. She is particularly feared by men, though she is also, surprising to some, best served by them. For when a man, be he boy or elder, once finds a place in her heart, he will never lack for a home, or a woman by his side. All his natural talents will be enhanced and so he will become a man of compassion and a father to all hurt by the world's turning.

This Mother is good for bitter, disappointed women who have entered Cailleach-hood prematurely, for she is the Mother of Sorrows, and women like to mourn a great loss properly and for a reason greater than they can personally find. Even if it is only one of those days when the door slams shut and the keys are still inside, whether the washing-machine has flooded the floor again, or whether the need is deeper and the lover's place is cold beside you, or the child that was to have been has fled the womb untimely, she is the one you need to weep with for the sheer comfort of tears shed and a deep bosom to shed them against.

She is the companion of lost, broken souls who have strained the boundaries of their senses till something burst like an overwound toy. Such people eventually find her through the regular, natural rhythm which she maintains for, though she abhors clocks, she holds times, tides and seasons in her sure hand. In the quiet passing of time, of regular, healing activity, she is present as a friend. She brings slow healing and release from traumatic memory to those who have suffered violence, and if life would become a torture prolonged then gentle death is her cure, loving received.

Though she is frequently envisioned as a kind of malevolent female demon with dire punishments dangling from every arm, she is other. Those who fear her, fear themselves, fear to live, fear to hope, because tomorrow might be the death and no return on the wheel of birth for them. Death and birth seldom happen at home any more and the great gates which once swung open in full view of the whole family, furtively click open and shut in sterile chambers, watched only by professional strangers. The Mother is familiar with this problem and she stands closer to the gates of death, the better to help those newly crossing over. She needs no payment in coin like Charon; her joy is to help us recapitulate our old life and help us reintegrate the new one.

If she has begun to appear apocalyptically in the last century and a half, it is timely. For her body is threatened and even her beautiful faces are withdrawn for a few last tries to reach our stony hearts. There is nothing so appealing to the pride of a powerful man than a beautiful woman on her knees begging. Well, that is not the way the Mother does it, I'm afraid. She is of the sound, practical school of necessity. There is nothing more appalling to governments than the sight of their people reduced to starvation and the stark face of the Mother announcing austerity and prophesying the end of the world. The eschatological Virgins of Fatima and Medjugorge are not sweet, insipid madonnas with the full backing of the Church's hierarchy, but angry, importunate appearances of the Dark Mother telling us where the world is at. Her face also peers out of television screens in every home: no longer Sheba in sables and quartz, adorned like the Queen of the South, but gaunt, empty-breasted Ethiopia, eyes heavy with a terrible wisdom that needs no Solomon to interpret.

The Dark Mother is the Goddess of our age, but she is not so far-distant from the people who worshipped here. We all came out of her, we all return to her. And that is why we stand here first to kindle her fire which is life and sharing. The world is her body and I, who have walked it, feel only great wonder and pride in being a daughter, among other sons and daughters.

At the Threshold Stone

Set foot, bound eye,
A hand blind.
Yet, a light discovered,
A welcome found.

I stand at the threshold stone. It seems a long time since memory was first activated in me. For many of us the real threshold is earlier than that first fearful, expectant hovering on the edge of the circle. It happens in childhood or adolescence.

The opening, the way through, is a fortuitous crack through which we may pass unaware. It takes only a bar of music, a single, shining sentence and we are through into the Otherworld. After this experience, we are changed forever and, although we put it aside as precious, or just forget about it, the experience remains to haunt us. Our unconscious lives are lived in its pursuit, but because we seldom notice our motivations, this also escapes us. It is the irrational quest for the glory of the Otherworld which draws us. Any hint of it, the merest, mediocre echo will quicken our blood. But the way through and in is not so easy.

This unconscious quest must, at some point, be acknowledged and pursued purposefully. Then difficulties begin. What we touch in the inner world is unfindable in earthly terms and, although we find like-minded people who may give us a ritual framework to further pursue our obsession, their inner image and their practical expression are not only different from our own but often wildly astray from the intrinsic reality we have sensed. The frustration and disappointment are deep and abiding challenges to find something better.

Those who join groups and teaching circles invariably find

their membership of short duration because of these reasons and often never seek another group again, but remain alone, learning solitary wisdom in dreams, seasonal ritual and inner communion with the Otherworld.

Then there are others who desperately seek a kind of earthly ratification of innerworld empowerment through initiation ceremonies — often conducted by people least qualified to transmit or witness such a contract. All that happens in that situation is a kind of ritual gratification. Those who are empowered to initiate, know that the real initiations are those which life deals us. The thresholds over which we pass are to do with inner maturity and there are a great number of them to negotiate. We go forward blithely assuming that great forces will be on our side, invocable by a curt gesture or a mystic word. The truth is sadly different. Going with the flow of life is easy and there are indeed times when our inner lives are totally harmonious, so that everyday life takes on a synchronicitous patina. The outer verifications of such harmony are comforting, but do not denote a permanent state of affairs. Life moves us speedily from one crisis to another. We find it harder to cope until we either crack or adapt.

Adapting to life's curve is a skill. Initiation is about going beyond self-imposed limitations, finding new, practical ways of living. One of the major initiations is to discover that without a balanced everyday life, inner realizations are about as much use as a leaky hose at an inferno. Coping without the props of pride, alcohol, drugs, vanity and self-importance — the props vary — is another initiation.

A ritual initiation is a verification of something the individual has already undergone. But even here, fasting, self-purification and preparation are required first. The threshold stone is where we expect to find the broom, always ready on hand to clear away the debris that sometimes strays into the circle. For nobody ever stops stepping over this stone; we are ever learning anew, bringing our dirt or our blessings in with us.

At the Stone of Memory

The stones remember,
And the last sheaf
Sprouts eternally.

This stone is most challenging for modern Native believers. Here the wealth of ancestral memory is gathered and its guardian makes me all too aware that in the world of reinvented tradition which many of us have chosen to inhabit, there is a fine distinction between making it up and re-remembering. I have written about such analepsis as a valid means of restimulating the latent memories of the foretime, not with a view to living in the past but as a method of creative recall.

We all have memories rooted in another age which rise from the back of our brains to astound us with their vivid recall, but such memories do not validate that life-pattern for our age. We no longer sacrifice prisoners to our gods or dispose of unwanted children by exposing or eating them, for example. The Native wisdom is about living skilfully and in harmony with our circumstances. If the practice of our tradition does not help us to do this, then it is worthless.

The question of valid traditions divides the neo-pagan world today in exactly the same way that, say, branches of Christianity are divided. As the guardian beside me affirms, there are no rightful bearers of tradition, only bearers of tradition. However we are welcomed into our tradition — whether it be by formal training, ritual initiation or long personal meditation — we become bearers of that tradition by desire, aptitude and dedication.

It is very easy to judge the real vessels of tradition. They are people rooted in their living way, yet who use it creatively; they guard the wealth of memory and freely give it to those who are worthy; their way of life *is* their tradition. These are people in whom the deep speech and the eternal song well up endlessly because they have dedicated their lives to their tradition, meditated hard to bore the rocky strata which keeps us from that living water. The thieves of memory — those fake masters of tradition — are equally easy to judge; they are people void of tradition, in whom only the empty echo is heard in all its bombastic self-importance; they are known by their stage-props, and their short-lived spotlit 'ministry'; their life-style is vastly at odds with their avowed tradition. When they open their mouths, the emptiness of their soul becomes apparent to the listener, for they cannot give drink to the thirsty if they too have never experienced drought; they pour from a dry pitcher because they have never found the source.

The stone of memory marks our ancient springs which are

yet defended by guardians old and new. If any find their way to the wells of memory then no one can prevent them from drinking, if that is their desire.

At the Stone of Combat

Who stands at the stone?
— A maiden, a marryer, a moaner.
Who threewise threaded you?
— Catcher, Caller, Cut-the-Thread.
Enter the ring, riddler.

The guardian who stands at this stone is an opponent to the initiate's development, the defender of tradition, the one whose riddles and tests make us look ever-deeper into our motivations. But this is an opponent who, after we have grappled with him or her, becomes a friend and guide.

Celtic stories tell of the pillar stone set up in the tribal village centre where a single champion might come and strike sparks out of it with his sword, challenging the tribe's champion to a combat. It is by such struggle that we gain our acceptance within the tradition we have chosen; it is also the means by which we test that tradition's suitability for our condition.

Whoever makes an Otherworldly journey by means of deep meditation finds that similar border-guards surround the periphery of that archetypal country whose timeless, dimensionless wisdom interfaces with our own world. An interesting process emerges as each seeker approaches the wilderness which borders the home of wisdom. As each responds to the guardian at the Stone of Combat, answering and setting questions, seeking and finding ways in, a certain familiarity with the inner landscape is established. Those who find the source of wisdom and drink from it find, on the return journey, that there is no way out of this land except by replacing the guardian who let them in in the first place.

So the initiate *becomes* the guardian, who is freed for other duties. So it was at these stones through many generations of guardianship, so it is within our spiritual pagan traditions today. The apprentices become the journeymen and women; and these, released from their practical duties, assume those of the master or mistress of tradition, revealing wisdom to the worthy.

As one who has been handed a small part of this guardianship, I admit occasional reluctance, lethargy and self-interest; as one who has to stand and fight at the between-lands with oncoming challengers, I continually rediscover the roots of my tradition as the hard questions are fired mercilessly, and I am reactivated, refocused, made worthy to share this guardianship once more.

At the Stone of Gathering

In the beginning of the world
all men had knowledge cheerfully,
all had leisure,
all thoughts were pleasant,
at that time all creatures were friends.

Not all of life is challenge, the guardian here reminds me. There is the restoration of play, recreation and festival, when the glories of tradition are celebrated by everyone. This is not always so today where, though the Western traditions are striving to reintegrate the family and the idea of sacred play, believers are mainly single adults so entrenched in a last ditch battle to gather the necessities of life by means of their job, that they miss the release of festival.

We are redeeming the time when we prepare for festival, for these are the spaces outside time wherein we are recreated and realigned to the things which really matter — home, family, our relationship to the primal order and to the fellow creatures, organisms, rocks under nature's hand. Festival is the time when all created life is in-gathered and faces the Otherworld: a true communion of mind, body and spirit.

The Native Pagan traditions are noted for their proximity to nature and the natural cycles of life, and this pattern is reflected in the seasonal calendars which shape the festivals. Many have castigated the revival traditions for striving to adhere to an outmoded agricultural calendar in which few now play a major part, in terms of sowing the seed and harvesting the crops. Our survival is now based on a complicated set of food-chains, tied to world economic policies, but we are no less dependent upon nature whether we slaughter our own pig or buy pork loin ready wrapped in the supermarket. Nor are we less dependent upon each other.

Though there is much glib talk about our belonging to a global village, we would do well to bring this idea into the circle at festival time, as many are indeed doing, and make a resolution to consider our family or tribe as belonging to the world family. We need to work together at this crucial crossing point in our history in order that the world's peoples receive the living necessities.

Festivals are times of sharing and recreation, times when inessential work is set aside and the games begin. The original idea of sacred games, celebrated when the tribes gathered together at a festival, such as at the great cursus on Salisbury Plain, is now mainly lost. Although the modern Olympics valiantly attempt to keep the Classical concept functional, it is doubtful whether many people would appreciate the poet Pindar's odes on the games. For although his poems are dedicated to players, the lines are addressed directly to the purpose of the games — the gods themselves.

If we need to discover anything to keep our sanity and humour it is this very concept of sacred time, sacred play; to give time to the gods for their sport among humanity, to allow ourselves to be refreshed and invigorated by the archetypes which animate our traditions.

At the King's Stone

Iron on the king's thigh,
Plough in the loam.
Call the maidens to the dance
At the King's Stone.

Each young man or woman comes at some point to an understanding of the indwelling inspirer, giving them a unique insight, for men, of the Divine Feminine, and for women, of the Divine Masculine. Maidens flocked here to this stone to seek that very experience in dances and revels not unlike those Dionysian orgies so abhorrent to the 'civilized' mind. But adolescence is a time of ecstasy and, besides, who said that learning should be dull?

As I retrace my own steps to this stone I recall with what difficulty I arrived at an understanding which would have been obvious in a more primitive society. The touch of the inner inspirer is a magical secret in one's youth; at first it was easy to draw off his generous gifts and assume that this wonderful face would be that of my future lover. How many men and women frustrate their lives by falling into this snare, overlaying the image of the inner beloved onto the human partner who has neither the wit to realize nor the ability to reflect such ideals? Redeeming such mistakes brings wisdom, but how hard it is!

The Inspirer, as master, taught me discipline, technique, application of my creative skills. He also initiated me into sexual fulfilment. Beyond the reciprocal love which enveloped our inner relationship, I sensed also an awesome perspective and received a deeper understanding of the Mother which as a woman I instinctively drew upon. The Inspirer was also *her* inspiration and she *his*. What matchless partnership was I engaged upon?

The true polarities are like this and so subtle and so easily missed or misinterpreted. We need to focus on this deep dimension so urgently. So many human relationships misfire because of such misunderstanding.

Latterly the Inspirer has shown me another face, that one of the Youth, Mabon, Son of the Mother, who is both brother and son to me also; child of joy and strong talisman against despair and imprisonment of all kinds. When sunk in a ditch of uncreative unlovingness, my fingers clamped across my despairing eyes, he has shone through, plaguing me with his music till I opened up enough to laugh or cry. Like a child who prises his mother's fingers from some grim daily task for an instant game, he has restored me. He is a younger version of the Inspirer and though is old as the first dawn, he keeps me young.

All young women dream of dark lovers under this stone's shelter, just as all young men dream of endlessly various mistresses under the Queen's Stone. These inner inspirers are dream-keys to a wider realm of being and also correctives to an increasingly less creative world.

At the Queen's Stone

Barley in the queen's lap,
Honey in the comb.
Call the young men to the dance
At the Queen's Stone.

I have never stood at this stone, at least not in this lifetime, for it is the place of men's initiation into the mysteries of the Divine

Feminine, although I have often played the part of its guardian and so my understanding is completed by reciprocation of energies.

We miss the many-splendoured thing of a polarized relationship which transcends the partnership of a magically or sexually conjoined couple. The levels of polarity go on beyond this in a spiral of interrelationship which is obscure to us. These things are seldom spoken of; though some circle elders murmur darkly about Western tantra, they do little to enlighten the obscurity for younger seekers sitting with them.

Young men come to this stone with the same eagerness that young women show at the King's Stone. They are looking for initiation into the mysteries of their own abounding sexual energy which runs at such a head that it seems likely to take over their lives totally. The initiator may, as for women, be a human partner or, more likely at first, an inner one. The inspirer who appears in the psyche is invariably a dream-woman, a muse, bearing the lovely features of the Goddess in her first beauty. Her features appear in every love-poem and idealized icon of belief as the Ultimate Woman — an image which feminists have been quick to reject because its projection upon the female gender has been persistently obsessive and depressingly oppressive.

The need for the known, loved, inner inspirer is a driving compulsion for men, as for women, although men feel the need more urgently to manifest the image than women have done. Where we fail in these two crucial initiations today is all too plain: who initiates the initiators? is the question. Unless the adolescent man or woman is exposed to their inner inspirer and so learns the intermeshing of polarities which extend from physical human relationships into psychic and spiritual ones also, there are bound to be problems. Our society does not encourage such subtle investigation, preferring an 'only-safe-when-touched' policy about the inner worlds. If our inner inspirer is conceived of only as an ideal image which must be sought in a human partner, then no wonder the sexes are embattled.

At the Crossing Stone

Where night is bright as day
Where the twinlights gleam
Where reality is realer
— Between the worlds.

The realms within have many names. This guardian has known many appellations, but the co-ordinates for the Crossing Stone are always the same. Most children know their way here and step between the worlds with no difficulty whatever. But the world of play which we all once inhabited in childhood is one of our greatest lost resources and we are being bullied out of it, cajoled into adulthood far earlier than ever before.

The Otherworld, like the world of childhood, is now continually diminished in many minds, dismissed as 'imaginary' or 'childish'. The devaluation of the Otherworld is an indictment on our creativity. Whether people say it exists or not, it is perceived and experienced not only by artists and musicians, but by all peoples in touch with their creative roots.

Native wisdom comes from the ancestral Otherworldly dimension and it is available to us always and everywhere. We can tap into it at any given point, with practice. In primitive cultures, the facility to play and to enter the Otherworld is not lost, nor do people confuse the realities of everyday life with the Otherworldly realms, as some naïve anthropologists have assumed.

The loss of an inner cosmology, the realms within, which Gerard Manley Hopkins called 'the inscape' of a thing, has created many confusions in the modern mind. Part of the task of Western Native Traditions is to map this lost territory, entering its environs during meditation and ritual, meeting its denizens, correlating findings for the benefit of all earth's children bereft of this dimension. Such people become the real walkers-between-the-worlds, the modern shamans and shamankas of our society, whose task is to synthesize the inner urgings of the Otherworld and translate the ancient wisdom to be found therein for modern use.

The ways in vary with each person. For me music has been the knife which keeps the Otherworldly gates open, in the manner of travellers to Faery who go armed with iron. I have found it the source of my spiritual nourishment, the eternal welling up of freshness and the gift of life itself. If at the end of this life I have enabled others to find their own ways into these realms then I will consider my task accomplished.

At the Stone of Telling

In the times before the times,
This song was singing.
In the times after the times before,
They'll sing it still.

At this stone the nights draw in, the fires are fed, the tribe and any strangers welcomed to the hearth, sit closer and listen, as the story-teller spreads his hands and the singer shapes her mouth to sound the notes.

It is the time for the sharing of wisdom and everyone listens; children dozing against their mother's knee; hunters refurbishing their weapons; women weaving and plaiting new decorations for festival-time; elders seemingly alert and upright, ready to swear they were awake the whole time but whose inner hearing is tuned to the story and the song as the blood vessels are tuned to the circulation of the blood.

The song and the story are at the heart of our tradition, they are never marginal, optional entertainments for those who sit at this circle. In an age divorced from traditional wisdom, where people become fidgety when spirituality raises its head, the song and the story are joint means of re-establishing a rapport between themselves and living spiritual wisdom. People may vow that they are not religious, when challenged, but there are few who will not willingly listen to a song or story.

What is hidden, because it is mystical and therefore considered nowadays to be detrimental to the common life, can be approached through story. Story works so simply that it is overlooked. To *become* a story while it is being told is to experience by analogy. It is one of the best keys for the reluctant seeker whose intellectual faculty totally refuses to obey the simple natural responses to the Otherworld. To bypass this blockage, one has to be cunning. Song and story are one means of slipping between the cracks of the all-too-vigilant mind. Modern psychology has discovered this open secret and employed many folk-tales in its therapeutic practice, but it has become altogether adept at dissecting the story rather than transmitting it.

However, we need to have authorized story-tellers and singers, those who are *personally* in touch with their tradition in such a way that what they practice is not an entertaining performance nor a psychological exercise but a real communication of traditional wisdom by means of their art.

At the Lintel Stone

Dryghten, I am lifting your lintel,
I am raising your light.
In the name of your peace,
In the name of your love,
In the name of your compassion
May all who come here feel your indwelling presence.

As I prepare to leave the circle, I must pass under the Lintel Stone which is the place of the God, the Divine Masculine principle. There are currently many immature realizations about him. It is hard to call him Father, for that word seems devalued by so many betrayals of the spirit. Indeed, at this time, it is hard for a man to be a man, a condition deemed by some to be a shame and misfortune. But we should not confuse levels here, carefully considering how we see the Lord.

He is often known as the Son, and this is not surprising, for little boys are loveable and not threatening — at least not until they abandon Superman pyjamas and laser swords for y-fronts and machine guns. The Son is an easy sacrifice to accept, riven on so many altars, victim and saviour both; perhaps too easy. The awesome and sometimes casual acceptance of his immolation — in whatever mythos — needs pause.

He is not a weak, etiolated image at all. It is only the dilution of traditional wisdom which has made him appear so. In the Craft he is Dryghten, the power-wielder, the power of the forest; for the shaman, he is the Lord of the Beasts and Master of Totems, but all these archaic faces do not hide the fact that he is strong through creative wielding of life-energy. Hence the terrible sorrow when, like Christ or Cuchulainn, he goes bare to the elements to grapple with the *geasa* of the world — those unquenchable dark waves which stand to overwhelm every generation.

His action is on behalf of the tribe and is motivated by his love of his people. His is an initiation for us all and so his sacrificial struggle becomes precious to remembrance because all succeeding generations have imprinted in them forever afterwards the heroic sacrificial pattern. And relics are preserved, even though it be one leaf from the windy tree on which he hung to gain knowledge, Prometheus-like, for humanity, or a splash of the hero's blood soaked into a cloth, for it is our blood too. Native Americans remember the struggle of the God for the benefit of the tribe in their sun-dances, when one of their number represents the people before the Otherworldly gates.

He is also a provider. The Greeks called him Plutus, 'wealthy', because he gives of the treasures of wisdom. Those inexhaustible treasuries are laid down in the Otherworld, the accumulations of aeons of wisdom. Yet he is also a giver of material gifts, providing us with food for our bellies and clothes for our backs. He especially is the one who gifts us with skills to provide for ourselves — that is a father's responsibility as well as a mother's.

It is a pity that the God, and by inference, men, should have been associated with the demon, technology. The forging of metals, the shaping of verse, the nurture of beasts are all skills under his patronage. He is also a skilful husbandman, selecting stock, conserving land and reading the signs of the seasons, when to sow and reap.

There is one aspect of his many faces and personas which few chose to call upon — The submerged god-form of the Sleeping Lord, the King of the Underworld. His power has been confused with that of evil entities, but he is not malefic. He sleeps beneath the land to guard it and he comes forth at need. He is committed to his guardianship and has the words of empowerment at his command. Like the Green Knight, he challenges us at solstice-time, where, in the deep snows, he still wears evergreen in token of his renewal.

Those who pass under his lintel can meet him, but only on his terms. By answering his exacting riddles, by challenging him, we enable him to be reborn over and over, his skills alive in us, his empowerment our initiation.

At the Watch Stone

Dawn, day, twilight,
What does midnight say? —
The setting moon
Shall kiss the rising sun.

The circle is behind and I stand at the Watch Stone, the place where the lone guardian watched the heavens and the fall of their patterns upon the circle. I am no astrologer, nor diviner. Prophecy is quiescent in me, though I feel the pulse that animates these times.

There has been a long night and a longer dawning for the people of this century, who have seen the dying of many facets of traditional spirituality. The traditions themselves are deathless, on one level, but they need reanimation. This century has seen the longest and most daring leap across the aeons, not only forward in technology but also backwards to the roots of tradition themselves. But this was no retrograde movement, only a *réculer pour mieux sauter.*

The living tradition which we inhabit by our practice and meditation is firmly rooted and is already bearing fruit. Its diverse groups are all part of a greater circle in which there is room for guests and strangers. In our diversity there is hope for confederated unity — not that individual groups will conform to some projected mean, but that the Western Pagan and Native traditions will regard themselves as part of a larger family sitting together and sharing.

If I open my eyes once more and look back at the circle I no longer see grey lichened stones but the known, loved companions of my tradition who are the Guardians of the West. It is in this company that I shall choose to be numbered and, though new guardians come to take their places, I shall pray to be among them wherever the circle gathers.

Contributors' Biographies

Gwen Blythe lives with her husband and family in mid-Wales. She is an artist and harpist, finding the Welsh landscape, myth and history a constant source of inspiration. She makes no distinction between Paganism and Christianity, amusing and outraging friends of both persuasions

Philip Carr-Gomm is Chief of the *Order of Bards, Ovates and Druids*, which celebrates the eight seasonal festivals, organizes workshops and publishes a correspondence course on Druidry, (obtainable from The Secretary, OBOD, 260 Kew Road, Richmond, Surrey TW9 3EG.) Philip has two sons and lives in Primrose Hill. He has a B.Sc. in Psychology from University College, London, and trained at the Institute of Psychosynthesis, and with the Children's Hours Trust. He now has a private practice in psychosynthesis psychotherapy for adults and play therapy for children.

Imogen Cavanagh has studied Goddess mythology for the past 16 years. She celebrated the seasonal festivals for many years alone, relating them to her experience of the living in the country. She now works in London as an alternative healer and writer, and celebrates the seasonal festivals in a mixed group with Beth Neilson. She meets with an all-woman group to meditate and celebrate the monthly phases of the moon, and teaches Goddess mythology to a small evening class. She is equally committed to evolving a strong Goddess-oriented spiritual tradition with women, and to discovering how men and women may draw on inspiration from ancient mythological themes to improve their interrelationship in contemporary society.

Dr Vivianne Crowley is a High Priestess of the Gardnerian and

Alexandrian traditions of Wicca, the Old Religion. As a young child, she experienced dreams and visions of the Pagan Gods and Goddesses, and mystical states of unity with nature. However, it was not until she read Margaret Murray's *The God of the Witches* that she realized that Paganism had survived in the witch covens of Europe. Shortly afterwards, she discovered that Paganism was alive and well in England in the form of Wicca, a mystery religion, and she knew that this would be her path. At the age of 19, she was initiated into Alexandrian Wicca by Alex and Maxine Sanders. She was later initiated into the Gardnerian tradition. She believes that there are many paths to the one centre which is the goal of all religious, magical and mystical systems. For some, but not all, this goal is to be reached through Wicca and the path of Paganism, which speaks in the powerful archetypal symbols of the collective unconscious of humanity. She believes that Pagan religion, with its respect for the Goddess and the feminine aspect of divinity, its emphasis on personal growth and the development of the latent powers of the human mind, has an important message for those attempting to make sense of their place in the modern world. Vivianne Crowley lives in London, where, for the past 10 years, she and her husband have run a Wiccan coven. In addition to teaching Wicca and running seminars and workshops in the UK and Germany, she has a private practice as a psychologist and healer. She is the author of *Wicca: the Old Religion in the New Age* published by Aquarian Press.

Prudence Jones read philosophy at Girton College, Cambridge. Her research into Classical logic and mathematics revealed the contemporary world of the Greek mystery religions, whose recognition of the feminine principle and whose respect for nonrational thought processes exposed by contrast the hidden lopsidedness of later Western culture. She subsequently came across modern esoteric Paganism, and later trained in humanistic psychotherapy as a means of reawakening the Pagan outlook constructively in the Judaeo-Christian West. Because of the as yet inadequate articulation of the feminine principle in Western culture, she believes, a resurgence of Goddess religion will be the next step forward for the West. She speaks for the native European tradition, disguised but not obliterated in folk custom, legend, and the pervasive eightfold symbolism of the agricultural year, believing that it has much to teach us about reintegration with the natural world. Her publications include *Eight and Nine, Sundial and Compass Rose* (1982), and *Time and Tide* (forthcoming), on north European calendration, plus many articles in Pagan, Earth Mysteries and astrological journals; and *The Path to the Centre* (1988) on Goddess mysticism and the symbol of the Holy Grail. She is a key organizer in the Pagan Federation, the co-ordinating body for British revived Paganism, and in 1985 founded, (with Nigel Pennick), the *Pagan Anti-Defamation League.* She works as an astrologer and therapist in Cambridge and London.

Caitlín Matthews is a writer, singer and harpist working within the multi-faceted Western Spiritual Tradition. She is the co-author, with John Matthews — her partner in the Arthurian and mythic fields — of the seminal two-volume study *The Western Way*, as well as *The Aquarian Guide to British and Irish Mythology.* Together they have designed and written *The Arthurian Tarot* and *Hallowquest* (both Aquarian Press 1990), which combine their knowledge of the Arthurian legend with traditional teachings on the Hallows of Britain. She is an authority in the field of esoteric Celtic studies, and has written a two-volume study of the *Mabinogion* which deals with the gods, goddesses and traditional lore of this mythic cycle: *Mabon and the Mysteries of Britain, Arthur and the Sovereignty of Britain.* She is the co-editor, with Rachel Pollack, of *Tarot Tales*, a collection of short stories. She is primarily interested in mining the deepest core of the ancient spiritual traditions and finding applicable and practical uses of these traditions within contemporary society.

John Matthews is a writer who has made the Arthurian world his special province. He is an expert on the Grail legends, publishing three books on this subject: *The Grail — Quest for the Eternal, At the Table of the Grail* and *The Grail Seeker's Companion* (with Marian Green.) His *Warriors of Arthur*, written with Bob Stewart, explored the earliest legends of King Arthur. His anthology *The Arthurian Reader* shows his wide interest in the popular and scholarly fields of Arthurian studies. He is presently working on a major study of Gawain as Knight of the Goddess, and a book on the shamanic Celtic heritage of the bard Taliesin. He retains a lively interest in both the primal and hermetic ends of the Western Mystery Tradition.

Kaledon Naddair ('The Pictish Serpent': literally, the hard, severe but upright and fertile Adder), has his research and writing base in Edinburgh. His practically-lived shamanism takes him and his group off into the wilds of Alban as well as round the megalithic sites of Britain. From earliest childhood, he had pronounced psychic abilities which developed into especial, though undisciplined talents by the age of 16-18. From this age he embarked upon an extensive study of many ancient religions, mythologies and wisdom traditions. From 1979-89, he has been President of the Keltic Research Society. In 1982, he founded the College of Druidism — a Keltic-based initiatory organization with branches in Great Britain and abroad — and became its Director of Studies. Since 1982, he has amalgamated the Qabalah group with the College of Druidism's Kaer Eidyn Mother Group. In 1984, he was appointed General Secretary of the European Pan-Keltic League. Over the last 10 years, he has given many workshops and lectures to individual groups and major conferences throughout Great Britain and abroad. These workshops and his many books testify to his passionately outspoken commitment to profound and well-researched expositions of Keltic and Indo-European Lore. His publications include: *Druidism Ancient and Modern* (due 1989/90); *Pictish Art: its Shamanistic Symbolism, Sacred Geometry and Applied Aesthetics* (due 1989); *Keltic Shamanistic Calendar* (2 vols); *Keltic Tree Lore* (3 vols); *Keltic Bird Lore; Names for Trees in Keltic, Indo-European, Semitic and Other Languages; Pictish and Keltic Art Symbolism* (1984-87); *Cup and Ring Marks and Sacred Rock Art; The Shaman and Ritual Drumming* and *Keltic Folk and Faerie Tales* (Century, 1987). *Keltia; The Pictish Shaman; Awen.* Details of these and other publications from:

Keltia Publications, PO Box 307, Edinburgh EH9 1XA, Alban (Scotland).

Greg Stafford was born in Hartford, Connecticut in February 1948. As is typical among Americans, he moved six times in the 18 years preceding his high school graduation. In 1966 he began a period of wandering, broken by intermittent stints at various colleges, and has travelled throughout most of the continental United States. He married in 1974, and is the father of three children: a step-son aged 17, a daughter aged 14, and an adopted son aged six. In 1975 he published his first game *White Bear and Red Moon* and established his games company, Chaosium Inc. He publishes mainly role-playing games and art books. In 1981 he consciously entered the shamanic path with his first sweat-lodge ceremony and vision quest. In 1985 he helped to found the Cross Cultural Shamanism Network, now best-known for the publication of *Shaman's Drum*, a quarterly magazine, and has served as president since then. He also co-ordinates a shamanic network, gives workshops, conducts rituals and continues in the transformation of our society to assist in the healing of Grandmother Earth.

R.J. Stewart is a Scottish author and composer living in England. He has over 20 books in publication and translation world-wide and has written and recorded original music for feature films, television, radio, theatre and for concert tours and albums. In addition to writing on music and consciousness, magical arts, Celtic traditions and folklore, and mythology, he has made a special study of the figure of Merlin in medieval literature, including two books on the *Vita Merlini* and the *Prophecies of Merlin* by Geoffrey of Monmouth. In 1988, working with artist Miranda Gray, he published the *Merlin Tarot* (Aquarian Press) which draws upon imagery in the ancient Merlin texts and traditions and restates it for modern use in meditation, visualization, prevision and story-telling.

Felicity Wombwell has followed the native British Pagan path and the spiral of the Goddess since 1980. She has been a member of several groups along the way. These have included Ceremonial Magic groups, a Dianic group and a Women's Mystery group. She is an artist following the philosophically-based tradition of Cecil Collins. Felicity now gives workshops in the Creative Arts and Spirituality. These involve finding our sacred self through art, music, drama, play and movement. Her interest in things mystical started with an interest in astrology, an interest she retains. The idea of the circle or mandala is strong in all aspects of her work, because for her it is the symbol for the creative self. Her ideas have come through the study of alchemy and dreams. Felicity believes that one's true path is found when one tries to find the self. The path to the self is the path to discovery and freedom.

Glossary

The following is a short glossary of proper or mythological words which may be unfamiliar to the reader. Some words have been idiosyncratically employed by the writers in this collection and occasionally their normal use may be more general or more particular depending upon the context. The following is thus intended as a brief guide for use with this book only, not as an encyclopedic explanation.

Æsir In Norse myth, the warrior gods who dwelt in Asgard.

Aether The sacred fifth element, representing the spirit.

Alban The ancient name for Scotland.

Alban Arthuan lit. 'The Light of Arthur'; Druidic name for the winter solstice.

Alban Eiler lit. 'The Light of the Earth'; Druidic name for the spring equinox.

Alban Elued lit. 'The Light of the Water'; Druidic name for the autumn equinox.

Alexandrian Craft The brand of witchcraft founded by Alex Sanders (1926-1988).

Analepsis A method of remembering events, lore and wisdom of the past.

Apollo Greek god, particularly associated with music, poetry and mystical illumination. His famous oracle at Delphi was consulted by many.

Apuleius A north African Latin writer who flourished in the first century AD. His chief work, *The Golden Ass*, is the source of many myths concerning the Goddess, including the myth of Cupid and Psyche. The book describes the initiatory course of

Apuleius into the Isiac mysteries.

Arawn British god of the Underworld. His title was Pen Annwn, 'Lord of the Underworld', and was associated with the Wild Hunt which he is said to lead in some parts of Wales.

Ariadne In Greek myth, she was the daughter of the King of Crete. It is she who guided Theseus through the labyrinth of the Minotaur by means of a clew of thread. She was later married to the god Dionysus, who awarded her the Crown of the North, or Corona Borealis, as her starry diadem.

Asgard In Norse myth, the world of the Æsir.

Astraea In Greek myth, she was the Goddess of Justice. She was the last of the immortals to withdraw from the earth at the time of the Golden Age; she was later associated with the constellation of Virgo.

Atropos The last of the Fates, called 'Unchangeable'; the sister who cuts the thread of life.

Baba Yaga In Russian folklore, the hag-like goddess who has a house on chicken's legs.

Baubo In the Greek Eleusinian myth, the crude antics of Baubo divert **Demeter** from her grief over the loss of **Persephone**.

Belle Dame Sans Merci In the poem of this name by John Keats, the hero is beguiled into entering the domain of La Belle Dame Sans Merci, only to wake up 'on the bare hillside' alone.

Beltane The Celtic fire festival celebrated on 30 April or May Eve.

Beorn A character from J.R.R. Tolkien's **The Hobbit** who guarded the pass over the Misty Mountains from the depredations of orcs. He frequently assumed a bear-like persona.

Beowulf The Scandinavian hero whose exploits are told in the Anglo-Saxon epic of the same name.

Besom A broom of twigs.

Black Annis The **Cailleach** or hag-aspected goddess associated with the Dane Hills in Lincoln; she is said to eat unwary travellers after dark.

Bladud This legendary British king attempted to fly from the roof of the temple of Minerva and crash landed.

Blodeuwedd In British myth, she is the wife of **Llew Llaw**

Gyffes, formed out of flowers by **Gwydion** and Math.

Book of Shadows The collected rituals, rules and spells of a Gardnerian coven are written in a book called the Book of Shadows, which individual initiates of that coven are permited to copy 'in their own hand of write.'

Brighid or **Brigit**. Celtic Goddess of Wisdom. In Ireland, she was one of the Tuatha de Danaan and was the patron of women, Druids and smiths. She was later conflated with the fifth-century saint, Brigit of Kildare. Her cult in the Western Highlands of Scotland shows a perfect comprehension of both figures.

Cailleach Gaelic term meaning 'old woman'; it is a reverent way of referring to the dark or hag-aspect of the Goddess.

Callisto In Greek myth, the daughter of Lycaon. She bore Zeus a son called Arcas. Artemis, angered at Callisto's forsaking the state of maidenhood transformed her and her son into bears. Zeus raised Callisto to become the constellation of the Great Bear and her son to be the Little Bear.

Candlemas The alternative name for the feast of **Oimelc**. In the Christian calendar it is celebrated on 2nd February and commemorates the Purification of the Virgin.

Carlos Castañeda (1925-) Peruvian anthropologist and writer whose fictional writings about the shamanic Yaqui Indian, Don Juan, have had a formative effect upon the development of the Native traditional resurgence.

Ceridwen In British myth, she was the Goddess who prepared a cauldron of inspiration for her ugly son, Afagddu. Its contents were imbibed accidentally by the cauldron's guardian, Gwion Bach, who was subsequently reborn of her womb as **Taliesin**.

Cernunnos Celtic god, protector of the forest and its animals.

Charge, the In the Craft, the Charge is the instruction of the Goddess which is normally recited by the High Priestess who, at that point, is understood to represent the Goddess. It describes the mystical and all-pervasive nature of the Goddess, and it exhorts her followers to revere her and to abide by the natural laws.

Charon In Greek myth, the ferryman who bore the dead to the realms of Hades. The toll to Charon was the coins placed on the eyes of the dead.

Clotho The first of the Fates, literally 'the Spinner' who spun the thread of life.

Craft, the A popular name for **witchcraft**, sometimes called 'the Craft of the Wise'.

Cretan maze This maze is unicursal in form, there being only one defined path to the centre.

Daimon A Greek term for a helping or indwelling spirit, the transpersonal source of creative power. It has nothing whatever to do with the word 'demon'.

Demeter In Greek myth, the goddess of the earth's fertility. When **Persephone** was abducted to Hades, Demeter withdrew her gifts so that perpetual winter reigned. She and Persephone were the chief deities of the Eleusinian Mysteries.

Dervishes Sufi mystics, known as dervishes, whirl and dance in order to enter ecstatic states in which they find their communion with Allah.

Despoina One of the names of **Persephone**, the Greek goddess of the Underworld. Despoina is the name of the aspect of Persephone to whom **Demeter** gave birth after having been raped by Poseidon. She is generally depicted as horse-headed and is similar in many ways to the Celtic goddess, Epona.

Dianic Craft A form of witchcraft practised solely by female groups. It originated in America and has been heavily influenced by the feminist witch, Z. Budapest.

Don Juan The Yaqui Indian shaman of whom **Carlos Castañeda** wrote in his many books.

Dryghten The Saxon name for 'Lord' is frequently given by many in the Craft as a title of the male principle of the God.

Ereshkigal In Babylonian myth, the Goddess of the Underworld.

Eumenides 'The Kindly Ones' is the propitiatory name given to the Erinyes, or 'Angry Ones', the Furies of Greek myth.

Fogu lit. Fo-gi or below ground; man-made caves used as special dwellings and initiation caves. Cognate with Kymraeg (Welsh), Ogof and Gogof — 'cave'.

Foretime The primal, prehistoric period.

Frey In Norse myth, one of the **Vanir**. He was a god of plenty.

He was brother to **Freya**.

Freya In Norse myth, one of the **Vanir**. She was particularly associated with acts of love and war, and was said to be mistress of magic and witchcraft.

Gardnerian Craft The brand of witchcraft founded by Gerald Gardner (1884-1964).

Geasa In Gaelic, the prohibitions which bound the individual. These geasa were like taboos; whoever contravened them endangered his or her existence.

Gnosis Is the inner wisdom of any mystical tradition. Historical Gnosticism was an idiosyncratic mystical divergence of early Christianity.

Gnostic Mass Written by Aleister Crowley (1875-1947). As a ritual it is frequently performed by many groups of pagan affiliation or magical adherence.

Great Work The Great Work is undertaken by the magician who seeks to align the macrocosm and microcosm in perfect harmony.

Green Knight The Green Knight appeared at King Arthur's Christmas court to play the beheading game which only Sir Gawain would play. Gawain subsequently undertook a quest to find the Green Knight and offer his own head for decapitation. This ancient mythos has been taken to imply the combat between the old and new years.

Gruagach Translated as 'wildman-giant-wizard'; faerie being with supernatural knowledge and abilities. Cognate with Kyraeg, Gwragach or Gwrach.

Gwydion In British myth, the magician who fostered **Llew Llaw Gyffes** and who created **Blodeuwedd** out of flowers.

Gyre Carlin In Scottish tradition, the old wife or **cailleach** who shakes down the snows of winter and rides upon the elements bringing rough weather.

Hathor One of the most ancient goddesses in Egyptian religion who had a variety of attributions, including patronage of the dead and fertility. She was known as 'Mistress of the Sycamore', her symbolic appearance. Women very much associated themselves with her, as is revealed from extant Coffin Texts.

Hecate In Greek myth, the triple Goddess of the crossroads, of the Underworld and of witchcraft.

Hereditary Craft Hereditary witchcraft is perhaps the least accessible brand of the Craft since one has to be born into it in order to belong to it. A few hereditary families still exist, utilizing local and familial practices which are generally vastly different from the popular brands of witchcraft.

Herne Saxon god of the Wild Hunt. His stamping ground is Windsor Forest.

High Priest and **Magus** Titles given to the male leader of an Alexandrian coven.

High Priestess and **Witch Queen** Titles given to the female leader of an Alexandrian coven. These titles are not favoured by other brands of the Craft.

Human Potential Movement A term given in the 1960s and 1970s to a group of humanistic thinkers and psychologists interested in the correlation of rational and ecstatic states. It explores mystical experience as a valid method of human experience.

Hymehosts Storm Writer of North Cheyenne extraction whose seminal book *Seven Arrows* helped opened up the lore of the Native American to the white West. His exposure of tribal lore was considered controversial in the early 1970s.

Icarus In Greek myth, the son of Daedalus who, to escape the captivity, made wings to fly away. He flew too near the sun and his waxen wings melted.

Imbolc or **Oimelc**. Celtic fire festival, celebrated on 31 January.

Inanna Sumerian Goddess, cognate with **Ishtar**, who underwent a redemptive descent to the Underworld.

Inner Planes Sometimes also called 'the Inner'. Most Westerners acknowledge only one plane of consciousness — the physical, manifest world about them. The Inner Planes are the successive levels of awareness which lie beyond the physical world. Different traditions perceive them in varying ways. The Inner Planes are usually seen to be the abode of the gods and helping spirits.

Ishtar The Babylonian Goddess who was Queen of Heaven.

Jacob's Angel In Biblical tradition, the patriarch Jacob wrestles with an angel.

Kali Hindu Goddess, who represents in full measure the Dark Aspect of the Goddess's nature. She is revered as the most caring mother, for though some of her images depict her with severed heads or trampling upon her consort, Shiva, she always holds up two of her many arms in the gestures of fearlessness and spiritual strength.

Koed Kaledon The Caledonian Forest that initially covered much of Highland Alban, as well as Dumfries, Galloway and the Borders.

Koelbren lit. 'Omen-trees' or 'divination-twigs', constituting the Kymraeg (Welsh) alphabet.

Lachesis The middle sister of the Fates, 'the Disposer of the Lots', who chose how the thread of life should be apportioned.

Lammas Alternative name for the feast of **Lughnasadh**.

Leuchairpins Beings with a 'radiantly light face/head or countenance'; they became later known as leprechauns.

Lughnasadh The Celtic fire festival celebrated on 31 July.

Mabon The Celtic god Mabon was always known as Mabon ap Modron — titles which mean respectively Youth, Son of Mother. He was taken 'from between his mother and the wall when he was three nights old' and it is the quest of the British hero, Culhwch, to discover him in his place of imprisonment where he has been from the beginning of creation. Mabon is the patron of innocence and justice.

Macrocosm lit. 'The Great World'. It is used to designate the archetypal world of pre-existence or potential inner universe.

Maeve In Irish myth, the Queen of Connacht, an ecstatic goddess associated with battle. She renewed herself periodically in a lake and had numerous lovers. It is she who was responsible for Cattle Raid of Cooley, during which Cuchulainn's notable exploits are performed.

Mediation An esoteric function whereby an individual communicates or is a channel for blessing, healing or the expression of an archetype. A priestess may be said to mediate the Goddess, for example.

Medicine Wheel In Native American lore, the Medicine Wheel is the earth wheel of the four directions upon which different qualities, totems and powers are designated. Each person or tribe has its own correspondences upon the Medicine Wheel. It corresponds to the magical use in Western esotericism of the circle of working.

Medusa In Greek myth, she was one of the Gorgons whose gaze could turn people to stone.

Menarche The time when a woman first menstruates.

Michaelmas A Christian feast commemorating St Michael, the archangel, celebrated on 29 September. It is associated also with the Pagan festival of the autumn equinox.

Microcosm lit. 'The Little World' — the world of manifestation or 'the real world' as we tend to call it. It is understood esoterically to be a miniature of the macrocosm.

Morgan le Fay In medieval Arthurian legend, she is the half-sister of King Arthur, an enchantress. In earlier British tradition, she is Morgen, the mistress of the Otherworldly island of Avalon, whereon she heals Arthur of his mortal wounds.

Narnia The magical, inner world created by C.S. Lewis in his sextet of children's novels. It corresponds to the Happy Otherworld where creation is largely unfallen, and it is peopled by mythical species as well as mortal kind. Lewis employed it as an analogue of paradise.

Native tradition Each country has its native or primordial aboriginal tradition of belief and practice. These have been mostly overlaid by other forms of spirituality, not usually native of that place, yet within which remnants of the Native tradition can yet be discerned.

Neith Egyptian Goddess of the Upper Heavens. She was later subsumed into the cult of the Goddess Isis, of whom it was said, 'no man has lifted my veil.'

New Age The esoteric ages of the universe are seen in terms of the Zodiac. In the current age or aeon, we are passing from the age of Pisces into the age of Aquarius. This is the source of the great change in consciousness which has been experienced world-wide, bringing a greater interest in practical applications of spirituality.

Niamh In Irish myth, she was an Otherworldly woman who

invited **Oisin** to Tir na n'Og, the land of the ever-young, where they lived in great happiness.

Numen A numen is an indwelling spirit of a place.

Nut or **Nuit** Egyptian Goddess, whose body stretches out over the heavens. Beneath her, lying upon the earth is her partner, Geb.

Odin In Scandinavian myth, the greatest of the gods, one of the **Aesir** particularly associated with wisdom and prophecy.

Oimelc see **Imbolc**.

Oisin In Irish myth, the son of Fionn mac Cumhail. He went with **Niamh** into the Land of Youth and lived with her, but grew homesick for his own country. Niamh begged him to go but not to dismount. Oisin's saddle broke and he fell to earth an aged man.

Orpheus In Greek myth, the great singer under the aegis of **Apollo**. By the power of his music, he was able to win back his wife, Eurydice, from the realms of Hades.

Oshun Nigerian Goddess of the healing waters.

Otherworld The Native traditions each have their own name for the realms which lie beyond the physical world. The Otherworld is usually conceived as a place of primal peace and power.

Ouspensky, Peter Demianovich (1878-1947) the Russian philosopher who combined mathematics, religion and mysticism into an original and coherent system.

Oya Nigerian Goddess, associated with the elements. She is a special patron of women.

Pagan Derived from the Latin *paganus* or country-dweller. Its current use denotes a follower of a Native tradition, as opposed to a member of an orthodox religion. Within this book, Pagan has been used as a convenient word for all contemporary witches, shamans, and wise people who derive their spirituality from the Native traditional basis.

Persephone In Greek myth, the daughter of **Demeter**.

Plutus The Greek god of riches, frequently conflated with the god of the Underworld, Dis or Hades.

Pretanoi/Qretanoi/Kruithny All names for the Picts, the aboriginal inhabitants of Prydain (Britain). Their name is derived from the 'Kruiths' (geometric shapes and creature forms) that they painted or tattooed (Peik) upon their bodies, hence they were also known as Picti/Ffichti. In support of this, a carved wooden head showing facial tattooing has recently been dug up from a bog in Ireland.

Prometheus In Greek myth, one of the Titans, famed for stealing fire from heaven for the use of mortals.

Prydain One of the ancient names for the isle of Britain.

Puck In British folklore, an Otherworldly being, frequently associated with Robin Goodfellow. The name probably derives from the Irish word 'pooka'. He is generally considered to be a helpful spirit.

Queen of Elphane The Queen of Elfland, like the Faery Queen, is a British folk tradition variant of the Queen of the Otherworld.

Ragnarok In Norse myth, the battle at the end of time between giants and monsters, gods and humankind.

Samadhi A Hindu term, also employed in Jainism and Buddhism, to denote the highest state of yogic meditation. This stage leads to self-realization.

Samhain / Samhuin The Celtic fire festival celebrated on 31 October. This feast marks the beginning of the Celtic year.

Shaman/shamanka An Altaic word which is now used to indicate a man or woman who works within a native traditional system, acting as a walker-between-the-worlds of the gods and the manifest realms. Many shamanic practices are paralleled in Craft tradition.

Spider Woman In Native American tradition, Spider Woman — sometimes called Thought Woman — sits, thinks, names, while weaving her stories, and the world takes shape from her.

Sun Bear Chippewa medicine chief of the Bear Tribe, Spokane, Washington. His popular teachings have familiarized many with the wisdom of the medicine wheel.

Taliesin Sixth century British poet who also has a mythical persona. As Gwion Bach, he tended the goddess Ceridwen's cauldron and obtained a synthesis of wisdom from the drops which landed upon his fingers. He is one of the great bardic initiates of British tradition.

Tam Lin In Scottish folk-ballad tradition, Tam Lin went into faeryland with the Queen of Faery. He was rescued by the love of Janet who pulled him from his steed at Hallowe'en and held him fast until all Tam Lin's enchanted shape-shifting ceased.

Thomas the Rhymer Thomas of Ercledoune was an historical Scottish character who went into Faeryland with the **Queen of Elphane**. After his sojourn there, he was given 'a tongue which could not lie'. His many prophecies are recorded.

Totem Algonquian word, used originally to denote the emblem/ancestor of a tribe. It is now in general use to represent the power animal or spirit beast of an individual.

Traditional Craft Traditional witchcraft is defined as being a brand of witchcraft existing without contact with either Gardnerian or Alexandrian groups. Usually existent in country areas, with adherents from the locality, it has its own local appearances and practices.

Troja In Norse myth, an alternative name for **Asgard**.

Vanir In Norse myth, the fertility gods who warred with the **Æsir**, until they were reconciled.

Virgins of Fatima and **Medjugorge** The late nineteenth and twentieth centuries have been marked by numerous apparitions of the Blessed Virgin Mary. She appeared to three illiterate children at Fatima, Portugal in 1917. Recent apparitions of Our Lady at Medjugorge in Yugoslavia seem to reinforce the Fatima apparitions, and are much concerned with the state of the world and its people.

White Buffalo Woman In Sioux tradition, the being who brought the sacred buffalo calf pipe from the Great Spirit to the tribe. At the ritual of the sun-dance one mature woman is usually chosen to embody this being. Although White Buffalo Woman appeared first as a woman, she is also a buffalo; white buffalo hide is a talisman of great virtue.

Wicca An alternative name for witchcraft or the Craft of the Wise, as it is often known. The word probably derives from the Old English word 'wic' or wisdom.

Witchcraft The practice of the Old Religion, part of the Native tradition of north-west Europe. Within Paganism it has no negative connotation, but is seen as a religion which exercises its ancestral lore for the good of all.

Woodwoses Term for the shaggy wildfolk of the forests.

Wyeem/Wemys Pictish for 'cave', also associated with the passage of the egg down the fallopian tube.

Yemaya African goddess, known as 'Mother of Fishes'.

Yule In Norse and Anglo-Saxon tradition, the festival of Midwinter.

Bibliography

Fiction

Andrews, Lynn V., *Medicine Woman*, Routledge & Kegan Paul, London, 1984.

____*Flight of the Seventh Moon*, Routledge & Kegan Paul, London, 1984.

Anthony, Piers, *Tarot*, Ace Books, New York, 1987.

Bradley, Marion, *The Mists of Avalon*, Michael Joseph, London, 1983.

Caldecott, Moyra, *Guardians of the Tall Stones*, Arrow Books, London, 1986.

Cameron, Anne, *Child of Her People*, Siren Books, London, 1987.

____*Dzerlarhons*, Harbour Publishing, Madeira Park, BC., 1986.

Campbell, J.F., *Popular Tales of the Western Highlands*, Wildwood House, London, 1983-4.

Crowley, John, *Little, Big*, Gollancz, London, 1982.

Fortune, Dion, *Moon Magic*, Aquarian, London, 1956.

____*The Sea Priestess*, Aquarian, London, 1957.

Gardner, Gerald, *A Goddess Arrives*, Stockwell, London, 1941.

____*High Magic's Aid*, Michael Houghton, London, 1949.

Garner, Alan, *The Owl Service*, Collins, London, 1967.

Kay, Guy Gavriel, *The Darkest Road*, Unwin & Hyman, London, 1987.

____*The Summer Tree*, Allen & Unwin, London, 1985.

____*The Wandering Fire*, Allen & Unwin, London, 1986.

Kurtz, Katherine, *Lammas Night*, Severn House, London, 1983.

Matthews, Caitlín & Pollack, Rachel ed., *Tarot Tales*, Century, London, 1989.

Middleton, H., *Son of Two Worlds*, Rider, London, 1987.

Ross, Anne, *Druids, Gods and Heroes*, Peter Loewe, London, 1986.
Skelton, Robin, *Fires of the Kindred*, Porcepic Books, British Columbia, Victoria, 1987.

General

Bohm, David, *Wholeness and the Implicate Order*, Routledge & Kegan Paul, London, 1980.
Chatwin, Bruce, *The Songlines*, Picador, London, 1987.
Fraser, J.G., *The Golden Bough*, (abridged), Macmillan, London, 1957.
Graves, Tom, *Needles of Stone*, Turnstone Books, London, 1978.
Jeffreys, Richard, *The Story of my Heart*, Longman, London, 1979.
Jones, Prudence, *The Path to the Centre*, Wiccan Publications, London, 1988.
Keller, W., *The Etruscans*, Cape, London, 1975.
Lovelock, James, *The Ages of Gaia*, Oxford University Press, Oxford, 1988.
Marshall. S., *Everyman's Book of English Folk Tales*, Dent, London, 1981.
Matthews, John, with R.J. Stewart, *Legendary Britain: An Illustrated Journey*, Cassell, London, 1989.
Mead. G.R.S., *Orpheus*, Watkins, London, 1965.
____*Thrice Greatest Hermes*, Watkins, London, 1964.
Michell, J., *New View Over Atlantis*, Thames & Hudson, London, 1983.
Pennick, Nigel, *Earth Harmony*, Century, London, 1987.
Purce, Jill, *Mystic Spiral*, Thames & Hudson, London, 1974.
Russell, J.B., *The Devil, The Perception of Evil From Antiquity to Primitive Christianity*, Cornell University Press, Ithaca, N.J., 1977.
____*Satan, the Early Christian Tradition*, Cornell University Press, Ithaca, N.J., 1981.
____*Mephistopheles, the Devil in the Middle Ages*, Cornell University Press, Ithaca, N.J., 1984.
____*Lucifer, the Devil in the Modern World*, Cornell University Press, Ithaca, N.J., 1986.
Stewart, R.J., *Music and the Elemental Psyche*, Aquarian, Wellingborough, 1987.

Watkins, Alfred, *The Old Straight Track*, Garnstone Press, London, 1970.
Weston, Jessie, *From Ritual to Romance*, Cambridge University Press, Cambridge, 1920.

Goddess and Women's Spirituality

Durdin-Robertson, Lawrence, *Juno Covella: Perpetual Calendar of the Fellowship of Isis*, Cesara Publications, Enniscorthy, 1982.
Graves, Robert, *The White Goddess*, Faber, London, 1952.
Hall, Nor, *The Moon and the Virgin*, Women's Press, London, 1980.
Harding, M.E., *Women's Mysteries*, Rider & Co., London, 1935.
Harrison, Jane Ellen, *Prolegomena to the Study of Greek Religion*, Merlin Press, London, 1961.
____*Themis*, Merlin Press, London, 1963.
Johnson, Buffie, *Lady of the Beasts: Ancient Images of the Goddess and her Sacred Animals*, Harper & Row, San Francisco, 1988.
Luke, Helen, *Woman: Earth & Spirit*, Crossroad, New York, 1981.
Matthews, Caitlín, *The Elements of the Goddess*, Element Books, Shaftesbury, 1989.
____*Sophia, Goddess of Wisdom: From Black Goddess to World Soul*, 1990, forthcoming.
____*Voices of the Goddess: a Chorus of Sibyls*, Aquarian Press, Wellingborough, 1990.
Mookerjee, Ajit, *Kali: the Feminine Force*, Thames & Hudson, 1988.
Neumann, E., *The Great Mother*, Princeton University Press, New Jersey, 1963.
Olson, Carl ed., *The Book of the Goddess*, Crossroad, New York, 1987.
Paxson, Diana, *The Liturgy of the Lady: the Fellowship of the Spiral Path*, MZB Enterprises, P.O. Box 72, Berkeley, CA. 94701, USA.
Pereira, Sylvia, *Descent to the Goddess: a Way of Initiation for Women*, Inner City Books, Toronto, 1981.
Whitmont, E., *The Return of the Goddess*, Routledge & Kegan Paul, London, 1983.

Magic

Ashcroft-Nowicki, Dolores, *The Ritual Magic Workbook*, Aquarian Press, Wellingborough, 1986.
Gray, William G., *Magical Ritual Methods*, Helios, Toddington, 1971.
____*Seasonal Occult Rituals*, Helios, Toddington, 1970.
____*Temple Magic: Building the Personal Temple*, Llewellyn, St Paul, MN., 1988.
Green, Marian, *The Elements of Natural Magic*, Element Books, Shaftesbury, 1989.
____*The Path Through the Labyrinth*, Element Books, Shaftesbury, 1988.
Matthews, Caitlín & John, *The Western Way: vol. I The Native Tradition*, Arkana, London, 1985.
____*The Western Way: vol. II The Hermetic Tradition*, Arkana, London, 1986.
Stewart, R.J., *Advanced Magical Arts*, Element Books, Shaftesbury, 1988.
____*Living Magical Arts*, Blandford Press, Poole, 1986.

Native American Traditions

Bierhorst, John ed., *The Sacred Path: Spells, Prayers & Power Songs of the American Indians*, Quill, New York, 1983.
Erdoes, Richard & Ortiz, Alfonso, *American Indian Myths & Legends*, Pantheon Books, New York, 1984.
Lincoln, Kenneth, *Native American Renaissance*, University of California Press, Berkeley, CA., 1983.
Sams, Jamie & Carson, David, *Medicine Cards: the Discovery of Power Through the Ways of Animals*, Bear & Co., Sante Fe, 1988.
Steiger, Brad, *Indian Medicine Power*, Para Research. West Chester, PA., 1984.
Sun Bear & Wabun, *The Medicine Wheel: Earth Astrology*, Prentice-Hall, New York, 1980.
Tedlock, Dennis & Barbara, *Teachings from the American Earth*, Liveright, New York, 1975.
Waugh, R.H. & Prithipal, K.D. et al., *Native Religious Traditions*, Waterloo, Ontario.
Ywahoo, Dhyani, *Voices of our Ancestors*, Shambhala, Boston, 1986.

Northern Traditions

Caesar, Julius ed. S.A. Handsford, *The Conquest of Gaul*, (De Bello Gallico), Penguin, Harmondsworth, 1982.

Crossley-Holland, *The Norse Myths*, André Deutsch, London, 1980.

Dronke, Ursula, *The Poetic Edda*, Oxford University Press, Oxford, 1969.

Evans-Wentz, W.Y., *The Fairy Faith in Celtic Countries*, Lemma Pub. Co., New York, 1973.

Foote, P. & Perkins, R., *The Law Book of Iceland*, University of Manitoba Press, Manitoba, 1980.

Gantz, J. ed & trans., *The Mabinogion*, Penguin, Harmondsworth, 1976.

Goulstone, J., *Summer Solstice Games*, Privately printed, 10 Haslemere Rd., Bexleyheath, Kent.

Jones, Prudence, *Eight and Nine: Sacred Numbers of Sun and Moon in the Pagan North*, Fenris-Wolf, Cambridge, 1982.

____*Sundial and Compass Rose: Eightfold Time Division in Northern Europe*, Fenris-Wolf, Cambridge, 1982.

Le Roux, Françoise & Guyonvarc'h, Christian-J, *Les Druides*, Ouest France. Rennes, 1986.

Matthews, Caitlín, *Arthur & the Sovereignty of Britain: King & Goddess in the Mabinogion*, Arkana, London, 1989.

____*The Elements of Celtic Tradition*, Element Books, Shaftesbury, 1989.

____*Mabon & the Mysteries of Britain: an exploration of the Mabinogion*, Arkana, London, 1987.

Matthews, Caitlín & John, *The Aquarian Guide to British and Irish Mythology*, Aquarian Press, Wellingborough, 1988.

____*The Arthurian Tarot: A Hallowquest*, Aquarian Press, Wellingborough, 1990.

Matthews, John, *The Arthurian Reader*, Aquarian Press, Wellingborough, 1988.

____*Elements of Arthurian Tradition*, Element Books, Shaftesbury, 1989.

____*Elements of the Grail Tradition*, Element Books, Shaftesbury, 1990.

____*Gawain, Knight of the Goddess*, Aquarian Press, Wellingborough, 1990.

Matthews, John with Bob Stewart, *Warriors of Arthur*, Blandford Press, Poole, 1987.

Naddair, Kaledon, *Keltic Folk and Faerie Tales*, Century, London, 1987.
Palsson, H. & Edwards, P., *Settlement Book (Landnâmabók)*, University of Manitoba Press, Manitoba, 1972.
Pennick, Nigel, *Practical Magic in the Northern Tradition*, Aquarian Press, Wellingborough, 1989.
Rees, Alwyn & Brinley, *Celtic Heritage*, Thames & Hudson, London, 1961.
Reuther, Otto Sigfrid, *Germanische Himmelskunde*, Lehmann, Munich, 1934.
Ross, Anne, *Pagan Celtic Britain*, Sphere, London, 1967.
Snorri Sturluson, *The Prose Edda*, trans. J.R. Young, Bowes & Bowes, Cambridge, 1954.
Stewart, R.J., *The Merlin Tarot*, Aquarian Press, Wellingborough, 1988.
____*The Mystic Life of Merlin*, Arkana, London, 1986.
____*The Prophetic Life of Merlin*, Arkana, London, 1986.
____*The UnderWorld Initiation*, Aquarian Press, Wellingborough, 1985/9.
Tacitus, *The Agricola and the Germania*, trans. H. Mattingley, Penguin, Harmondsworth, 1970.
Tille, Alexander, *Yule & Christmas*, David Nutt, London, 1896.

Shamanism

Doore, Gary ed., *Shaman's Path*, Shambhala, Boston, 1988.
Guss, David M., *The Language of the Birds*, North Point Press, San Francisco, 1985.
Harner, Michael, *The Way of the Shaman*, Harper & Row, London, 1980.
Jamal, Michele, *Shapeshifters: Shaman Women in Contemporary Society*, Arkana, London, 1987.
Kalweit, Holger, *Dreamtime and Inner Space*, Shambhala, Boston, 1988.
Nicholson, Shirley ed., *Shamanism: an Expanded View of Reality*, Theosophical Publishing House, Wheaton, Ill., 1987.

Witchcraft

Adler, Margot, *Drawing Down the Moon*, Beacon Press, Boston, 1986.
Bracelin, Jack, *Gerald Gardner, Witch*, Octagon, London, 1960.
Buckland, Raymond, *Complete Book of Witchcraft*, Llewellyn, St Paul, MN., 1986.
Crowley, Vivianne, *Wicca: The Old Religion in the New Age*, Aquarian Press, Wellingborough, 1989.
Farrar, Janet & Stewart, *The Life and Times of a Modern Witch*, Piatkus, London, 1987.
Gardner, Gerald, *The Meaning of Witchcraft*, Aquarian Press, London, 1959.
____*Witchcraft Today*, Rider, London, 1954.
Leland, Charles, G., *Aradia, The Gospel of the Witches*, C.W. Daniel Co., London, 1974.
Murray, Margaret, *The God of the Witches*, Sampson Low, London, 1931.
____*The Witch-Cult in Western Europe*, Oxford University Press, Oxford, 1921.
____*A History of Witchcraft, Sorcerers, Heretics and Pagans*, Thames and Hudson, London, 1980.
Starhawk, *Dreaming the Dark*, Beacon Press, Boston, 1982.
____*The Spiral Dance*, Harper & Row, New York, 1979.
____*Truth or Dare*, Harper & Row, New York, 1988.
Valiente, Doreen, *ABC of Witchcraft*, Robert Hale, London, 1988.
____*Where Witchcraft Lives*, Aquarian, London, 1962.
____*Witchcraft for Tomorrow*, Robert Hale, London, 1978.

The Pagan Federation

BM Box 7097 London WC1N 3XX, England

The Pagan Federation was founded in 1971 (as Pagan Front) by elder members of four Wiccan paths of the Old Religion of Pagan Europe. Its primary aim is to provide contact between the Craft of Wicca and genuine seekers of the Old Ways; also to promote contact and dialogue between the various branches of the European Pagan religion which have re-emerged in the 1980s; and to provide practical and effective information on Wicca and other branches of Paganism to members of the public, the media, public bodies and the Administration. Being a Pagan is neither illegal nor antisocial, but from time to time our legislators need reminding of this fact. Article 18 of the Universal Declaration of Human Rights, to which Britain is a signatory, states:

> *Everyone has the right to freedom of thought, conscience and religion; this right includes freedom to change his religion or belief, and freedom, either alone or in community with others and in public or private, to manifest his religion or belief in teaching, practice, worship and observance.*

The Pagan Federation publishes a quarterly journal, *The Wiccan* (f. 1968), price £5 p.a. (£8 overseas airmail, sterling funds only please), and other publications as required. It holds members-only and public gatherings as appropriate, and maintains personal contact by letter with individual members and with the wider Pagan community. Membership costs £5 p.a., including free receipt of the journal, and is open to anyone over 18 years old who finds sympathy with the three principles of Paganism listed below. These principles are:

1. Love for and kinship with Nature, rather than the more customary attitude of aggression and domination over Nature. Reverence for the life force, and the continuing renewing cycle of life and death.

2. The Pagan Ethic, 'Do what thou will, but harm none'. This is a positive morality, not a list of thou-shalt-nots. Each person is responsible for discovering their own true nature and developing it fully in harmony with the world around them.

3. Acceptance of the polarity of deity, the reality of both Goddess and God. Active participation in the cosmic dance of Goddess and God, female and male, rather than the suppression of either the male or the female principle.

To join the Pagan Federation, send details of yourself and your interest in Paganism to us at the address above. Please include an s.a.e. (UK), or 2 IRCs (overseas) to cover postage. We welcome all genuine seekers.

Of further interest...

Wicca

The Old Religion in the New Age

Vivianne Crowley

Witchcraft is said to be the oldest religion in the world. Its adherents have been sorely persecuted and publicly ridiculed, yet on a deeper, more intuitive level, many people view witches with a sort of fearful respect, furtively seeking them out to buy magical spells, potions and talismans.

Vivianne Crowley here explains the 'way of the witch', the quest for the self, showing how Wicca — rapidly regaining its former popularity — has real relevance in today's world. Includes:

★ Witchcraft as a non-dogmatic New Age religion
★ The misunderstood concepts of black and white magic
★ Why witches have initiations
★ The meaning of magic
★ The God and Goddess within us
★ Sex and nudity
★ Making sense of the life cycle
★ The future of witchcraft

Complete with an explanation of the relationship of witchcraft to Jungian psychology, this intriguing volume aims to shed light on what has traditionally been seen as a shadowy and slightly malevolent religion.

Magical Tales

The Story-Telling Tradition

R. J. Stewart

Story-telling is one of the most enduring and important magical traditions, yet it is represented the least in the twentieth-century revival of New Age disciplines. In *Magical Tales* R. J. Stewart deals in depth with the tradition of magical story-telling, found in various forms throughout the world. He shows how such tales are essential to psychic health and how, on a deeper level, they contain the keys to profound inner transformation.

The book begins with a discussion of the traditional ancient roots of magical tales and epics. The author then moves on to suggest how this powerful imaginative process might be reinstated for the modern individual without attempting to mimic or falsely restore the lost oral traditions of past cultures. He also compares modern fantasy literature with genuine magical or spiritual tales and points out that a story is not magical simply because its author selected 'occult' events and characters—magical tales are always embedded within spiritual traditions. By way of example, a series of original magical tales by the author is featured, with line drawings by Stuart Littlejohn.

With this book the reader will learn many ways of working with magical stories, including visualization, meditation and methods of using story-telling for personal development.